Maren Lickhardt, Gregor Schuhen, Hans Rudolf Velten (eds.)
Transgression and Subversion

Gender Studies

Maren Lickhardt, Gregor Schuhen,
Hans Rudolf Velten (eds.)
Transgression and Subversion
Gender in the Picaresque Novel

[transcript]

We thank the Vice Rectorate for Research at Leopold Franzens University Innsbruck for the support with the printing costs and Gestu_S: Zentrum Gender Studies Siegen.

Bibliographic information published by the Deutsche Nationalbibliothek
The Deutsche Nationalbibliothek lists this publication in the Deutsche Nationalbibliografie; detailed bibliographic data are available in the Internet at http://dnb.d-nb.de

© 2018 transcript Verlag, Bielefeld

Cover layout: Maria Arndt, Bielefeld
Printed and bound in Great Britain by Marston Book Services Ltd, Oxfordshire
Print-ISBN 978-3-8376-4400-5
PDF-ISBN 978-3-8394-4400-9

Contents

Transgression and Subversion. Far from Gender?
An Introduction
Maren Lickhardt/Gregor Schuhen/Hans Rudolf Velten | 7

The Parent Trap
Mothers and Others in the Spanish Picaresque
Anne J. Cruz | 17

Between Subject, Object, and Abject
Masculinities in the Spanish Picaresque
Gregor Schuhen | 33

The Charms of Circe
Narrative Persuasion in *Guzmán de Alfarache*
Timo Kehren | 47

Gender Trouble Without Subversion
Libro de entretenimiento de la Pícara Justina
Hanno Ehrlicher | 65

Genealogy, Gender, and Genre in Alonso de Castillo Solórzano's *La Garduña de Sevilla* (1642)
Frank Estelmann | 85

Body and Gender in *Till Eulenspiegel*
Inversions of Masculinity in the 16th century
Hans Rudolf Velten | 111

Subversion and Stabilization of the Sexes by Transgression in Grimmelshausen's *Courasche* (1669)
Maren Lickhardt | 131

Role Switching and Gender Marking in the Picaresque Novel
Matthias Bauer | 147

**Picaresque Narrative and Gender Construction
in Wilhelm Raabe's *Lorenz Scheibenhart* (1858) and
Aus dem Lebensbuch des Schulmeisterleins Michel Haas (1860)**
Hans-Joachim Jakob | 163

Masks to Mock the Light
The Authentic Pícara in Marivaux's *La Vie de Marianne*
Alexandra Schamel | 181

Virile Maturity, Female Linearity, and the Transformation of the Picaresque Novel
Tobias Smollett's *Roderick Random* and Daniel Defoe's
Moll Flanders
Jens Elze | 201

Contributors | 217

Transgression and Subversion.
Far from Gender?
An Introduction

MAREN LICKHARDT / GREGOR SCHUHEN / HANS RUDOLF VELTEN

The picaresque universe is without any doubt a patriarchal and phallogocentric construction, in which most of the characters are male, where physical and non-physical violence is omnipresent, and where femininity is depicted as a constant threat to the male identity of the adolescent anti-hero, the pícaro. Even though the collective ethical norms in this "great wolves' game" (Bauer 1993: 85) work in accordance with the narrative pattern of *mundus inversus*, which means that feudal social hierarchies are – to quote Bachtin – "carnivalized", the prevailing patriarchally determined gender norms in the picaresque diegesis do not seem to be inverted at all, not even in the female picaresque (cf. Cruz: 1999).

This general observation serves as a starting point of our volume and leads us to the crucial question why the transgressive and subversive potential of the picaresque narrative challenges and criticizes the feudal hierarchy of the social strata without subverting and transgressing gender norms. Moreover, if the gendered norms of the picaresque novel really perpetuate the misogynist tradition of medieval treatises on the hierarchy of the sexes, which role does the genre-specific device of picaresque irony or satire play? And finally: Does the fact that female characters are so uncommon in the picaresque novel automatically suggest that womanliness is of minor importance to the genre? Especially the appearances of the pícaro's mothers and their doubles in several key scenes of the texts might complicate this assumption, as Anne J. Cruz suggests in her contribution to this volume. That gender issues are rarely located in the center of the rich scientific reception history of the picaresque genre makes analyzing "Gender in the Picaresque" even more challenging.

The Spanish Picaresque

Shortly before the end of his long journey through the cities of early modern Spain and just before getting married, Guzmán de Alfarache informs his readers about the preferences of young women when choosing the ideal husband. This chapter is written in a manual style and is explicitly addressed to young women. According to the narrator, most of the inexperienced girls make poor decisions because they mostly rely on the wrong parameters. Following the arguments of the narrator, only money and social status should be taken into account. The passage begins with the stereotypical attribution of *inconstantia* to his female readers: "Haces como mujer: eres mudable" (Alemán 2010: 388); ("You act like a woman: you are inconstant"). What follows is a long list of examples why women usually choose the wrong husband: They marry in order to escape their parents' houses, they marry because of love, they marry to avoid social isolation by losing their honor, they marry because they have read the wrong romantic books, or they marry because of their lovers' physical appearance. All of these points touch on the relationship between the two sexes, and they reveal much about the image of women. Only the last point does not focus on stereotypes of femininity or develop a binary typology of male and female, but provides insight into images of masculinity as it describes how to look like a 'real man'. Women should not choose young men who care too much about their physical appearance (Alemán 2010: 393): "mocitos engomados" ("tarted up young men"), "pulidetes más que Adonis" ("smoother than Adonis"), "aderezados para ser lindos" ("prepared to be beautiful"). The playful use of "goma" / engomado" hints at the true character of these young men: "goma" usually means 'rubber' or 'pomade', but it is also – according to contemporary dictionaries (cf. Covarrubias 1611: 441) – a familiar expression for syphilitic tumors (by the way, also the term *fuentes* has this double meaning: it means 'fountains', on the one hand, and purulent wounds, on the other). Both meanings of *goma* are usually attributed to women: women who fix their hair with pomade or the syphilitic prostitute, such as Úbedas *Pícara Justina* (cf. Hanno Ehrlicher's paper in this volume). This is because syphilis as a venereal disease is closely related to sexual debauchery, which is stereotypically regarded as a female vice. This shows clearly that in the gendered picaresque universe sexual excesses – or sexual activities in general – constitute a bodily practice which serves as a mode of differentiation between the two sexes. Such a corporeal practice which constitutes masculinity is the excessive use of physical violence, as for example the first half of *Lazarillo de Tormes* (1554) demonstrates (cf. Gregor Schuhen's contribution to this volume). In short, it is not the narrative depiction of the body itself which establishes binary sexual differentiation, but corporeal practices in the strictest sense of *doing gender*.

Returning to Guzmán's remarks on women, it is not only the sexual double meaning of *goma* which refers to issues of gender difference, but also the fact that practices such as hair dressing ("copetes") and makeup ("las colores y buena tez") are clearly attributed to women "que lo han menester y se han de valer dello" (Alémán 2010: 393-94); ("who need them and have to make use of them"). This passage echoes a similar phrase from the beginning of the novel where the narrator states that these practices depict "actos de afeminados maricas" (Alémán 2012: 140) ("acts of effeminized faggots").

If it is true that this excerpt also serves as a manual on how to behave like a 'real man', this becomes clear in the exclamation "Sea la mujer, mujer, y el hombre, hombre [...]. Bástale a el hombre tratarse como quien es. Muy bien le parece tener la voz áspera, el pelo recio, la cara robusta, el talle grave y las manos duras" (Alemán 2010: 393-94). A man should remain natural, should abstain from female practices, which are moreover judged as morally reprehensible.

Interestingly enough, passages dealing explicitly with sexual differentiation are scarce, at least in the male picaresque (Frank Estelmann examines the relationship between gender and genre in the *female* picaresque). The picaresque sexual discourse seems mainly to consist of misogynist addresses by male narrators or characters. Even in the passage quoted above, female practices are portrayed as morally odious, and feminization has been classified as one of the main and most dangerous threats to masculinity (cf. Solomon 1997), an observation questioned in this book. Moreover, gender constitution is strictly related to different corporeal performances. Men mainly use physical violence to prove their masculinity, whereas women act as strongly sexualized characters. According to the inverted social framing of the picaresque narrative, both modes of gender constitution are presented as moral antitheses to Renaissance humanism and official Christian values. One might expect that the ironic literary depiction of the picaresque *mundus inversus* not only refers to social hierarchy and moral values but also includes gender norms in terms of subversion or transgression, as the title of this book suggests. As far as we can see, this is not the case. The passage just discussed, by mentioning classical queer aspects such as effeminacy and cross-dressing, reveals that these phenomena are unambiguously marked as abnormal in a strictly heteronormative discourse. Therefore, we have to add a question mark behind the title of our book. Furthermore, if the gendered body can be conceived only as a performative construction, we have to ask which specific roles the excessive amount of corporeal imaginary plays, since bodily excesses undoubtedly belong to the typical ingredients of the picaresque narrative.

The passage quoted at the beginning of this introduction evokes the double meaning of *goma* and *fuentes*. Both terms refer to rather disgusting physical phenomena: syphilitic tumors and purulent wounds. This leads to a theoretical approach by Julia Kristeva that can be regarded as crucial in the picaresque representation of gender constitution: In her essay *Pouvoirs de l'horreur*, written in 1980, Kristeva analyzes the mechanism of abjection. Among other things, the abject is described as body fluids which cause disgust and nausea, but which are vitally important for the organism's survival. The paradox of abjection is that it enables the body to remain healthy, on the one hand, and that it reminds the body of its own boundaries and its transience, on the other. The abject is neither subject nor object, as Kristeva states: "Pas moi. Pas ça. Mas pas rien non plus. Un 'quelque chose'" ("Not me, not that. But not nothing, either. A 'something' that I do not recognize as a thing") (Kristeva 1980: 10). In the picaresque aesthetics, fecal imaginary and scatological speech are omnipresent and can be related to Kristeva's thoughts on abjection. Cruz distinguishes two ways of abjection that both belong to the gendered order. First, the abjection of the *pícaro* himself as being a non-hegemonic, liminal male "something" which is visually demonstrated by his contamination with all kinds of body fluids. Second, the abjection of the feminine, which is not only constitutive for the pícaro's precarious masculinity (cf. Schuhen 2018), but for the constitution and the continuation of the patriarchal system depicted in the picaresque novel as well:

> The patriarchal system in which [the pícaro] remains enclosed is paradoxically supported by its rejection of the other, by its abjection, not only of [the pícaro] but, conspicuously, of the feminine. As scapegoat for the social ills of the time, [the pícaro] shares with the abjected feminine what Kristeva names the embodiment of the remainder; that is, that which escapes symbolic identification, and which is emphasized in the later picaresque narratives' profuse scatological references (Cruz 1999: 131).

In the passage from *Guzmán*, neither the pícaro or the mother nor any other female character is stigmatized with purulent wounds and syphilitic tumors. The excerpt belongs to the long reflective, mostly moralistic passages that constitute more than half of the novel. The narrator therefore explicitly informs his readers about general social problems in a rather abstract, almost sociological manner. It is the "mocito engomado" or the "afeminado marica" who is in the focus, thus a 'queer' figure *avant la lettre*, or at least a male character who did not perform the abjection of femininity successfully, but rather integrates female practices and desires in the conception of his male identity. Once more this indicates that the feminine or the queer is regarded as a threat to the formation of masculinity or, generally speaking, to the patriarchal system itself: Feminization automatically leads to abjection – a misogynist stereotype that is not only valid for premodern gender configurations. Therefore, transgressions of boundaries between the sexes are sanctioned as long as male-to-female switching is concerned, because male-to-female marks a synonym of social degradation, as Timo Kehren observes in his contribution to this volume. We will consider the queerness of the picaresque figure and its consequences in this book.

EUROPEAN HEIRS

So far, we have exclusively discussed the Spanish picaresque novel, which was adapted quite early in France and England, where the transmission was altered by intermingling with other genres so that we can speak of semi- or neo-picaresque texts (Bauer 1994). The French version of Quevedo's *Buscon* by Sieur de La Geneste shows some modifications of the genre which, as such, greatly influenced the European picaresque tradition. The English picaresque novel – or the rogue novel – can be considered as a genre of its own that was especially popular in the 18th century. It already started as an original genre with Thomas Nashe's *The Unfortunate Traveller* in 1594. In contrast, the early modern German picaresque novel was adapted and translated relatively late. The first translation of *Lazarillo* into German is a manuscript dating from the year 1614; a newer, printed version dates from 1617. The much modified German *Gusman* by Aegidius Albertinus was published in 1615, and *Buscón* did not appear in German until 1671 by Johann Michael Moscherosch, based on the French *Buscon*.

As we are dealing with intricate traditions and as these texts have been adapted to the German cultural context and set new accents in various respects, they deserve special attention by German literary historians. Especially the relevance of picaresque texts as media of the reformation and counter-reformation leads to a disambiguation of the picaresque narrator, who is, more or less credibly, chastened and has converted to Catholicism at the end. In addition, the picaresque encounters already existing literary traditions, like early German printed jest books, for instance *Dil Ulenspiegel*, and a widespread jester literature (*Narrenliteratur*), which preceded and influenced the reception of the picaresque novel. Hans Rudolf Velten discusses this German pre-history of the picaresque and the interconnections with the jest novel to question the thesis that masculinity is weakly marked and to ask how gender relations and sexuality shape the male protagonist.

However, an original German picaresque tradition did not start until 1668, when Johann Jacob Christoph von Grimmelshausen's *Simplicissimus* – which has only a few picaresque traits – and Hieronymus Dürer's *Lauf der Welt und Spiel des Glücks* were published, soon followed by Grimmelshausen's *Courasche* in 1699 (*Courasche* of course refers to *Pícara Justina*). The novel primarily deals with female sex and gender in any respect and shows the transgressive and subversive potential of the picaresque handling of gender. We encounter a female narrator who has lived in sin and in the end regrets nothing. Concerning the male picaresque figure, many aspects of the Spanish picaresque novel also appear in German picaresque texts, although we confront modifications of the genre formula (Bauer 1994). These aspects will be discussed in the following in connection with Hieronymus Dürer's *Lauf der Welt und Spiel des Glücks*.

Once again, the male pícaro remains rather volatile, for masculinity appears as a performative category. Where Dürer's anti-hero Tychander shows traits of a picaresque figure, hardly any markers of gender are visible. Tychander is at the mercy of Fortuna and suffers physically from her ups and downs (Heßelmann 2007), but his body is sexually unmarked. While the female figures are fixed according to current ascriptions to femininity like gentleness and fickleness and are staged as beautiful, physically attractive women, a male physicality or physical masculinity remains elusive. We learn from a story within the story that Tychander's father even manages the typical early modern cross-dressing – which is also performed in Grimmelshausen's *Simplicissimus*. He can easily pretend to be a pregnant woman simply by putting on women's clothes and a pillow. "Er verkleite sich in weibes-kleidern und weil ihm doch von natur der bart langsam wuchse / soo ließ er die wenigen milchhaar / die noch übrig waren / mit einem schwermeßer vollends abnehmen." ("He disguised himself in women's clothes and because his beard was sparse by nature / he had the few fine hairs / that still showed / shaved off with a shear knife.") (Dürer 1984: 116). What marks his manhood is the barely expressed physical sign of the beard – which can simply be shaved off. The father also puts on makeup. But this is not necessarily to pretend femininity. The pale face merely insinuates that he is not feeling well. So pretending to be pregnant and sick requires a greater effort than pretending to be feminine Again, gender is staged as a performative category restricted to men. Women are marked as such, and they are object of othering, which is the topic of Grimmelshausen's *Courasche*. But, ultimately, her sex is staged to be undermined in the novel. Maren Lickhardt focuses on the female picaresque figure Courage in Grimmelshausen's novel and shows how she not only transcends gender norms as a self-determined subject but is also the object or result of male ascriptions and valuations.

If we ask more precisely what shapes the masculinity of *Tychander*, it gets more complicated. The novel mixes various genres, which significantly impacts the staging of the sexes. In fact, we encounter a hybridization of the picaresque, historical, chivalric, and pastoral novel in which the genres not only overlap but comment on each other (Mayer 1970, Unsicker 1974: 226). Only where chivalric narration dominates in the text, the main character performs masculinity. Through forms of gallantry, Tychander stabilizes his gender role, which simultaneously means that the picaresque is challenged as a genre by other genres. Only when the genre comes into motion, the sex of the figure is fixed against the background of a heteronormative framework, whereby the latter is never transgressed or subverted as such (cf. Lickhardt 2016). But sex is not only fixed in terms of stereotypical male practices and behavior. It also becomes disambiguous because the picaresque figure now has sexual relationships with women, from farce-like affairs to romantic love stories. Tychander is not only definitely not impotent, but also even possessed by love (Mayer 1970: 30). "Diesem nach wurde ich nicht von der liebe algemach eingenommen / sondern plözlich überfallen / und zwar mit solcher macht / daß ich nicht wuste / was ich weiter antworten solte / und stund eine weile ganz erstarret und gleichsam entzückt und betrachtete mit verwundern dieses kunst-stücke der Natur." ("In this way I was not captured gradually by love / but ambushed by it /indeed with such force / that I did not know what to answer / and stood thunderstruck and at the same time enraptured and regarding these wonders of nature with amazement.") (Dürer 1984: 208). And love is not a flash in the pan. It leads to a desire for stabilization, "the virtue of constancy, which is totally foreign to the picaro [...]. With love he announces most emphatically his intention to be at home in the world" (Mayer 1970: 30).

Overall, it is remarkable that gender relations extend the more basic picaresque body discourse of hunger and other corporeal requirements. Sexuality in many senses of the word belongs to Tychander and forms a strong motif that underlies the notion of just surviving. The struggle for survival supports and from time to time is replaced by the struggle for sexual or romantic contact, which might not only result from genre transgression and hybridization but also allegorizes them. Moreover, the genre mixing means that Tychander develops a memory, which is the first step for a general personal development (Friedrich 2014).

In the German picaresque novels, the transgression and subversion of role models go hand in hand with those of genre. As this can be described as a process of 'becoming bourgeois' (Hirsch 1979), it corresponds with figures that are socially less limited than the ones in the Spanish picaresque novel – which obviously leads to a wider range of masculine registers. Dürer delivers just one example that shows the dynamics of the picaresque universe, where all parameters are fleeting, being transgressive and subversive in dynamic interrelations. Gender is only one of the categories questioned and challenged. Alexandra Schamel discusses in this volume to what extent the pícaresque practice of dissimulation is reactivated in

Marivaux's novel *La Vie de Marianne*; she conceives the domesticated female body as a set of masks of authenticity, playing with the indexical codes of established discourses and genre differentiation. Here, the subversion of the protean male body of the pícaro is transformed into a non-readable mask of authenticity which exceeds gender. In a different approach to genre blending in the 18th-century English picaresque novel, Jens Elze troubles the transgression of female gender roles in a comparative study of Daniel Defoe's *Moll Flanders* and Tobias Smollet's *Roderick Random*. Whereas the casuistry of sex and gender schemes in *Moll Flanders* continues the precarious picaresque forms, Smollet's *Roderick Random* shows a similar stability in order to enforce satirical and genre transformation and classification.

Returning to later examples in German Literature, Hans-Joachim Jakob focuses on picaresque elements in Wilhelm Raabe's *Lorenz Scheibenhart* and *Aus dem Lebensbuch des Schulmeisterleins Michel Haas*. Jakob shows how the masculine identity of the itinerant vagrant is stabilized and destabilized by the intermingling of different genres, which appears as a travestying form of the pícaro novel which becomes highly dysfunctional in an age dominated by historicism. Matthias Bauer, concluding the volume, follows the tracks of the German and English picaresque novel from the 17th to the 20th century – e.g. John Barth' *The Sot-Weed Factor*, Irmtraud Morgner's *Leben und Abenteuer der Trobadora Beatriz nach Zeugnissen ihrer Spielfrau Laura* – to show how the inverted world of each different German and American picaresque variation reveals the contingency of gender constructions, which simultaneously leads to a liberation of gender roles and to gender trouble.

Bibliography

Alemán, Mateo. *Guzmán de Alfarache*. 2 volumes. Ed. José María Micó. Madrid 2010 (vol. 2), 2012 (vol. 1).
Bauer, Matthias. *Im Fuchsbau der Geschichten. Anatomie des Schelmenromans*. Stuttgart/Weimar 1993.
Bauer, Matthias. *Der Schelmenroman*. Stuttgart, Weimar 1994.
Covarrubias Horozco, Sebastián de. *Tesoro de la lengua castellana o española*. Madrid 1611.
Cruz, Anne J. *Discourses of Poverty. Social Reform and the Picaresque Novel in Early Modern Spain*. Toronto 1999.
Dürer, Hieronymus. *Lauf der Welt und Spiel des Glücks* [1668]. Hildesheim 1984.

Friedrich, Udo. "Wahrheit und Wahrscheinlichkeit. Zur Paradigmatik und Syntagmatik des Glücks in Hieronymus Dürers *Lauf der Welt und Spiel des Glücks*." *Syntagma des Pikaresken*. Ed. Jan Mohr and Michael Waltenberger. Heidelberg 2014. 315–347.

Heßelmann, Peter. "Picaro und Fortuna. Zur narrativen Technik in Hieronymus Dürers *Lauf der Welt Und Spiel des Glücks* und Grimmelshausens *Simplicissimus Teutsch*." *Simpliciana* 29 (2007): 101–118.

Hirsch, Arnold. *Bürgertum und Barock im deutschen Roman. Ein Beitrag zur Entstehungsgeschichte des bürgerlichen Weltbildes*. Köln, Wien 1979.

Kristeva, Julia. *Pouvoirs de l'horreur. Essai sur l'abjection*. Paris 1980.

Lickhardt, Maren. "Gattungshybridisierung und Geschlechterausdifferenzierung in Hieronymus Dürers Schelmenroman *Lauf der Welt und Spiel des Glücks* (1668)." *Simpliciana* 38 (2016): 562–576.

Mayer, Jürgen. *Mischformen barocker Erzählkunst. Zwischen pikareskem und höfisch-historischem Roman*. München 1970.

Schuhen, Gregor. *Vir inversus. Männlichkeiten im spanischen Schelmenroman*. Bielefeld 2018.

Solomon, Michael. *The Literature of Misogyny in Medieval Spain. The Arcipreste de Talavera and the Spill*, Cambridge 1997.

Unsicker, Karin. *Weltliche Barockprosa in Schleswig-Holstein*. Neumünster 1974.

The Parent Trap

Mothers and Others in the Spanish Picaresque

ANNE J. CRUZ

Although the genealogy of the Spanish picaresque novel has been ascribed to various literary traditions, such as St Augustine's *Confessions* and saints' lives, and as a forebear of the *bildungsroman* or formation novel (Stone 1998: 371), its purpose as social satire has never been in doubt (cf. Guillén 1971). While the novel's main protagonist often assumes a solitary position alienated from society, the plots themselves abound with multiple characters, beginning with the pícaro's own birth parents, whom the protagonists inevitably satirize and deride. Following the *bildungsroman* convention by starting with what has been called their "pre-history" (Rico 1984: 64), the Spanish novels give primary narrative space to the reporting by the pícaros of their degraded parentage. Indeed, the outsider's family origins are considered of such import that the various Spanish novels that constitute the genre – from the anonymous *Lazarillo de Tormes* to the pseudonymous *Estebanillo González*; and, in the female picaresque, from Francisco Delicado's *Lozana andaluza* to the seventeenth-century courtesan novels whose protagonists perform as pícaras – all have the narrator begin by reciting his or her genealogy. Lázaro is the only one who vocalizes his purpose for doing so: "Your Honour has written to me to ask me to tell him my story in some detail" (Alpert 1969: 26) ("Y pues Vuestra Merced escribe se le escriba y relate el caso muy por extenso") (1987: 10).[1] He clarifies why he will narrate his life from its beginning: "I think I'd better start at the beginning, not in the middle, so that you may know all about me" Alpert 1969: 26) ("parecióme no tomalle or el medio, sino del principio, porque se tenga entera noticia de mi persona") (1987: 10-11). Although Francisco Rico has attributed this beginning to Lazarillo's

---

1   All translations by AC.

canny defense (Rico 1987: 9-16), as we will see, the "case" as presented serves also to satirize and disparage conventional family and social values.

Throughout Lázaro's telling of his life, from the earliest episode with the blind man in Salamanca to his employment with the Archpriest in Toledo, where he acts as cover-up to the master's adulterous relationship, Lázaro blames his miscreant behavior on the abuse he received as a child, detailing how his parents and his masters mistreated him. The picaresque novels that follow incorporate as part of their protagonists' family history the same trauma of childhood abuse. According to Edward Behrend-Martínez, "early modern Spanish culture defined child abuse as 1) violence that permanently scarred a child's body, 2) the material neglect of a child (food and clothing), and/or 3) an authority other than a parent who employed illegitimate violence against a child." (2014: 251-52). While physical violence was perceived as abuse only by non-blood relations, since parents had the right to castigate their children, the material neglect by fathers was taken very seriously. As his pre-history alleges, Lazarillo endured both physical suffering from his masters and abusive neglect from his parents. As a rhetorical ploy, the anonymous author's beginning with the protagonist's family origins is closely aligned with the familiar genealogical trope of literary birth, which Cervantes will later parody when he calls *Don Quixote* not his son, but his stepson (cf. Cruz 2014). While the novels of chivalry – a genre whose male heroes never stop propagating sequels and clearly lampooned as well by *Lazarillo* – celebrate exotic elements and royal births, the narrators-pícaros instead claim authority by identifying both parents by their common toponyms. Picaresque novels thus mock the many proliferating tales of Spanish knights, whose generative function was intended to ensure both the fiction's heroic heritage and, beyond the individual narratives, their literary continuity.

Unlike the chivalric novels' textual obsession to engender literary progeny, the picaresque genre contrasts its own proliferation and popularity with the young protagonists' mistreatment and abandonment. The paternity satirized by the genre thus retains a social, and not merely a genetic function, as Lacan asserts: "the attribution of procreation to the father can only be the effect of a pure signifier [...] not of a real father, but of what religion has taught us to refer to as the Name of the Father" (1977: 199). Lazarillo goes so far as to invalidate not only his biological father's name, rejecting his patronymic "González" and calling himself "de Tormes".[2] As the first Spanish picaresque novel, *Lazarillo de Tormes* initiates the genre's convention of simultaneously claiming and ques-

---

2 Although several names have been proposed for its author, the book itself elides the author's name, and remains anonymous to this day.

tioning its paternal pedigree. In the novel, the name of the father is erased by the many male masters that usurp the father's place. Lázaro paints a highly ambiguous portrait of his biological father, who, he tells us, is falsely accused of being a thief and who courageously goes to war as a muleteer. His ironic discourse, however, implies otherwise: the father is not only a thief and a coward, but most likely a Morisco, as the occupation of muleteer was held mainly by this group. Lázaro's dubiously Moorish father is then substituted by an actual one: the Moor Zaide takes over the role as his stepfather, another thief whose petty crimes, unwittingly denounced by a still-innocent Lazarillo, land him in jail. The *pícaro*'s unreliable narration nonetheless informs us that since his birth, Lazarillo is surrounded by debased male figures, such as his father and his masters, all of whom end up abusing him. However, they furnish him with an excellent rogue's education: the mistreated child soon transforms into an amoral and cynical adult who will know better than to tell the truth. While its protagonist produces no offspring of his own, this radical – and radically new – novel engendered two sequels, also titled *Lazarillo*, and, in less than fifty years, would also spawn an unlikely "monster" of a novel.[3]

The first edition of Mateo Alemán's *Guzmán de Alfarache*, whose Part I was published in 1599, was followed nine weeks later by the reedition of *Lazarillo*'s expurgated 1573 version, thereby launching *Lazarillo*'s fame as a picaresque novel (Ruan 2011: 32). The birth of *Guzmán* through *Lazarillo*'s rebirth thus twice tropes the paternal metaphor, as Alemán's novel assigns its protagonist two fathers. Indeed, Guzmán praises his mother for serving two masters: "she pleased two gentlemen equally [...]. Both acknowledged me as their son: one called me thus, and so did the other" ("agradó igualmente a dos señores [...]. Ambos me conocieron por hijo: el uno me lo llamaba y el otro también") (2006: I.157).[4] Yet neither of the two fathers performs his paternal duty: Guzmán's legal father – his mother's aged, cuckolded husband – dies too soon to take care of

---

3 The anonymous *Segunda parte de Lazarillo de Tormes* was published in 1555 in Antwerp, followed in 1612 by the Protestant Juan de Luna's *Segunda parte de Lazarillo de Tormes*, published in Paris. Alemán's awareness of his book's "monstruosity" is evinced in Guzman's narration of the story of the hermaphrodite monster of Ravenna (2006: I.141. Such births were believed to predicate social disruptions (Covarrubias 1943: 812).

4 The novel produced an illegitimate second part by a pseudonymous author, Mateo Luján de Sayavedra. Recently, the authorship of this apocryphal novel has been attributed to the Valencian professor and printer, Juan Felipe Mey (cf. Laguna Fernández 2012: 18).

the boy through adolescence. His biological father, moreover, functions as a negative role model, as he embodies all the social evils that apparently had befallen Spain. A Genoese *converso* and merchant swindler who, on fleeing from the authorities, is taken captive by Moors to Algiers, he reneges his Christian faith and becomes a Muslim. After marrying a wealthy Muslim woman, he steals her jewelry and monies, abandoning her to return to Spain, where he reconverts to Catholicism. In line with his devious behavior, his effeminate looks are heatedly defended by Guzmán, whose ironic description, however, belies his assurance of their natural beauty, with no help from cosmetic aids:

He had large, turquoise-colored eyes. He wore a high pompadour with long curls by his temples [...]. If it's true he applied creams and cosmetics, and that his white teeth and hands, praised by so many, were due to powders, astringents, soaps, and other filth, I'll confess to everything you say about him and turn into his worst enemy [...] since these are doings of effeminate queers.

(Traía los ojos grandes, turquesados. Traía copete y sienes ensortijadas [...] Si es verdad que se valía de untos y artificios, que los dientes y manos, que tanto le loaban era a poder de polvillos, hieles, jabonetes y otras porquerías, confesaréte cuanto dél dijeres y seré su capital enemigo [...] pues son actos de afeminados maricas.) (Alemán 2006: 140).

In spite of his implied homosexuality, the father aggressively seduces Guzmán's mother in a scene worthy of a tale from Boccaccio's *Decameron* (cf. Ricapito 2002: 128). Born of this adulterous relationship, Guzmán sets about rejecting his progenitor's name (which is never mentioned in the novel) to assume his mother's purported surname: the lofty-sounding Guzmán, the family name of the prominent dukes of Medina Sidonia, grandees of Spain (cf. Giles 2013). Like *Lazarillo de Tormes*, whose protagonist is given as his oxymoronic toponym, the river over which he was born, Guzmán adds "de Alfarache," the name of the Edenic garden where he was adulterously conceived. Ironically, the garden's luxurious surroundings are admired in the novel for their recreational value, masking Mateo Alemán's censure of such aristocratic playgrounds, as their fallow lands contributed to Spain's agricultural crisis.[5]

---

5   An estimated 40% decrease in Castilian cereal production had been due to poor harvests, adverse weather and depopulation, with the grain price index reaching its highest level between 1598 and 1601 (cf. García Sanz 1995). The crisis, which also seriously affected grain prices in Andalucía, when the *Guzmán*'s Part I was published,

In another, perhaps unwitting critique of the aristocracy, the novel's eponymous title was soon disregarded by its readers in favor of Guzmán's epithet of "pícaro," the name by which the book also became known. As pícaros, Lazarillo and Guzmán mirrored the uselessness and sterility of their low social position, even as their narratives gave impetus to the genre's continuation. Shortly after the *Guzmán*'s publication, a young Francisco de Quevedo wrote his own picaresque novel, bombastically titled *Historia de la vida del Buscón, llamado Don Pablos, ejemplo de vagamundos y espejo de tacaños* (*History of the life of the Swindler, called Don Pablos, model for hobos and mirror of misers*). Quevedo chose not to imitate his predecessors' cunning critique of those in power, but instead selected his own subversive mode of social criticism, excoriating social climbers. The pícaro's paternity, therefore, remained at stake: the *Buscón*'s prehistory begins by condemning the father as a thief, a drunkard, a cuckold, and a converso, as his mother does not deny the insult thrown at him of being a son of a whore and witch ("hijo de una puta y una hechicera") (2005: 70). Taking his father's surname as his first, he pluralizes it to Pablos in an attempt to hide his converso origins, alluding ironically to the redemptive conversion of Saul into the apostle and evangelist Paul (*Acts* 9:4-6). Rejected by Pablos for his despicable office of hangman, his uncle displaces the pícaro's father by hanging and quartering him. Quevedo's contempt of conversos is revealed by the narrative's portrayal of Pablos as a Christological figure: the son's refusal to consume his father's remains in a meat pie informs the narrative with sacrilegious Eucharistic significance, as he cannot escape the stain of converso blood foisted on him by the author.

The picaresque's fatalistic worldview is enforced by the father figures that embody corrupt patriarchal society and by the protagonists who subsume the characteristics of their debased progenitors. The mother figure in the picaresque, however, has tended to be overlooked by critics, despite her substantial narrative function. Her lack comes about because the theme of motherhood itself – whether in literature or in actual social settings – endured in a constant state of anxiety and ambivalence. Although moralists held virginity to be a woman's greatest virtue, its elevation to a higher state than marriage did not diminish the necessity to procreate in a society that was continuously vulnerable to depopulation. Marian devotion stressed motherhood through the Virgin's own role as mother of God, acknowledging childbirth and childrearing of utmost importance to the aristocracy and royal families, since descendants were needed for inheritance purposes,

---

spurred economists to urge for an increase in agricultural labor and production (cf. Cruz 1999: 91-92).

and marriages arranged with the woman's potential fertility in mind. This need was also visited on the emerging middle class, but not on the poor, who were the overwhelming majority in early modern Spain. Even if, as Teófilo Ruiz rightly states, infant mortality and death by childbirth struck the rich and poor evenly, childbirth proved far more of a burden on the latter (2014: 167). Like Lazarillo's mother, impoverished women were often abandoned by their children's father, complicating their finding work and pushing them into deeper poverty. Possible solutions were either methods of abortion or infant abandonment (*expósitos*), and it is at this time that the majority of hospitals for foundlings are opened, such as those of the Piedra in Toledo in 1499, the Hospital de Niños Expósitos in Burgos in 1525, and the Inclusa in Madrid in 1579 (cf. Sherwood 1988).

Because abortion and child abandonment were viewed as shameful and condemned by moralists, however, there was great reticence in the cultural imaginary to deal openly with anti-maternal and, by extension, anti-family behavior.[6] Even when depicted as protective, maternal images carried traces of the bad mother – what Freud would later call the phallic or castrating mother – awakening anxiety-producing emotions that then necessitated containment. Medieval Spanish songbook lyrics, for example, often elaborated on a daughter's amorous confessions to a loving, albeit vigilant mother (Walters 2002: 108). References to the figure of Medea in chivalric novels highlight her magical powers and books; when she is depicted for her vindictiveness, it is Jason who is blamed for his cruelty (cf. Campos García Rojas 2011). Even in folktales and ballads, women who are spiteful toward children are depicted as stepmothers, not birth mothers. The compulsion to exalt maternal virtue was reinvigorated by the visual arts, which extended positive features to both parents. The image of the Holy Family gained importance during the Renaissance, as it mirrored the Counter Reformation concept of both the Holy Trinity and the Holy Family. Two versions of the Holy Family were frequently represented: the Virgin and Christ child with St Anne, and the Virgin, Christ child, and St Joseph. This second version granted St Joseph increasing importance: earlier depictions, in fact, had portrayed Joseph as an old man, negating his biological parentage to Christ (cf. Chorpenning 1997). By the seventeenth century, as St. Joseph became equally as important as Mary, he was depicted as a younger, more virile man. Yet in both representations, Mary's bond with her infant son retained the greatest power.

Against this backdrop of both an idealized and socialized motherhood, Lazarillo's narrative surely takes the unsuspecting reader by surprise. Among the

---

6 An exception is Lope de Vega's play, *El hierro de Madrid*, which deals with a pregnant woman who is unmarried besides (cf. Sánchez 2015).

many revolutionary aspects of this tale, not least its first person narrative, is the blasphemous depiction of an *unholy* family. Having already signposted his thievery and cowardliness, the narrative discharges the father early on, leaving Lazarillo's mother to bring the impious comparison to completion. After living in sin with Lazarillo's father, Antona Pérez breaks Alphonsine law by procreating with an infidel. When the Moor is tortured, she moves on, by implication, to a life of prostitution. No mention is made again of the child she has had with Zaide; her worst behavior, therefore, is evinced when she gives away her older child to the blind man. This episode is seen by some critics as a heartbreaking moment; Pilar Puig Mares describes the incident in these terms: "The scene of the separation between Lazaro and his mother moves us by its force and restrained emotion" (2000: 38), and María V. Jordán Arroyo also interprets the mother's last words to her son as sincerely felt (2010: 143). When approaching the novel ironically, however, it is difficult for the reader not to accept the mother's tears as a charade meant to disguise her urge to quickly get rid of the boy: "I know I will never see you again. Try and be good and may God guide you. I've raised you as best I know and I've put you with a good master. Now you must look after yourself" (1969: 27) (Hijo, sé que no te veré más. Procura ser bueno y Dios te guíe. Criado te he y con buen amo te he puesto: válete por ti) (1987: 22).

Like the Moor Zaide, who only apparently jokes to his son, "your mother's a whore" (*hideputa*) (1969: 26), in order to reveal the truth, the mother's parting words, voiced indirectly by an unreliable narrator, connote exactly the opposite of a loving mother's lament, as Lazarillo will have no choice with the blind man but to survive by his wits. Similarly to Lázaro's other recollections, this episode is sufficiently ambiguous to ask whether it might be yet another ploy on his part to manipulate the reader's sympathies. While not as physically cruel as exposing a newborn on church steps – and quite possibly introducing the author's criticism of the practice of sending off young children as apprentices or servants to abusive masters – the mother's abandonment of her child is a sign of maternal lack, especially because she hands him to a folkloric type well known for extreme callousness toward young guides. Lázaro's relations with all women – from his mother to his wife – are therefore negatively marked from the outset. Lazarillo's adulterous wife substitutes metonymically for his absent mother, since by conflating the wife's sexual excess with her desertion of her three children, the novel retraces the mother's behavior: both his mother and his wife assume the dual roles of prostitute and unnatural mother (cf. Cruz 2010: 8-9).

The picaresque novel's focus on the maternal imago in shaping the protagonist's behavior is most evinced in the *Guzmán de Alfarache,* despite the pícaro's imitation of his father's proclivities. As we have seen, Guzmán is conceived through the mother's immoral sexual relations with the merchant reprobate, which determines his actions throughout his life. Her prehistory harks back to her grandmother's ability to trick men into believing that each was her daughter's biological father: "If my mother tricked two, my grandmother tricked two dozen [...]. With this daughter, she claimed a hundred lineages, swearing to each father that she was his, and each one believed it" (Si mi madre enredó a dos, mi abuela dos docenas. [...] Con esta hija enredó cien linajes, diciendo y jurando a cada padre que era suya; y a todos les parecía" (2006: I.160). Unlike Lazarillo, whose mother soon left him with no emotional or material support, Guzmán is spoiled and indulged by his mother, who has lavishly fed the young boy all sorts of delicacies. The food metaphors thinly conceal the powerful character of a devouring, phallic mother. Guzmán leaves his maternal house, he tells us, because his mother can no longer support him, as she has spent all the inheritance left by the old gentleman and is now too old to prostitute herself. Yet when he abandons her, he cries "rivers of tears" (dos Nilos reventaron de mis ojos) (2006: I. 163-64).

Moralists like Juan Luis Vives claimed that good mothers should not spoil their children; Vives insisted they must forsake their inclination to nurture and coddle them, and gives his own mother as an example of a mother who never demonstrated her love (cf. Bergmann 1992: 130). Psychoanalysts perceive the force behind such apparent maternal abnegation: Justine Chasseguet-Smirgel, for instance, sustains that the child "will maintain a terrifying maternal image in his unconscious, the result of projected hostility deriving from his own impotence" (1998: 121). Fully understanding the paradox posed by Vives's and other moralists' claims, Alemán created a mother whose excess of maternal devotion instead stands for a manifestation of her lack, one that, as in Lazarillo's case, will carry over in Guzmán's own dysfunctional relations with women. His diatribe in Part II against women who marry for money anticipates the fundamental cause of his own marriages' undoing: of his first wife, he complains that

[she] was a spendthrift, improvident, extravagant, used to seeing me come always, laden with gifts. [...] When there was no more to eat nor where to find it, we had to sell our possessions. [...] She could no longer stand me. She came to hate me, as if I was her worst enemy.

(Era gastadora, franca, liberal, enseñada siempre a verme venir como abeja, cargado de regalos. [...] Cuando no habiendo qué comer ni adónde salirlo a buscar, se sacaban de casa las prendas para vender [...] Nunca más me pudo ver. Aborrecióme, como si fuera su enemigo verdadero) (2006: II.384).

Yet when Guzmán widows, he marries yet again, this time to an innkeeper's daughter who is actively trying to marry off her own daughters for pecuniary purposes.

The mother's role as procuress of her own children will be exploited by the female picaresque in such novels as Alonso de Salas Barbadillo's *La hija de la Celestina y la ingeniosa Elena*[7] and Alonso de Castillo Solórzano's *Las harpías en Madrid*. These novels trace their origins to the old bawd, Celestina, in *La tragicomedia de Calisto y Melibea*, whose invention of "whoring virgins,"[8] as Jean Dangler so well puts it, is highly incriminating, as it shows the go-between's ability to deceive and disrupt social stability (2001: 114). Go-betweens are not mothers, however, and as grievous as Celestina's behavior is, it does not achieve the same perversity as the later picaresque novels, in which biological mothers actually attempt to sell (and resell) their daughters to the highest bidders. One example is that of Elena's Moorish mother, Zara, known by the slave name of María, and like Celestina, a witch and a hymen mender. Fittingly named after the infamous old bawd, she mends her daughter's hymen three times in order to sell her to rich husbands: "I was sold three times as a virgin: the first, to a rich ecclesiastic, the second, to a titled lord, and the third to a Genoese who paid the most and ate the least" (Tres veces fui vendida por virgen: la primera a un eclesiástico rico, la segunda a un señor de título, la tercera a un ginovés que pagó mejor y comió peor) (1983: 47). The mother's efforts are doubled in Alonso de Castillo Solórzano's *Las harpías en Madrid*, where a crone recommends to Teodora, the penurious mother of two attractive young daughters, to move from Seville to Madrid to try her luck at placing them as courtesans:

Heaven gave you two daughters that, were they mine, with such beauty as they've been given, I would find in each one a Potosí silver mine of riches; no, that's not enough, an entire Indies of silver, pearls, gold, and precious stones, which is what one can get with beauty.

---

7 The novel was first published in 1612 as *La hija de Celestina* and as *La ingeniosa Elena* in 1614. I cite from the Fraderas edition, "doubled and synthesized", as he calls it. For its publication history, see García Santo-Tomás 2008: 186-87.

8 "When the French ambassador was here she sold him the same servant girl three times as a virgin" (quando vino por aquí el embaxador francés, tres vezes vendió por virgen una criada que tenía) (cited in Dangler 2001: 115).

(Diote el cielo dos hijas que, a ser mías, con la hermosura de que las ha dotado, pensara llevar en cada una de ellas un Potosí de riquezas; poco he dicho, una India entera con plata, perlas, oro y piedras preciosas, que esto se alcanza con la belleza) (1985: 48).

Despite its comparison to exquisite treasures, the young girls' beauty, exploited for its sexual commerce by the mother, becomes nothing more than sordid capital.

In the *Guzmán*, such mothers serve as a warning to men of predatory women who marry solely for their material gain, demeaning its sacramental value. But the *Guzmán* also repeats the demeaning lesson from the *Lazarillo*: he becomes a pimp to his second wife, who, in full irony, is named Gracia ('grace').[9] Guzmán's return to Seville with this second wife to exploit the "peruleros" or those who returned rich from Peru, retraces his initial departure from the city, as he again passes by the hermitage of St. Lazarus. Most important, however, is that by returning to Seville, the place of his birth, he is drawn to find his mother, yet his search uncovers a repulsive reality that he had not expected: "I found her emaciated, old, toothless, wrinkled, and her appearance entirely changed" (Halléla flaca, vieja, sin dientes, arrugada y muy otra en su parecer; 2006: II.462). According to Roger Scruton, Mary's images are a tribute to human beauty: the Virgin is "a woman whose sexual maturity is expressed in motherhood and who yet remains untouchable, barely distinguishable, as an object of veneration." The Virgin's beauty, he states, symbolizes purity, distinct from the realm of sexual appetite. He argues that the notion harks back to the Platonic concept of beauty, not solely an invitation to desire, but also a call to renounce it (Scruton 2011: 45). The mother's physiognomy contrasts with the many Renaissance portraits of the Virgin Mary, who even when depicted as the crucified Christ's grieving mother, reflects an unassailable spiritual beauty. By contrast, Guzmán's mother displays the signs of defilement and old age; she is a symbol of female corruption, both external and interiorized.

If, in *Lazarillo de Tormes*, the pícaro's mother vanishes only to be supplanted by his wife, Guzmán's mother has passed the age of sexual attraction, deteriorating into the visual specter of a witch. Literalizing their mirror image, both his wife and mother come face to face: in keeping with her aberrant past, Guzmán's mother immediately begins to teach the wife how to attract the right kind of client for a prostitute. The duplication of mother and daughter-in-law soon diverges, however, as the wife leaves Guzmán for a sea captain, taking along their jewels and money, her actions serving as a reminder, in reverse gender, of Guz-

---

9   Regarding the irony of the name Gracia see Kehren (this volume).

mán's father's desertion of his Moorish wife. Guzmán's life thus comes full circle: he now remains with his mother only to be abandoned by her, as she sets up shop with a young prostitute, repeating the life cycle of the aging prostitute who then becomes a procuress. In both Lazarillo's and Guzmán's case, in spite of the abundance of paternal figures and the son's Oedipal entry into the world of the father, the *pícaros* are unable to detach themselves from their pre-Oedipal relationship with the mother, whose desexualizing control keeps the sons from sustaining any kind of mature relationship with women.

The force field of the phallic mother will be intensified in Quevedo's picaresque novel, *El buscón*. Pablos's mother is not only suspected of having converso or Moorish blood, her literary ancestry again descends from the old bawd, Celestina:

She was rumored to be able to construct virgins [...] Some said she could arrange any pleasure, others called her a satisfier of unsatisfied desires [...] and others, on the bad side, a procuress and a hole in the pocket for everybody's money (1969: 86).

(Hubo fama que reedificaba doncellas [...] Unos la llamaban "zurzidora de gustos", otros "algebrista de voluntades desconcertadas" [...] Para unos era tercera, primera para otros, y flux para los dineros de todos) (2006: 64-65).

The mother's emasculation of the father is clear when she claims to have sustained him economically through her witch's arts. Her hold on Pablos is equally so strong that he is taken *for* his mother by others: when he is seen wearing a plumed hat, the vegetable sellers throw turnips at him, making him cry out that he is not his mother. Just as he never breaks away from his paternal origins, he is unable to shake off his maternal attachment. Like the two pícaros he emulates, Quevedo's Pablos cannot develop any lasting relationship with women; his attempts to court women are fated to fail, and his only successful connection with a woman occurs in the final episode with the prostitute Grajales, who dresses Pablos in her clothing.[10] In contrast to his claims to the vegetable sellers, he has indeed been transgendered into a duplicate of his mother, with whom he shares the underworld life of a pícaro. The novel's ending, at which point Pablos admits to the failure of his plans in abandoning Spain, his mother country, for a new and supposedly better world, just as he is impeded from operating any change in

---

10 The name Grajales may allude to the bird "graja" or crow, which is supposed to represent conformity in marriage (Covarrubias 1943: 358).

himself, confirms the plot's circularity and the impossibility of breaking with his past.

For these three pícaros, then, as for the pícaras, the phallic mother never fully disappears from the narrative. Although she may physically abandon the child, she remains a symbolic presence in the adult pícaro's imaginary order, blocking any attempt at establishing relationships with others. Surely influenced by these early modern novels, the most graphic example of a pícaro's unbreakable bond with the maternal imago appears almost four hundred years later in Camilo José Cela's *La familia de Pascual Duarte* (*The Family of Pascual Duarte*), published in 1942 and banned shortly afterward for its seemingly gratuitous violence. The protagonist, whose name ironically recalls the sacrificial Paschal lamb, has his own prehistory: his unholy family is constituted by a vicious father, and a thin, filthy, and angry drunkard of a mother, with syphilitic sores around her mouth.[11] He describes their relationship as one of constant fights brought on by her taunts at his father: "he would scream as if mad; he called her ignorant and a witch [...], she responded by calling him a miserable, hairy, hungry Portuguese, at which point he would come after her with a belt" (el oírla esa opinión le sacaba de quicio; gritaba como si estuviera loco, la llamaba ignorante y bruja [...] Ella le llamaba desgraciado y peludo, lo tachaba de hambriento y portugués y él [...] se sacaba el cinturón y la corría todo) (2002: 38). The only person who shows any concern for Pascual is his sister Rosario, who, like their younger brother, also suffers from lack of their mother's care, and soon leaves the house to work as a prostitute.

Pascual marries a young girl he has impregnated who resembles his sister; any happiness the couple experiences, however, is quickly dissipated by the premonition of bad luck that hangs over them. She miscarries the first pregnancy, and a second child dies at eleven months. Pascual abandons his wife for several years only to return and find her pregnant; wresting the truth from her that his worst enemy, his sister's lover, is the father, he blames his mother for bringing the two together and kills the man. Like the protagonists of other picaresque novels, who attempt to escape their fate only to fall back into the circularity of the genre, Pascual dreams of leaving his house, where he lives with his new wife, Esperanza, whose name means hope, and his mother. Yet the latter becomes an unbearable and hateful burden to him:

---

11 Like Guzmán, Pascual also has a sister to whom he is attached, and who becomes a prostitute and surrogate mother figure.

My mother felt an insistent satisfaction in arousing my bad temper, which kept getting worse, like the numbers of flies drawn to the smell of dead bodies. The bile that I drank poisoned my heart, and I had such vile thoughts that I was afraid of my own rage.

(Mi madre sentía una insistente satisfacción en tentarme los genios, en los que el mal iba creciendo como las moscas al olor de los muertos. La bilis que tragué me envenenó el corazón y tan malos pensamientos llegaba por entonces a discurrir que llegué a estar asustado de mi mismo coraje) (2002: 172).

After thinking that he will escape to the Spanish coast, he meticulously plans her death and waits until she falls asleep. Pascual's grotesque matricide, one of the most disturbing episodes in Spanish literature for its cold-bloodedness, is worth citing in full:[12]

I threw myself at her, holding her down. We wrestled; it was the most monstrous battle you could imagine. We roared like beasts, spit coming out of our mouths. My clothes were torn, exposing my chest. The damn woman had more strength than a demon. I had to use all my masculine power to keep her down. Fifteen times I held her, and fifteen times she broke from me, scratching, kicking, hitting, and biting me. At one point, she caught my left nipple with her mouth, yanking it off. This was when I stuck the knife in her throat... the blood spilled out without stopping, hitting me in the face. It was as hot as a woman's womb and tasted the same as lamb's blood. I let her go and fled [...]. Taking to the countryside, I ran and ran without resting for hours on end. The country was cool, and I felt a sense of relief run through my veins. I could breathe.

(Me abalancé sobre ella y la sujeté. Forcejeó [...] Luchamos; fue la lucha más tremenda que usted se puede imaginar. Rugíamos como bestias, la baba nos asomaba a la boca [...] llegué a tener las vestiduras rasgadas, el pecho al aire. La condenada tenia más fuerzas que un demonio. Tuve que usar toda mi hombría para tenerla quieta. Quince veces que la sujetara, quince veces que se me había de escurrir. Me arañaba, me daba patadas y puñetazos, me mordía. Hubo un momento en que con la boca me cazó un pesón—el izquierdo—y me lo arrancó de cuajo. Fue el momento mismo en que pude clavarle la hoja en la garganta...

---

12 The mother figure in this novel has elicited various interpretations: Ziamandanis sees her as a Christ figure that allows Pascual to blame and sacrifice her for his ills (1996-97: 444). Pérez-Sánchez contends that by painting the mother as an evil character, Pascual "manipulates his readers into believing in the moral necessity of the crime" (2007: 73). She further allegorizes her as Spain, the mother-nation that emasculates its male children.

La sangre corría como desbocada y me golpeó la cara. Estaba caliente como un vientre y sabía lo mismo que la sangre de los corderos. La solté y salí huyendo [...] Cogí el campo y corrí, corrí sin descanso, durante horas enteras. El campo estaba fresco y una sensación como de alivio me corrió por las venas. Podía respirar.) (2002: 176-77).

With those last words, Pascual confesses to the reader that he has finally managed to free himself from his mother's grasp. Yet the novel's irony, as in the previous picaresque novels, is that he does not escape, as he has internalized her rejection as self-hatred; he will kill again, be imprisoned, his final ambiguous ending to be understood as either victim or perpetrator.

Indeed, the novel shows us in graphic detail his abortive effort to be set free from the phallic mother by reversing the image of giving birth: the warm womb, the blood, even the ripped nipple all symbolize the momentous struggle to attempt to separate from maternal control.[13] Arguing from the side of motherhood, Julia Kristeva has said that pregnancy "is followed by the mother's passion for the new subject that will be her child, provided he/she ceases to be her double, but from whom the mother detaches herself to allow the child to become an autonomous being. This motion of expulsion, of detachment, is essential" (2013: 86). In the picaresque novels, the relationship of the pícaro to his mother is one that fails to allow his extrication from the maternal, which in turn stymies his autonomy and sexual maturity. The pícaro's wives revert incessantly to the maternal imago, supplanting the mother. The novel's circularity compels the pícaro to duplicate by his actions his vitiated paternal genealogy; in the final analysis, however, it is the phallic mother who bears him, yet who will not let him go.

BIBLIOGRAPHY

Alemán, Mateo. *Guzmán de Alfarache*. 2 vols. Ed. José María Micó. Madrid 2006.

Alpert, Michael (Tr.). Two Spanish Picaresque Novels. Lazarillo de Tormes, The Swindler. London 1969.

Behrend-Martínez, Edward. "The Castigation and Abuse of Children in Early Modern Spain." Ed. Grace E. Coolidge. *The Formation of the Child in Early Modern Spain*. Farnham, UK 2014. 249–72.

---

13 The narrative ironically predicts Pascual's violent matricide in his ferocious rape of Lola, his first wife, instigated by the comparison she makes of him to his less-than-human brother.

Bergmann, Emilie L. "The Exclusion of the Feminine in the Cultural Discourse of the Golden Age. Juan Luis Vives and Fray Luis de León." Ed. Alain Saint-Saens. *Religion, Body, and Gender in Early Modern Spain*. San Francisco 1992. 124–36.

Campos García Rojas, Axayácatl. "Medea en los libros de caballerías hispánicos. Libros, mito y ejemplaridad." *Acta Poética* 32.2 (2011): 115–43.

Castillo Solórzano, Alonso de. *Las harpías en Madrid*. Ed. Pablo Jauralde Pou. Madrid 1985.

Cela, Camilo José. *La familia de Pascual Duarte*. Barcelona 2002.

Chasseguet-Smirgel, Janine. "The Female Castration Complex and Penis Envy (excerpt)." Ed. Nancy Burke. *Gender and Envy*. New York 1998. 119–30.

Chorpenning, Joseph. *The Holy Family in Art and Devotion*. Philadelphia 1997.

Covarrubias, Sebastián de. *Tesoro de la lengua castellana o Española*. Ed. Martín de Riquer. Barcelona 1943.

Cruz, Anne J. *Discourses of Poverty. Social Reform and the Picaresque Novel in Early Modern Spain*. Toronto 1999.

Cruz, Anne J. (2010): "Figuring Gender in the Picaresque Novel. From Lazarillo to Zayas." *Romance Notes* 50.1 (2019): 7–20.

Cruz, Anne J. "Fathers and Sons in *Don Quixote*." Ed. Grace E. Coolidge. *The Formation of the Child in Early Modern Spain*. Farnham, UK 2014. 65–92.

Dangler, Jean. *Mediating Fictions: Literature, Women Healers, and the Go-Between in Medieval and Early Modern Iberia*. Lewisburg, PA 2001.

García Santo-Tomás, Enrique. *Modernidad bajo sospecha. Salas Barbadillo y la cultura material del siglo XVII*. Madrid 2008.

García Sanz, Ángel. "Castile 1580-1650. Economic crisis and the policy of reform." Ed. I.A.A.Thompson and B. Yun. *The Castilian Crisis of the Seventeenth Century*. Cambridge 1995. 13–31.

Giles, Ryan D. "Picaresque Fatherhood: Racial and Literary Heritage in 'Guzmán de Alfarache 1.1'." *Neohelicon* 40.1 (2013): 227–44.

Guillén, Claudio. *Literature as System: Essays toward the Theory of Literary History*. Princeton 1971.

Jordán Arroyo, María V. "Has Charity Gone to Heaven?' The Women in *La vida de Lazarillo de Tormes*." Ed. Reyes Coll-Tellechea and Sean McDaniel. *The Lazarillo Phenomenon. Essays on the Adventures of a Classic Text*. Lewisburg, PA 2010. 138–60.

Kristeva, Julia. *Hatred and Forgiveness*. New York 2013.

Lacan, Jacques. *Écrits. A Selection*. Tr. Alan Sheridan. New York 1977.

Laguna Fernández, Juan Ignacio. *La "Philosophia Moral" en el "Guzmán" apócrifo. La autoría de Juan Felipe Mey a la luz de nuevas fuentes*. Ciudad Real 2012.

Mañero Lozano, David. *Segunda parte de la vida del pícaro Guzmán de Alfarache*. Madrid 2007.

Pérez-Sanchez, Gema. *Queer Transitions in Contemporary Spanish Culture. From Franco to La Movida*. New York 2007.

Puig Mares, María del Pilar. *Madres en la literatura Española. Eros, honor y muerte*. Caracas 2000.

Quevedo, Francisco de. *El buscón*. Ed. Pablo Jauralde Pou. Madrid 2005.

Ricapito, Joseph P. "En la mente de Mateo Alemán." Ed. Pedro M. Piñero Ramírez. *Atalayas del "Guzmán de Alfarache". Seminario internacional sobre Mateo Alemán*. Seville 2002. 113–40.

Rico, Francisco. *The Spanish Picaresque Novel and the Point of View*. Tr. Harry Sieber. Cambridge 1984.

Rico, Francisco. *Lazarillo de Tormes*. Madrid, Cátedra 1987.

Ruan, Felipe E. *Pícaro and Cortesano. Identity and the Forms of Capital in Early Modern Picaresque Narrative and Courtesy Literature*. Lewisburg 2011.

Ruiz, Teófilo F. Spanish Society. 1400-1600. New York 2014.

Salas Barbadillo, Alonso Jerónimo de. *La hija de Celestina y la ingeniosa Elena*. Ed. José Fradejas Lebrero. Madrid 1983.

Sánchez, Jelena. "Illness and Pregnancy: Female Agency in Lope de Vega's El acero de Madrid." Ed. Adrienne Martin and María Cristina Quintero. *Perspectives on Early Modern Women in Iberia and the Americas. Studies in Law, Society, Art, and Literature in Honor of Anne J. Cruz*. New York 2015. 286–98.

Scruton, Roger. *Beauty. A Very Short Introduction*. Oxford 2011.

Sherwood, Joan. *Poverty in Eighteenth Century Spain. The Women and Children of the Inclusa*. Toronto 1988.

Stone, Robert S. *Picaresque Continuities. Transformations of Genre from the Golden Age to Goethezeit*. New Orleans 1998.

Walters, D. Gareth. The Cambridge Introduction to Spanish Poetry. Spain and Spanish America. Cambridge 2002.

Ziamandanis, Claire M. "La redención de la madre en La familia de Pascual Duarte." *E.L.U.A.* 11 (1996/97): 439–45.

Between Subject, Object, and Abject
Masculinities in the Spanish Picaresque

GREGOR SCHUHEN

The researches on conceptions of masculinity in the picaresque novel are more than scarce so far. One might get the impression that the picaresque fictional universe is as androcentric or as "overpoweringly patriarchal" (Cruz 1999: 99) that further studies obviously do not seem to promise intriguing insights into the gendered order of the picaresque *mundus inversus*. This impression – wrong or right – corresponds perfectly with Bourdieu's statement on the "masculine order":

La force de l'ordre masculin se voit au fait qu'il se passe de justification : la vision androcentrique s'impose comme neutre et n'a pas besoin de s'énoncer dans des discours visant à la légitimer (Bourdieu 1998: 22).[1]

Furthermore, one might consider as well Simmel's remarks on the hypostatization of the male principle to the generally human while discussing the relationship between gender and culture in an essay written in 1911, i.e. many years before second-wave feminists had taken issue with the identification of white men and objectivity and thus culture:

Daß das männliche Geschlecht nicht einfach dem weiblichen relativ überlegen ist, sondern zum Allgemein-Menschlichen wird, das die Erscheinungen des einzelnen Männlichen und

---

1 Cf. the English translation by Richard Nice: "The strength of the masculine order is seen in the fact that it dispenses with justification: the androcentric vision imposes itself as neutral and has no need to spell itself out in discourses aimed at legitimating it" (Bourdieu 2001: 9).

Weiblichen gleichmäßig normiert – dies wird, in mannigfachen Vermittlungen, von der *Machtstellung* der Männer getragen (Simmel [1911] 1985: 202).[2]

Paraphrasing Simmel, the so-called 'naive identification' of human with man produces a situation in which deficient performances in the most diverse areas are degraded as 'feminine' while outstanding performances of women are celebrated as 'thoroughly manly.'

To cut a long story short: It seems as if the male centered plots of the picaresque novels – according to Bourdieu and Simmel – paradoxically (or logically?) have been prevented scientists from analyzing them in a gender-focused way. On the other side, 'deficient performances' or rather 'deviations' from the androcentric norm, hence questions of the feminine, female representations and even queer aspects, are meanwhile well explored (cf. Hanrahan 1967; Alegre 1981; Gossy 1989; Jordán Arroyo 2010), whereas concrete examinations of the male picaresque figures *as* males are still missing. In this respect, my project of analyzing masculinity /-ies in the Spanish picaresque novel means to me as a researcher on masculinity issues a challenging task.

MASCULINITY STUDIES AND LITERATURE

As is generally known the beginnings of Masculinity Studies, formerly known as Men's Studies, emerged as a sub-discipline of gender-focused sociology. As a critical reaction to social changes and political crisis, such as the Vietnam War, the gay and lesbian movements and the second-wave feminism, representatives of the early Men's Studies – rather activists than scientists – claimed a critical re-thinking of outdated perceptions of masculinity, especially the WASP model. In the 1990s, due to the well-received works by Raewyn Connell and Pierre Bourdieu and strongly influenced by deconstructivist gender and queer theory as well as by cultural studies, the metamorphosis from essentialist Men's to more or less constructivist Masculinity Studies took place and remained standard until today (cf. Fenske 2012).

Above all, the works of the Australian sociologist Connell introducing a pluralistic view on masculinity affected the field of research worldwide – her well-

---

2   Cf. The English translation by Guy Oakes: "The male sex is not merely superior in relation to the female but acquires the status of the generally human governing the phenomena of the individual male and the individual female in the same way" (Simmel 1984: 103).

known typology of hegemony, subordination, complicity and marginalization, as established in her major study *Masculinities* (1995), inspired the interdisciplinary theoretical approach to masculinity in terms of a performative, culturally and historically variable and relational category. In simplified terms, Connell argues that masculinity merely exists in the plural form, which means by the acknowledgement of multiple masculinities, which not only constitute themselves in contrast to femininity, but in interaction with other forms of masculinity. As a consequence, masculinity – according to Connell – does not depict a biological matter of fact, but a highly dynamic and relational social practice, which varies considerably depending on its cultural or historical context.

Considering roughly the picaresque's historical context of the 16th, 17th and 18th century, one has to be careful not to adapt Connell's approach naively in an ahistorical manner. Connells model clearly refers to modern, democratic and capitalist structures of society, which means that particularly the competitive aspect of masculinity logically is quite different today than in premodern feudalistic societies as e.g. Spain's estate-based society of the *Siglo de Oro*. Today the barriers between different estates are much more permeable which is why the model of hegemony and subordination is much more dynamic today than in a system with rigid lines of social demarcation. Therefore, the possibility of social advancement today is much more realistic in contrast to premodern feudalism where birth is everything and achievements almost nothing. In a nutshell: not only literary texts have to be historicized thoroughly but as well the theoretic approaches we apply in analyzing them. Nevertheless, Connell's approach offers numerous connecting points in order to examine narrative structures of masculinity in premodern texts: first of all, the aspect of masculinity as a social practice, then the relations between the two sexes as well as between members of the same sex, which finally includes the pluralization of masculinity.

Talking about typical male narratives brings me to the last point of this part: With Walter Erhart, I understand masculinity basically as a "narrative structure" (Erhart 2005: 207) which has to be reconstructed by contextualizing literary texts in their socio-historical background. Erhart postulates that each period within literary history has its own typical male narratives and scripts. I just touched upon the possibility of social uplift in our times: the "American Dream: from dishwasher to millionaire" could without any doubt be evaluated as a good example of such a typical male narrative as well as Campbell's model of the "hero's journey" (cf. Campbell 1949). This approach – Erhart claims a "male narratology" (Erhart 2005: 176) – does not contest, but complement Connell's sociological model as narratives not only can be found in literary texts but are also – in a more general and abstract sense – inherent part of our cultural text. Erhart states therefore that masculinity *only* exists in form of narratives, scripts and patterns which means that *doing* masculinity and *narrating* masculinity cannot be separated, especially while analyzing literary texts with male protagonists such as the picaresque novel.

REPRESENTATIONS OF MASCULINITY IN THE SPANISH PICARESQUE NOVEL

The question "Is the pícaro a 'real' man"? seems to be quite simple. Still, if we take Connell's sociological and Erhart's narratological approach into account and combine them, there is obviously no problem in answering: We have a very young man from the lowest classes who, after having been separated from his single mother, starts working as a servant for different masters. His journey through the – to quote Mathias Bauer – "wolves' game" (Bauer 1993: 85) of the urban premodern society depicts not only a daily quest for food and survival but also for social status and recognition. Similar to the German *bildungsroman* of the late 18th century, the pícaro's wandering and constantly precarious existence is a hard school of life; unlike the optimistic humanist vision in the bildungsroman, we do not meet a socially accepted human being of moral integrity at the end of these novels but a corrupted individual who had learnt how to cheat and to betray in order to survive and, as it is the case in *Lazarillo de Tormes*, to advance socially within the very limited margins of the prevalent feudal system.

The picaresque narrative therefore can be described as a male narrative which – at least in the three classical novels *Lazarillo de Tormes* (1554), *Guzmán de Alfarache* by Mateo Alemán (1599/1604) and Francisco de Quevedo's *El Buscón* (1626) – basically functions according to the same pattern: childhood in a precarious milieu, separation from the mother, initiation, changing employments, career as a petty criminal, open end – so far the numerous commonalities in content. On the formal level, the similarities are even more evident: an unreliable auto-diegetic narrator (i.e. division into a narrating and a narrated I), episodic structure, ironic and vulgar speech. The comparability of both, content and form, allows us to identify a picaresque narrative, which is at the same time a narrative of becoming male because the textual formation of the pícaro depicts also a narrated formation of masculinity.

There are other male narratives in premodern Europe with quite similar structures, for instance the heroic pattern in knight's tales. Having a short glance on *Perceval* (ca. 1180) by Chrétien de Troyes, the hero is also separated by his mother in the beginning, then has to wander around and to pass several adventurous exams, proving his prowess and defending his chivalric honor before ending as a so-called hegemonic, that is *ideal* knight. The difference between the chivalric and the picaresque narrative, as far as contents are concerned, is not only grounded on historical and generic reasons but is due to the completely different social framing in which the formations of masculinity take place.

Referring to the title of my paper, we have to consider that the picaresque narration of becoming male is located in the – to quote Bachtin's well-known concept – carnivalesque *mundus inversus* of the urban lower classes, the socially depraved (cf. Bachtin 1995). When I conceptualize the pícaro as a *vir inversus*, an 'inverted man', this has of course nothing to do with sexual inversion. The introduction of the *vir inversus* serves me as a socio-literary figure of thought since mere sociological terms, such as the Connellian typology, prove inadequate to classify picaresque masculinity. Of course, the pícaro is somehow "subordinate" (Connell 1995: 78) or "marginalized" (80), sometimes even "complicit" (79), but these categories all seem insufficient to me as they obviously lack the genuine literary aspect of picaresque masculinity. In my opinion, the purely *formal* figure of inversion fits much better as it includes social as well as rhetoric, moral and even gender implications.

By describing the social sphere of the picaresque diegesis as a *mundus inversus*, as an arena of carnivalesque counter culture, the official culture remains intact as a point of reference, because the inversion naturally refers to it. One might say: The pícaro as narrator transmits the mirror-inverted and thus subversive image of the whole of society. Therefore the German notion of the 'Schelmenspiegel', the 'rogue's mirror', is double coded: On the one hand, the narrator delivers a mimetic mirror by portraying the precarious live and struggle for survival of the poor; on the other hand the pícaro's ironic mirror shows an unofficial culture in which the social order as well as moral and Christian values are completely inverted. This aspect of *desengaño*, of unmasking hidden truths, can only be adequately understood if we take into account that the picaro's learning process, hence his male socialization, is a process of imitating and adapting social practices, behavioral patterns he learns from his male masters which are, speaking in terms of social hierarchy, members of the higher classes: priests, certified beggars, *escuderos*, noble men, craftsmen, teachers. In short, the male secondary characters epitomize a *pars pro toto* of the whole androcentric society. Speaking about *official* ideal masculinity in premodern Spain, one might consider *honor* and *honra* as key values as well as moral integrity, prowess, *limpieza de sangre*, Catholicism, heterosexuality and sexual potency. Ideal clerical masculinity is focused on charity, wisdom, austerity and selflessness. However, what the pícaro learns from this male role models is hypocrisy, *engaño* / dissimulation, greed, adaptability and the readiness to use violence. The picaresque novel therefore makes the implicit, well-hidden moral codes visible by using the voice of a socially liminal figure that is not authorized to participate in the official discourse. In this respect, the 'vir inversus' is rather a figure of thought than a genuine literary character, or, more precise – a figure of *desengaño* as *desengaño* means – to quote the *Tesoro de la lengua castellana* (1611) – "hablar claro" (Covarrubias 1611: 309).

But the pícaro is not only an unmasking social critic of hypocritical male values but a literary character as well. This double function is in accordance with the narrative structure of the picaresque novel: The narrating I functions as social critic whereas the narrated I acts out as a literary character. In my example of *Lazarillo de Tormes*, this schizophrenic aspect is visualized by the use of two different names: The adult narrator's name is Lázaro while his adolescent alter ego is called Lazarillo. On this second level, masculinity plays a slightly different role: Here, the narrative focus is not on the androcentric order as such but on the masculinity of the socially disadvantaged. Obviously these two levels cannot be divided as the masculinity of the poor is constituted by social interaction and therefore is dependent on the handlings of the more powerful.

Two preconditions have to be taken into account which both refer to the general lack of psychologizing in the picaresque genre: As the picaresque novel, despite the first-person narrator, is on the whole waiving psychological depth, the construction of a male identity has to be analyzed rather from a praxeological point of view. Due to the absence of psyche, which is of course typical of premodern narratives, we can observe an excessive depiction of corporeal motives.

By combining these two preconditions, it gets clear that corporeal practices play an important role in the construction of picaresque masculinity. The pícaro's body itself is hardly marked as a gendered body. Its materiality can be described as grotesque in the Bachtinian sense as the pícaro's body is in a process of permanent exchange with its surroundings, which means that its borders are not well-defined at all (cf. Bachtin: 1990). Because this corporeal exchange is never – as for example in Rabelais or the medieval *Fabliau* – sexually motivated, the pícaro's body remains almost unmarked in terms of gender. This is of course a particular characteristic of the Spanish picaresque novel; the German picaresque is quite different. This matter of fact can be interpreted as being in accordance with Laqueur's controversially discussed one-sex-model which states that „[t]here was still in the sixteenth century, as there had been in classical antiquity, only one canonical body and that body was male" (Laqueur 1992: 63). Sexual differentiation, according to Laqueur, didn't take place until the end of the 18th century – until then "at least two genders correspond to but one sex"

(25). Therefore – again – gender differentiation, especially in the picaresque novel, has to be examined rather on the basis of corporeal practices and than anatomical conditions.

Coming back to the pícaro's masculinity, three types of body practices are relevant to me: physical violence, bodily excretions and the hunger motive. What these three aspects have in common is the dual structure of deficiency and abundance or excess. The pícaro is confronted with an excessive impact of physical violence. Furthermore, he has to cope with an abundant waste of bodily excretions – either his own or those of his antagonists. As far as food is concerned, the protagonists have to be located on the side of deficiency – paraphrasing the dictum "You are what you eat" the pícaro is almost nothing. Referring to physical violence, the pícaro is mostly condemned to play the victim role as an object. His body frontiers turn out to be permeable due to the excessive violent acts of his masters or other male characters of his social environment. According to Bachtin's conception of the grotesque body, the pícaro's body epitomizes the body of the intruded whereas his masters play the role of the intruder. On the whole, violence serves as a powerful practice to establish or defend masculinity as Ruth Mazo Karras states: "Violence was the fundamental measure of a man because it was a way of exerting dominance over men of one's own social stratum as well as over woman and social inferiors" (Mazo Karras 2003: 21): The fact that only the social inferiors, such as the pícaro himself, have to suffer physical violence and that physical violence is generally depicted as an exclusively male practice, makes clear that picaresque masculinity in this respect is constituted as objective and deficient. Bernhard Teuber also observes that, on the contrary, the only the bodies of noble men remain intact and unharmed (cf. Teuber 1989: 211). This contrast helps to better understand the role of physical violence as an intersubjective manner to either establish one's own masculinity or to deprive the other of his male status.

Dealing with the exchange and imaginary of bodily excretions, the representation of masculinity gets more complex, as Cruz has stated for Quevedos *Buscon*: In this case, masculinity is not the result of social objection, but of social abjection (cf. Cruz: 1999: 124-134). Bachtins interpretation of the scatological imaginary in the works of Rabelais as belonging only to the comical sphere and celebrating excrement as the "gay matter" (Bachtin 1995: 216) cannot be applied to the picaresque novel. The contamination of the pícaro with all kinds of body fluids and excrements may cause laughter on behalf of his offenders but the scenes don't evoke funny feelings on the part of the reader. Julia Kristeva has conceptualized the abject as provoking nausea and repulsion, such as bodily excretions, pus, carrion or corpses do. The abject is neither object nor subject but confronts the I with its borders und its fears. Kristeva writes in *Pouvoirs de l'horreur*:

> Tout en se rapportant toujours aux orifices corporels comme à autant de repères découpant-constituant le territoire du corps, les objets polluants sont, schématiquement, de deux types : excrémentiel et menstruel. Ni les larmes ni le sperme, par exemple, quoique se rapportant à des bords du corps, n'ont valeur de pollution. L'excrément et ses équivalents (pourriture, infection, maladie, cadavre, etc.) représentent le danger venu de l'extérieur de l'identité : le moi menacé par du non-moi, la société menacée par son dehors, la vie par la mort (Kristeva 1980: 86).[3]

This passage is highly instructive as it shows that not only the individual body is confronted with abjection, but the social body as well: "society threatened by its outside". Here, at the very latest, it becomes clear that the excremental motives in the picaresque not only show the contamination of the pícaro's body on the actual plot level, but reflects – once more – the way, in which the society deals with its weakest members: The liminal social status of the pícaro makes him socially abjected, neither subject nor object. Furthermore, the social body needs the poor in order to make sure its own integrity by excreting them, such as the biological body needs excretion to survive. For both "contamination by these despised elements cannot be averted or contained, since they originate precisely from within the social body itself." To quote Cruz: „The scatological excess discharged on the pícaro expresses the disquietude of a xenophobic society that simultaneously acknowledges and rejects the presence of the ‚other' in itself" (Cruz 1999: 126).

To resume at least the different meanings of these three corporeal practices and relating them to the construction of picaresque masculinity, it becomes obvious that they refer to different cultural localizations: the pícaro's social status between subject, object and abject. In his quest for food we can see also his quest for social status as Polly Wiesner has pointed out, i.e. his ambitions to become a socially recognized subject (cf. Wiesner 1998). The society replies these ambi-

---

3 Cf. The English translation by Leon S. Roudiez: "While they always relate to corporeal orifices as to so many landmarks parceling-constituting the body's territory, polluting objects fall, schematically, into two types: excremental and menstrual. Neither tears nor sperm, for instance, although they belong to borders of the body, have any polluting value. Excrement and its equivalents (decay, infection, disease, corpse, etc.) stand for the danger to identity that comes from without: the ego threatened by the non-ego, society threatened by its outside, life by death" (Kristeva 1982: 71).

tions with objection through physical violence and abjection via contaminating his body publically. Keeping in mind that hegemonic masculinity constitutes itself among other things by eating meat (cf. Reeser 2010: 94), by exercising physical violence and by securing the conservation of society by procreation, it becomes quite evident that the pícaro represents a completely anti-hegemonic type of masculinity, or: the *inversion* of the hegemonic.

Therefore, we can define the pícaro as a 'vir inversus' in a double sense: As a figure of *desengaño* he reveals the hidden truths of official male values, such as honor, prowess and moral integrity; as a literary character, he brings to light the social mechanisms of objection and abjection of the poor.

LA VIDA DE LAZARILLO DE TORMES (1554)

Already the narrative framework of the anonymous text reveals a structure of social imbalance: Adult Lázaro has to defend himself before a judge – "Vuestra Merced" – who decides not only about his future as a town crier ("pregonero") but implicitly about his masculinity since the delicate "caso" consists of the question whether or not his wife lives in a concubinage relationship with Lázaro's benefactor, a catholic archpriest. As the honor of a married man – especially in premodern times and especially in Spain – is dependent on the fidelity of his wife, the verdict of Vuestra Merced (which we never get to know) will evaluate not only Lázaro's social status in terms of profession but also in terms of masculinity. Therefore, it is not over-interpreted to state that the pícaro's masculinity is precarious from the start on. Or, in other words, his unreliable autobiography manifests his effort to stabilize or regain his threatened masculinity and is, at the same time, his only manner to act as a subject, as a *narrating* subject exercising full narrative control – so much for the narrative framework.

The core plot starts with the genre-specific separation from his mother. According to Erhart's conception of masculinity as a narrative structure, the first step in the construction of a male identity depicts the cutting of the maternal cord. It seems to me that not only the narrative framework introduces an unstable form of masculinity but the core narration as well by starting with the act of maternal loss which evokes autonomy whishes and melancholia at the same time. To quote Erhart:

Männlichkeit entsteht als Negation einer primären, durch die Mutter-Kind-Beziehung gegebenen Weiblichkeit, von der sich der Mann jeweils emanzipieren und losreißen muß; die Entfernung vom maternalen Ursprung erzeugt Unsicherheit und Angst auf der einen,

Sehnsucht und Nostalgie nach Verschmelzung und Wiedervereinigung mit der verlorenen Symbiose auf der anderen Seite (Erhart 2005: 177).[4]

Quevedo stages the maternal drama as a lifelong *trauma* of his Buscón and therefore as the prime mover of the plot. In *Lazarillo de Tormes*, the separation cannot be evaluated as a genuine trauma but by releasing his son to the hands of the blind beggar, his mother also "sets in motion the child's socialization according to masculine standards" (Cruz: 1997: 100).

The blind beggar is Lazarillo's first male role model and is thus responsible for the boy's initiation experience, i.e. the second step in his process of becoming male, which depicts one of the best-known scenes of the novel. The blind man asks Lazarillo to lay his head against the stone statue of a bull – Spanish symbol of masculinity *par excellence* – so that he will be able to hear a „gran ruido" (Lazarillo 23), a 'mighty sound' from within. When Lazarillo is close enough his new master beats his head with full fury against the monument so that his servant will feel the pain for the next three days. The first lesson, Lazarillo learns, is: "Necio, aprende, que el mozo del ciego un punto ha de saber más que el diablo" (23) –in other words: Don't trust anybody! Much more interesting than the fact, that physical violence is the starting point of Lazarillo's male socialization are his own reflection afterwards: „Paresciómе que en aquel instante desperté de la simpleza en que, como niño, dormido estaba" (23). It is hardly possible to describe an experience of enlightenment more clearly: The blind man has opened his servant's eyes.

This initiation experience manifests the cutting of the maternal cord not only in a performative way but also on the linguistic level: „Y fue ansí, que, después de Dios, éste me dio la vida y, siendo ciego, me alumbró y adestró en la carrera de vivir (24)." It is not the mother anymore who is recognized as having given birth to Lazarillo but the blind beggar – not only „me dio la vida" is central but also the verb „alumbrar" which means both: „to enlighten" and „to give birth". From now on Lazarillo is part of the androcentric and homosocial wolves' game, his *rite de passage* can be interpreted as the starting point of his process of becoming male. As already mentioned before, the forthcoming episodes and his future masters as well as the imitation of their unethical social practices mark the next steps of his male socialization. The lessons will be constantly extended:

---

4 Cf. my translation: "Masculinity comes into existence as a negation of a primary femininity the man has to become emancipated and get rid of; the growing distance to the maternal origin evokes insecurity and fear on the one hand and a desire and nostalgia for merging and reunion with the lost symbiosis on the other hand."

While the blind man, according to the principles of *desengaño*, teaches him fundamental mistrust in everyone, the clergyman epitomizes greed, avarice and hypocrisy as key values, whereas the *escudero* shows the pitfalls of social *engaño* in terms of an outdated understanding of *honor*, etc.

Conclusion

The construction of masculinity in the Spanish picaresque novel depicts a fruitful research field with many different facets which have to be taken into account. It would go beyond the scope of this paper to present them all. For example, I did not mention the pícaro's relationship to women, I merely touched the point, that Lazarillo – in contrast to his German successors – never has sexual relations, that he probably might be regarded as impotent.

What I wanted to demonstrate is that the conception of picaresque masculinity has to be, in spite of the age of the texts, classified as surprisingly modern. Masculinity is depicted as constituted by specific social practices long before Harold Garfinkel informed us in 1960s for the first time about the significance of 'doing gender' (cf. Garfinkel 1967). Moreover, these practices – here the picaresque novel as it were anticipates Connell's thoughts about the double relational character of masculinity – are mostly interactive and dependent on power relations or even create and manifest them.

What I try to describe with the concept of 'vir inversus' is that the picaresque novel creates a doubled perspective on masculinity, which is due to the genre's specific narrative structure. On the one hand, the pícaro as narrator and social critic who deliberately uses his marginalized position as well as his allegedly naïve voice to unmask the unofficial unethical values of the mighty. His pessimist vision delivers the perfect inversion of the official humanist ideal of noble, knightly or even Christian masculinity. On the other hand, the pícaro as literary character demonstrates the male socialization as learning individual, which means as an object that struggles each day for survival and social recognition by trying to avoid constantly social abjection. In the case of Lazarillo, his social ambitions are assuaged in the end within the very limited margins of his opportunities. Guzmán however ends as a prisoner and Pablos leaves Spain for the New World. But even though Lazarillo imagines himself living "en la cumbre de toda buena fortuna" (Lazarillo 135), we know it better: his social status and therefore his stabilized male status is only temporarily secure and massively endangered by social degradation. His wife turns out to be his mother's avenger, his symbolic capital of male honor lies in the hands of a woman which – in the gendered logic of premodern narratives – represents the incarnation of *inconstantia*. It is surely not by coincidence that the last word of the novel is "fortuna", the most inconstant of all ancient goddesses.

So after all, is the pícaro a 'real man'? To my mind, due to his literary status, he is even more than that: The pícaro is the incarnate mirror of well hidden truths, i.e. he is a *desengañador*, a critic of both, androcentric and feudal policy, as well as a member of the lowest classes whose minimum of male honor is constantly in danger as it is threatened by the more powerful, by his own imprudent actions and at least – by the women of this social environment.

Bibliography

Alegre, José María. "Las mujeres en el *Lazarillo de Tormes*." *Revue Romane* 16 (1981): 3–21.
Anonymous. *La vida de Lazarillo de Tormes y de sus fortunas y adversidades*. Ed. Francisco Rico. Madrid 1987.
Bachtin, Michail M. "Die groteske Gestalt des Leibes." Michail Bachtin. *Literatur und Karneval. Zur Romantheorie und Lachkultur*. Frankfurt a.M. 1990. 15–23.
Bachtin, Michail M. *Rabelais und seine Welt. Volkskultur als Gegenkultur*. Ed. Renate Lachmann. Frankfurt a.M. 1995.
Bauer, Matthias. *Im Fuchsbau der Geschichten. Anatomie des Schelmenromans*. Stuttgart/Weimar 1993.
Bourdieu, Pierre. *La domination masculine*. Paris 1998.
Campbell, Joseph. *The Hero with a Thousand Faces*. New York 1949.
Connell, Robert W. *Masculinities*. Cambridge 1995.
Covarrubias Horozco, Sebastián de. *Tesoro de la lengua castellana o española*. Madrid 1611.
Cruz, Anne J. "The Abjected Feminine in the *Lazarillo de Tormes*." *Crítica Hispánica* 19 (1997): 99–109.
Cruz, Anne J. *Discourses of Poverty. Social Reform and the Picaresque Novel in Early Modern Spain*. Toronto 1999.
Erhart, Walter. "Das zweite Geschlecht. 'Männlichkeit', interdisziplinär. Ein Forschungsbericht." *Internationales Archiv für Sozialgeschichte der deutschen Literatur* 30 (2005): 156–232.
Fenske, Uta: "Männlichkeiten im Fokus der Geschlechterforschung." Ed. Uta Fenske and Gregor Schuhen. *Ambivalente Männlichkeit(en). Maskulinitäts-

diskurse aus interdisziplinärer Perspektive. Opladen, Berlin, Toronto 2012. 11–26.

Garfinkel, Harold. *Studies in Ethnomethodology*. Englewood Cliffs, N.J. 1967.

Gossy, Mary S. *The Untold Story. Women and Theory in Golden Age Texts*. Ann Arbor 1989.

Hanrahan, Thomas. *La mujer en la novela picaresca. 2 Vol*. Madrid 1967.

Jordán Arroyo, María V. "'Has Charity gone to Heaven?' The Women in *La vida de Lazarillo de Tormes*." Ed. Reyes Coll-Tellechea and Sean McDavid. *The Lazarillo Phenomenon. Essays on the Adventures of a Classic Text*. Cranbury 2010. 139–160.

Kristeva, Julia. *Pouvoirs de l'horreur. Essai sur l'abjection*. Paris 1980.

Laqueur, Thomas. *Making Sex. Body and Gender from the Greeks to Freud*. Cambridge, Mass., London 1992.

Mazo Karras, Ruth. *From Boys to Men. Formations of Masculinity in Late Medieval Europe*. Philadelphia 2003.

Reeser, Todd W. "Theorizing the Male Body." Ed. Todd W. Reeser. *Masculinities in Theory. An Introduction*. Chichester 2010. 91–118.

Simmel, Georg. "Das Relative und das Absolute im Geschlechter-Problem [1911]." Georg Simmel. *Schriften zur Philosophie und Soziologie der Geschlechter*. Ed. Heinz-Jürgen Dahme and Klaus Christian Köhnke. Frankfurt a.M. 1985. 200–223.

Teuber, Bernhard. *Sprache – Körper – Traum. Zur karnevalesken Tradition in der romanischen Literatur aus früher Neuzeit*. Tübingen 1989.

Wiesner, Polly. "Introduction. Food, Status, Culture, and Nature." Ed. Wulf Schiefenhövel and Polly Wiesner. *Food and the Status Quest. An Interdisciplinary Perspective*. Providence 1998. 1–18.

The Charms of Circe

Narrative Persuasion in *Guzmán de Alfarache*

TIMO KEHREN

In a pioneering study of the Spanish picaresque novel, Peter N. Dunn draws attention to the inversion of the forms, devices and motifs of the epic in *Guzmán de Alfarache* (1599/1604) by Mateo Alemán (cf. Dunn 1993: 65). The break with the rules of the epic is nowhere more evident than in the love plot, which dominates the last book of the second volume of the novel. Guzmán deliberately uses ambiguous semantics here in order to appear in a favorable light. But behind these semantics we can detect a scandalous subtext that consists of a complex net of interconnected plot patterns. If *Guzmán de Alfarache* is a Christian epic, as affirmed by Michel Cavillac (cf. Cavillac 2007: 39-65), these plot patterns must emanate from the Christian tradition. But true to the picaresque *mundus inversus*, the Christian tradition is turned upside down: departing from his acquaintance with Gracia, Guzmán creates a teleology based on disgrace. This allows him to explain retrospectively how he has come to the galley, from where he writes his *confesión general*. In accordance with the principles of figurative typology, the pícaro's pursuit of profit or greed can be satisfied in his marriage with Gracia, a contrast to his precedent marriage with the daughter of a usurer. When Guzmán is finally sent to the galleys, a superordinate cyclic structure based on the logic of original sin is completed: the pícaro becomes guilty of the *peccatum nefandum*, in this way following in his father's footsteps.

DISGRACE AND PERDITION

The beginning of the love plot is marked by a moment of failure. The pícaro has turned his back to worldly life and has gone to the prestigious University of Alcalá de Henares in order to study theology. He spends the first years of his studies in devout seclusion until, during the last year of his studies, he goes on a pilgrimage to the hermitage of Santa María del Val, the local patron saint, where he spots Gracia and falls in love with her:

> Desta manera, con estos entretenimientos proseguí mi teología y, cuando cursaba en el último año, ya para quererme hacer bachiller, mis pecados me llevaron un domingo por la tarde a Santa María del Val. Romerías hay a veces, que valiera mucho más tener quebrada una pierna en casa. Esta estación fue causa y principio de toda mi perdición. De aquí se levantó la tormenta de mi vida, la destruición de mi hacienda y acabamiento de mi honra (Alemán 2010: 424).

The pícaro lets us know that his sins guide him to the hermitage, even though this is not so much the reason for his visit to the house of God than its outcome. He follows his father's example, going there for a *galanteo*; as we learnt in the first volume of the novel, his father met his wife on a similar occasion. By saying that this event is the "principio de toda [su] perdición", Guzmán identifies the encounter with Gracia as a crucial moment in his life: from this point on, he will not be able to find his way back to the 'right path'. The lexeme "perdición" is to be understood in the Christian sense as the result of the absence of divine grace, a meaning obscured from the reader by the name "Gracia". In this way, the following plot action is integrated into a *telos*, which the pícaro uses retrospectively to explain how he has ended up in the galleys, where he is still caught at the moment of narration. By means of a climax he finally outlines the stages of his upcoming fall: his torturous love will be followed by his financial ruin and the end of his honor.

The pícaro then begins to examine the first stage of his perdition. Instead of crossing himself with holy water when he enters the hermitage, as would be common, he immediately pays attention to a group of women, among whom are "algunas de muy buena suerte" (424). The episode quickly turns out to be a sideswipe at the school of Petrarchism, which dominates early modern love poetry. Its founding father Petrarch first caught sight of Laura during the Good Friday prayers in the church of Sainte-Claire d'Avignon, whereupon he praised her beauty and lamented her unattainability. But while the Petrarchans sublimate women in their poetry, the pícaro's words make it clear that his interests are of a very different nature. As the women leave the hermitage, he follows them to a blossoming meadow on the shore of the river Henares. When Guzmán reveals which of the women has broken his heart, it becomes evident that this *locus amoenus* is deceptive:

Eran una viuda mesonera con sus dos hijas, más lindas que Pólux y Cástor. Iban con otras amigas, no de poca buena gracia; mas la que así se llamaba, que era hija mayor de la mesonera, de tal manera las aventajaba, que parecía traerlas arrastradas; eran estrellas, pero mi Gracia el sol (425).

Guzmán once again emphasizes the women's beauty here but then lets us know that Gracia is the most beautiful of all. The ambiguity of the name of his chosen one with regard to grace and disgrace is reflected in another context here: at first sight, Gracia is the incarnation of gracefulness, which is stressed by the use of the conventional Petrarchan metaphor of the sun. But it must make the reader suspicious that Gracia is the eldest daughter of the *mesonera*. As it is known from the Spanish folklore tradition, the landlady is a topical character that is related to the business of prostitution (cf. Redondo 1987: 88-89). Consequently, Gracia is somewhat of a Charis or Grace who, like her antique role models, drives men out of their senses by her arts of seduction. Once again, a positive first impression turns out to be its very opposite.

The pícaro develops the question of grace in an extended narrative break. His starting point is the *caída*, the Fall of Man, as told in the Book of Genesis. Tasting the fruit of the tree of knowledge was an act of disobedience towards God, which led to the alienation of man and, subsequently, to the emergence of unnatural concupiscence:

Porque como después de la caída de nuestros primeros padres, con aquella levadura se acedó toda la masa corrompida de los vicios, vino en tal ruina la fábrica deste reloj humano, que no le quedó rueda ni muelle fijo que las moviese. Quedó tan desbarat[ad]o, sin algún orden o concierto, como si fuera otro contrario en ser muy diferente del primero en que Dios lo crió, lo cual nació de la inobediencia sola. De allí le sobrevino ceguera en el entendimiento, en la memoria olvido, en la voluntad culpa, en el apetito desorden, maldad en las obras, engaño en los sentidos, flaqueza en las fuerzas y en los gustos penalidades (Alemán 2010: 433).

The pícaro's language reminds us of a sermon, in which the theological line of argument alternates with the corresponding illustrations. But the religious commonplaces used here serve less to instruct the readers than to explain the speaker's sinfulness.

The Fall of Man leads the pícaro to *libre albedrío*, free will, and thus to the liberty of man to choose between good and evil. When the first man tasted the forbidden fruit, free will fell victim to *voluntad*, desire. Turning to good means fighting against *voluntad*:

> Porque como no sabemos o, por hablar en lenguaje más verdadero, no queremos irnos a la mano y, por la corrupción de nuestra naturaleza, flaqueza de la razón, cativerio de la libertad y débiles fuerzas, deslumbrados desta luz, vamos desalados, perdidos y encandilados a meternos en ella, pareciéndonos decente y proprio rendirnos luego, como a cosa natural, y tanto, como lo es la luz del sol, el frío de la nieve, quemar el fuego, bajar lo grave o subir a su esfera el aire, sin dar lugar a el entendimiento ni consentir a el libre albedrío que, gozando de su privilegios, usen su oficio, por haberse sujetado a la voluntad, que ya no era libre, y en cambio de contrastarla, le dan armas contra sí (435-436).

In accordance with Cavillac, Philippe Rabaté indicates that Guzmán's comments on the original sin are based on one of the cornerstones of Augustinian theology. In his writing *De libero arbitrio*, St. Augustine explains that while free will theoretically exists, it can only be used righteously if divine grace has manifested itself (cf. Rabaté 2009: 114, note 43). At the same time, we have to take into account, as Hanno Ehrlicher points out, that the picaresque prose cannot be completely identified with the writings of St. Augustine or any theologian of his tradition. It is not possible, he argues, to deduce any dogmatic position from the novel (cf. Ehrlicher 2010: 223).

That Guzmán spends so much time dealing with free will has to be understood in the context of the intensive theological debates on divine grace which attended the emergence of the novel. At the time, Martin Luther advocated a radical interpretation of St. Augustine's doctrine of predestination. Because of the sole efficaciousness of divine grace, he argued, man could not work for his salvation himself, which rendered the idea of free will untenable. According to Luther, the will of man is always already subjugated. Therefore, faith alone – *sola fide* – serves as a premise for divine grace. As a consequence of these ideas, a conflict on the question of divine grace between the Jesuit Luis de Molina and the Dominican Domingo Báñez broke out and went on until Pope Paul V suspended it. The core of this memorable debate was Molina's idea of a *scientia media*, in which God is omniscient, but man is free to decide whether to act in accordance with the divine guidelines. Consequently, divine grace is given to everyone (*gratia sufficiens*) but can only become efficacious if one's free will allows it (*gratia efficax*). Since these ideas implied the fallibility of God, Báñez contradicted his fellow believer, defending the unlimited omniscience of God. According to the Dominican, man acts freely, even though God necessarily guides him to his deeds. In spite of this disagreement, the two theologians shared the opinion that, because of the original sin, man could not do good deeds without divine grace; but once he has obtained it, he is capable of deciding freely whether to turn towards the side of the good, proof of which can be provided by his acts (cf. Ruhstorfer 2004).

Various critics have pointed out that Guzmán's statements cannot be assigned to either of these two positions (cf. Rabaté 2009: 116, note 54). As a matter of fact, his interest in the debate on grace is limited to his wish to examine and justify his personal destiny. By relating the general statements he has made before to his own situation, he turns himself into an *exemplum*. For this purpose, he introduces another element stemming from the Book of Genesis: all women are dangerous temptresses because they are the successors of Eve, who incited Adam to sin. True to this idea, the pícaro says about Gracia, who he finally marries: "cegáronme dotes naturales, diéronme hechizos, gracia y belleza, tan proprio de mi esposa y sin algún artificio" (Alemán 2010: 437). Guzmán argues that Gracia suspended his free will when she cast a spell over him, making use of her natural abilities.

But the idea of the dangerous temptress is still to be put into a greater context. The pícaro concludes his reasoning with a digression on Homer's *Odyssey*, in which the enchantress Circe turns the protagonist's crew into swine, keeping them from continuing their voyage (cf. Homer 2010: 305):

Dicen de Circes, una ramera, que con sus malas artes volvía en bestia los hombres con quien trataba; cuáles convertía en leones, otros en lobos, jabalíes, osos o sierpes y en otras formas de fieras, pero juntamente con aquello quedábales vivo y sano su entendimiento de hombres, porque a él no les tocaba. Muy al revés lo hace agora estotra ramera, nuestra ciega voluntad, que, dejándonos las formas de hombres, quedamos con entendimiento de bestias (Alemán 2010: 437-438).

Guzmán explains that Circe transformed men into animals, leaving them their human reason. In the time of Christianity, however, human desire causes exactly the opposite: men maintain their bodies, but their reason becomes bestial. The pícaro uses Circe as a cipher that operates on three different levels: first of all, the *ramera* represents an allegory for *voluntad* that blinds men, as it is emphasized here. Moreover, applied to the *exemplum* of the novel, she refers to Gracia, who troubles Guzmán's reason with her *dotes naturales*. Finally, the use of the name "Circe" can also be understood as a poetological reference to the pícaro's own narrative strategy. Circe attracts the attention of Odysseus's crew by singing charmingly while she makes a web at her loom (cf. Homer 2010: 303-305). As weaving has been a standard metaphor for story-telling since the *Iliad*, in which Helen of Troy weaves a pictorial representation of this very poem (cf. Kruger 2001: 76-77), we can say that the pícaro, bewitched by the charms of Circe, models himself on her. As a narrator, he also sings charmingly in order to ensnare the reader. By insisting on his perdition, for example, Guzmán wants to convince the reader of his innocence. In this way, he clears himself of his real *voluntad*, which consists of prostituting his wife. True to a common proverb, "[é]l se hace romero y ella ramera" (Alemán 2010: 367).

PURSUIT OF PROFIT

With the prostitution of his wife, Guzmán attains his major objective of coming to prosperity. The fortunate marriage with Gracia is preceded by a failed marriage with the daughter of a usurer. The father's occupation suggests that economic interests are central for Guzmán already at that moment. His lack of affection towards his wife is also stressed by the fact that he does not mention her name throughout the whole episode: until the end she remains the anonymous *hija del mohatrero*. While in his first marriage Guzmán fails to climb up the economic ladder, he is successful in this regard in his second marriage. This plot structure is based on a method that belongs to the field of biblical exegesis.

By distinguishing between *figura* and *implementum*, the early Christian Community was able to relate the Old to the New Testament typologically in order to establish a continuation in salvific history. In this way, persons and events from the Old Testament could be read as announcements which were provisionally fulfilled in the New Testament. The definitive fulfillment of the biblical events was projected onto a divine omnitemporality. Rainer Warning identified figurative typology in French chivalric romance (cf. Warning 1978), research that followed Erich Auerbach's ground-breaking study of *Divina Commedia* (cf. Auerbach 1967). In Chrestien de Troyes's *Yvain*, for instance, the eponymous hero suffers a loss of self in the first course but then regains it in the second course so that he is integrated into court society. In a study of Garcilaso's second eclogue, Stephan Leopold has recently shown that figurative typology continues to be used in early modern Spanish literature (cf. Leopold 2012).

In *Guzmán de Alfarache*, figurative typology is not only detached from salvific history but also undergoes a reverse development: instead of overcoming the primitive self, the pícaro experiences a regression of civilization. Guzmán's first marriage is based on a contract with the bride's father. The latter recognizes the pícaro's talent for trading, which is not really surprising because his own father has already come to prosperity through "cambios y recambios" (Alemán 2012: 133) in the trading city of Genoa. The usurer takes up this expression when he addresses Guzmán as a merchant: "si habéis de ser mercader, seáis mercader, poniendo aparte todo aquello que no fuere llaneza, pues no se negocia con ella y con dinero, cambiar y recambiar" (Alemán 2010: 369). For the usurer, trading means treating each other as equals. By saying that it is not social background but personal merit that matters among fellow merchants, he challenges the prevailing social order, which is God-given and thus untouchable according to scholasticism. True to this logic, he is primarily interested in trading with money, rather than a subsistence trading which deals in merchandise. According to Thomistic theology, pursuit of profit – *cupiditas lucri* – is to be attributed to the sin of avarice (cf. Geisler 2013: 32-39). This also explains why Guzmán's father could be denigrated through the reproach of profiteering ("infamándolo de logrero"; Alemán 2010: 131). Intending to make a pact with the pícaro, the usurer eventually offers his own daughter. Guzmán accepts all too willingly in view of the generous dowry that comes along with the girl. But true to the proverb "con dote de mujer pocos llegaron a enriquecer, y muchos a envilecer", this relationship will not come to a good end.

The usurer's daughter is used to a luxurious lifestyle, which is why she starts spending her husband's money without restraint: "[e]ra gastadora, franca, liberal, enseñada siempre a verme venir como abeja, cargado de regalos" (384). Guzmán expresses the end of his prosperity by saying that the bread which is traditionally offered to the bride and the groom was consumed after four years: "[p]adecí con mi esposa, como con esposas, casi seis años; aunque los cuatro primeros nos duró tierno el pan de la boda, porque todo era flor" (398). The pun on the lexeme "esposa," which means both "wife" and "handcuff" (cf. Covarrubias 2006: 839), identifies marriage with captivity. At the same time, this lexeme can be understood as a hint to check the complete sentence with regard to possible ambiguities. The lexeme "flor" must appear especially suspicious to the reader in the mouth of a pícaro because it is a synonym for "deception" and "fraud" among rogues (cf. Covarrubias 2006: 915). In its literal meaning of "flour" it is related to the actual *pan de la boda*, whereas in its allegorical meaning of "bloom" it stresses the idea of prosperity. Furthermore, in the Spanish folklore tradition, the production of flour is a metaphor for sexual activity, for it consists of grinding the "semen," meaning both "seed" and "sperm" in Spanish (cf. Vasvari 1983). However, when Guzmán says that "todo era flor," he insinuates that the marriage has not been consummated because "flor" also means "virginity" (cf. Covarrubias 2006: 915-916). Thus, instead of meeting her marital duties, the young woman throws money down the drain. When she has finally driven Guzmán into ruin, her father reappears on the scene. Since he is all too familiar with the "buena maña para saber engañar" (Alemán 2010: 375) common all over Castile, he succeeds in saving his son-in-law from difficulties with the law that he faces because of outstanding loan repayments.

The usurer's daughter is soon tired of her husband, which is why she starts looking for a reason to get a divorce. After getting Guzmán into financial difficulties, she now also compromises his honor, by claiming that he has a secret love affair: "lleg[ó] a tal punto su aborrecimiento, que contra toda verdad me levantase que estaba amancebado, que era un perdido y que con estas causas hallase favor con que tratar de apartarse de mí" (383). In spite of the pícaro's assurance that he is innocent, the reader may assume that he does betray his wife because of the chastity that she has forced upon him. When she realizes that she cannot reach her goals, she resorts to madness, which does not present less trouble to Guzmán. Her screaming and shouting attracts the neighbors' attention. They gather in a great number at his house, worried, but eventually they have to realize that he has not done her any harm. Finally, the woman falls ill and dies without receiving the sacrament of extreme unction. Guzmán is freed from his *esposa* but has to return the dowry, the only fortune his wife has not spent, to her father (399-400). Since there is no progeny, the widower has no right to keep the money, confirming that the marriage has been unproductive both from a genealogical and an economic point of view.

At the end of this episode, Guzmán interrupts the main plot for an anecdote that, at first sight, appears to be completely detached, serving only the reader's distraction. The narrative insertion deals with an incident between a married couple that took place during a voyage by sea. At the beginning of the anecdote, we learn that there was a thunderstorm gathering on the high seas. This is why a captain ordered his crew to throw the heaviest *burdens* overboard so that his ship would not sink. Without further ado, one of the crew members pushed his wife into the water. When he was about to be punished for it, he objected that he had only followed the captain's order; among all the cargo, nothing *burdened* him as much as his wife (400).

If we take into account the extradiegetic level of the narrator Guzmán and the intradiegetic level of the character Guzmán, we must situate the anecdote on a metadiegetic level. In this way, the anecdote mirrors the conflict of the main plot and closes an important information gap at the same time: it reveals the way the pícaro's wife died. Because of the identical conflict, the reader must assume that the usurer's daughter has had a destiny similar to the one of the seaman's wife. In both cases, the women are identified as worthless commodities, incompatible with the economic interests of their husbands. Since his wife becomes an unbearable weight for him, the pícaro apparently decides to kill her. Consequently, he seems far from being as innocent as he makes his neighbors believe. In this light, the anecdote turns out to be a cover-up through which Guzmán sweeps his crime under the carpet, but, paradoxically, he still remains within the logic of confession.

To some extent, it is the usurer himself who is responsible for his daughter's death; thanks to the lesson that he gave to his son-in-law on monetary economy, Guzmán realizes that his marriage represents an obstacle to his prosperity. As a matter of fact, neither love nor economy has a positive outcome within this relationship. In his second matrimony, however, Guzmán is able to combine these two components by making a profit from his wife's body. While the different body parts of the Petrarchan lady (to whom Gracia was related in the hermitage) were compared to alabaster, ebony and gold in order to stress her nobility, the body of the landlady's daughter is completely reduced to its own materiality.

After getting married to Gracia, Guzmán moves into her parents' inn. But soon the family runs into debt because of his father-in-law, and the pícaro finally decides to put the plan to prostitute his wife into operation ("hice del amor granjería"; 512). In comparison to the first marriage, the characters now play reversed roles: while in the first case it was the father who saved Guzmán from the ruin caused by his daughter, it is now the daughter who saves him from the financial problems caused by her father. This is also why it is not the daughter, but the father, who has to die this time, even though the circumstances of his death remain completely obscure, in contrast to the last bereavement (440). Willing to find an appropriate clientele for his prostitution business, Guzmán leaves the family and goes to Madrid with his wife:

Yo sabía ya lo que pasaba en la corte. Había visto en ella muchos hombres que no tenían otro trato ni comían de otro juro que de una hermosa cara y aun la tomaban en dote; porque para ellos era una mina, buscando y solicitando casarse con hembras acreditadas, diestras en el arte, que supiesen ya lo que les importaba y dónde les apretaba el zapatillo (442-443).

At this point, the pícaro gives an account of the destiny of married women in the so-called *Babilonia española*, which represents a genuine *topos* in baroque literature.[1] The courtiers are in search of women whose beauty and seductiveness

---

1 Cf. "Calles de aquesta corte, imitadoras / del confuso Babel, siempre pisadas / de mentiras, al rico aduladoras / como al pobre severas, desbocadas; / casas a la malicia, a todas horas / de malicias y vicios habitadas" (Molina 2009: 210-211); "Don Cleofás, desde esta picota de las nubes [la torre de San Salvador], que es el lugar más eminente de Madrid, malaño para Menipo en los diálogos de Luciano, te he de enseñar todo lo

may be exploited, as they are endued with no dowry or other means of income. The metaphor of the mine used in this context makes it clear that, similar to the pursuit of profit that pulled thousands of Spaniards to the New World, prostitution provides an opportunity to become rich for those who stayed at home. Guzmán's considerations close with the famous metaphor of the pinching shoe, which not only refers to the economic but also to the sexual necessities of men. As is commonly known in the Spanish folklore tradition, the shoe serves as a signifier of any orifice of the body, whereas the corresponding foot represents the phallus (cf. Ferrer-Chivite 1983). Going to Madrid with a woman who does not dispose of any *dote matrimonial*, but of *dotes naturales*, the pícaro becomes a procurer himself. The digression, which becomes a completely unusual *alabanza de corte* in the mouth of the pícaro, thus marks the transition from Alcalá de Henares to Madrid, on the one hand, and from usury to procuring on the other.

After Guzmán and his wife have settled down at the Royal Court, the news of the arrival of the desirable prostitute spreads like wildfire ("corrió la fama de la bienvenida"; Alemán 2010: 444). Soon the couple meets a clothing merchant, who finds them accommodation with a relative. Every time Gracia has her duties to fulfill, Guzmán leaves the house. As soon as he comes back, he is delighted to see the generous presents offered by the clothing merchant, without asking any further questions concerning the sort of job his wife has had to do. Shortly after, they get to know a gentleman who is introduced as an unspecified stranger. He also takes advantage of Gracia's services, whereupon a rivalry between him and the clothing merchant breaks out. In accordance with the correlation of supply and demand, this competition raises the value of the courtesan, and Guzmán's income increases to such an extent that he can finally move into his own *tienda* (447-448). The couple has soon forgotten the clothing merchant, but the stranger does not enjoy the exclusivity for long because some members of the Royal Court ("algunos príncipes y caballeros"; 451) take notice of Gracia and start wooing her with presents. The rivalry unleashed by this conduct drives the stranger into ruin so that he also falls out of the couple's favor. In the end, the two meet a minister of Justice, who wants to see Gracia so frequently that she starts to resist. Since Guzmán is unable to change her mind, the minister orders their expulsion. But the pícaro does not really care about his departure because it allows him to avoid yet another loan repayment (455).

---

más notable que a estas horas pasa en esta Babilonia española, que en la confusión fué esotra con ella segunda deste nombre" (Vélez de Guevara 1941: 30).

He then decides to return to his native town Seville, where his itinerary once started. He expects good business deals in the Andalusian trading town, which is the place of transshipment for the commerce with the New World. Guzmán calls Seville "tierra de Jauja" (459) because this is where the *peruleros*, the rich returnees from the Viceroyalty of Peru, arrive and spend their silver in the local brothels after a long period of sexual abstinence at sea. The procurer's and these people's economic interests, which were only compared to one another at the beginning of the Madrid episode, now coincide. This is emphasized by the pícaro's wish that his new home will be like one of the Sevillian trade houses ("el deseo [...] de ver nuestra casa hecha otra de la Contratación de Indias"; 459). The reference to the land of milk and honey is in fact little surprising because it has traditionally been considered a place of human depravity. With Guzmán's return to the origins of his existence, the plot seems to close, which is also suggested by the reunion with his mother. Anagnorisis is a typical element at the end of an epic-romance plot but has to be understood as a parody in this case because of the all-too-honest description of the mother as "flaca, vieja, sin dientes, arrugada y muy otra en su parecer" (462). The prostitute, who was once so desirable, has now become a repulsive being. The lexeme "parecer", however, makes the reader understand that the old woman only *appears* to have changed. In reality, she is as cunning as before. The pícaro also lets us know that she has employed a "mozuela". As in the case of the commonly known "mujercilla", the pejorative suffix used here is to be interpreted as a hint that the maid increases her mistress's income by prostitution. Thus, the mother seems to have transformed into a Celestinesque go-between.

Even though (or for the very reason that) his mother is in a comfortable economic situation, Guzmán wants her to live at his house. She first resists, telling her son that mother and daughter-in-law cannot possibly live under the same roof ("dos tocas en un fuego nunca encienden lumbre a derechas"; 461). But finally, she agrees, and what must happen, happens: when Guzmán's wife cannot stand his mother's presence any longer, the latter's warning becomes true. Gracia leaves Guzmán with all her valuable objects and follows a galley captain to the sea:

Fueme cobrando tal odio, aborrecióme tanto que, hallándose con la ocasión de cierto capitán de las galeras de Nápoles, que allí estaban, trocó mi amor por el suyo y, recogiendo todo el dinero, joyas de oro y plata con que nos hallábamos entonces, alzó velas y fuese a Italia, sin que más della supiese por entonces (464).

The pícaro explains that his wife has replaced his love with a galley captain's. Remembering the semantic field of navigation from the beginning of the novel, which euphemized the mother's erotic services in the cathedral of Seville ("mujer [...] cursada entre los dos coros y naves de la Antigua"; Alemán 2012: 153), the reader can easily guess which sort of tasks Gracia has to perform on board the galley. What is euphemistically called "amor" is nothing more than the relationship between a prostitute and her procurer, whether he be Guzmán or the captain.

As the pícaro announced it at the beginning of the love plot, his (supposed) torturous love is succeeded by his financial ruin. As a matter of fact, it is his insatiable greed that once again makes him lose everything. Before he also loses his honor, reaching the *cumbre de toda mala fortuna*, so to speak, he starts a rogue's life in the dark streets and filthy inns of Seville. Since he cannot earn money by procuring any longer, he decides to make a living by robbing and swindling.

Original Sin

Guzmán's roguery ends when he enters the service of a wealthy lady with the help of a clergyman in his confidence. His new mistress, however, is not immune to the pícaro's mischievous acts either. He soon wants to leave for the New World at her expense, but she finds him out before his departure and lays a charge against him. Guzmán is imprisoned and sentenced to public whiplashes as well as a six-years-sentence in the galleys. From this moment on, the pícaro becomes more and more feminized. The beginning of this development is marked by a statement that he has already made in the incipit concerning the reproach of sodomy addressed to his father: "[f]ueme forzoso hacer con los demás y andar a el hilo de la gente" (Alemán 2010: 486). The repetition of this statement in such explicit terms makes it clear that the plot structure is circular. True to the logic of original sin, Guzmán finally chooses the same path as his father.

This development starts when the pícaro disguises himself as a woman shortly after his capture; he shaves his beard and puts on make-up and women's clothing in order to flee from the prison in this dress (488). Thus, he travesties in a similar vein as his father, who committed "actos de afeminados maricas" by getting equipped with "cosas tan solamente a mujeres permitidas" (Alemán 2012: 140). Just like his father, who was exposed to mockery and jeers because of his travesty, the pícaro does not succeed in hiding his original identity under his disguise either. Even before he can leave the prison, he is recognized and locked up again. In response to his escape attempt he is condemned to life-long slavery in the galleys.

When the convicts leave the prison in order to go aboard the galley, the route that they have to take to the port is lined by prostitutes: "[d]esta manera salimos de Sevilla con harto sentimiento de las izas, que se iban mesando por la calle, arañándose las caras, por su respeto cada una" (Alemán 2010: 491). Guzmán makes use of the criminals' secret language of Germanía here, in which "iza" stands for prostitute and "respeto" for procurer (491, notes 14-15). In contrast to the other convicts, the pícaro is not given a farewell by any prostitute. By saying "solo fue, solo entre todos" (491), he stresses that Gracia is absent. The peculiar solemnity that arises through the conduct of the prostitutes expresses that the convicts are on a threshold between prison and galley. At the end of this process they will not only have lost their liberty, but they will also have to renounce the assets of the female body.

After the galley has been put to sea, Guzmán tries to win the favor of the master-mate in order to avoid the cruel conditions of detention. One day, the man asks him whether he knows why his comrade Fermín has grown so thin during his stay aboard despite obtaining sufficient nourishment, whereupon the pícaro tells him a parable that is set in Moorish Spain. In the parable, the emir Muley Almanzor challenged his servant Buferiz with an impossible task: take care of his well-nourished ram for a month and give it back to him all skin and bones, but while continuing to feed it. The servant put the animal into a cage that stood next to another one with a hungry wolf in it. The ram did eat its food, but as it was afraid of the wolf, it grew thin anyway, and Buferiz kept on enjoying his master's favor (500-501).

Guzmán uses the parable with a didactic intention that consists of telling the master-mate by means of the relationship between the wolf and the ram why Fermín has lost so much weight: "[m]i cuento sirve al propósito, acerca de haberse Fermín enflaquecido en la privanza" (500). However, the function of the story is not limited to this. As a matter of fact, the master-mate appears twice in the story: he is not only represented by the wolf but also by the emir. This implies that Buferiz is the pícaro's double. Thus, the story, which – like the anecdote about the seaman – is situated on a metadiegetic level, fulfills a poetological function: by means of the relationship between the emir and his servant, it makes an issue of the novel's narrative pragmatics both on the intradiegetic level and on the extradiegetic level in terms of a *mise en abyme du code* (cf. Dällenbach 1977: 127-128, note 2). On the intradiegetic level, the hierarchical relationship between the master-mate and the pícaro is reflected. Similar to the case of Scheherazade from the Persian tale collection *One Thousand and One Nights*, the pícaro makes use of the trick of story-telling in order to survive. On the extradiegetic level, it seems that Guzmán, whom we have already identified as a Circean narrator, ensnares his addressee the same way he ensnares the master-mate.

Maurice Molho has commented that the relationship between Guzmán and the master-mate does not seem to be limited to mere flattery (cf. Molho 1985: 211). According to Juan Diego Vila, there is evidence to believe that, because of the captivity in the homosocial space of the galley, Guzmán also satisfies the bodily needs of his master (cf. Vila 2015). Indeed, an enquiry into the inquisitorial reports of that time reveals that, in addition to whiplashes, being sent to the galleys was a typical punishment for young men who had been found guilty of sodomy (cf. Kamen 2014: 290). Thus, in the imaginary of that time, the galley was some sort of ship of fools, by which sodomites and other sinners were excluded from society (cf. Foucault 1972: 13-55).

The master-mate's reaction to the parable is illuminating in this respect: "[c]ayóle al cómitre tan en gracia lo bien que le truje acomodado el cuento que me hizo mudar luego de banco, pasándome a su servicio con el cargo de su ropa y mesa, por haber siempre hallado igual a todo su deseo" (Alemán 2010: 501). Guzmán's statement that every wish of the master-mate is his command must appear suspicious to the reader against the background of the pícaro's progressive feminization. Moreover, the expression "caerle en *gracia*" refers to the *galanteo*, where Guzmán first fell victim to Gracia's charms. However, the decisive difference in this episode is that the pícaro has now taken the place of the seductress.

There is growing evidence of the sodomitical relationship between Guzmán and his master if we take into account that the former decides to practice sewing on board the galley ("busqué hilo"; 498), which is a craft that used to be done by women (cf. Molho 1985: 211). Furthermore, we can establish a link with the *Celestina*, similar to the episode in which the pícaro's mother appeared as the old go-between's double. The *hilo* that Guzmán uses for sewing evokes the *hilado*, which is not only a medium for love spells but also a metaphor for sexual penetration in Fernando de Rojas.[2] Last but not least, the thread necessarily brings to mind the idiom "andar al *hilo* de la gente," which has been used in order to point out the sexual preferences of Guzmán's father. By means of this key lexeme, the reader understands that the pícaro ensnares the master-mate and fi-

---

2   Cf. "Pocas vírgenes, a Dios gracias, has tú visto en esta cibdad que hayan abierto tienda a vender, de quien yo no aya sido corredora de su primer hilado" (Rojas 2008: 298-299).

nally offers his body to him for sexual practices, in return for which he demands facilitations of the terms of his imprisonment.

When the pícaro admits that he is eager to find ways of flattering the mastermate in order to gain his favor ("ansioso [...] en buscar invenciones con que acariciarlo para ganarle la gracia"; Alemán 2010: 505) and expresses his satisfaction of being able to please the whole crew ("contento en saber que daba gusto"; 509), the reader has already understood what he is up to: following the example of Gracia, who offers her love service in another galley at the same time, the *remero* transforms into a *ramera*. When he becomes guilty of the 'unspeakable sin', Guzmán is dependent more than ever on the narrative strategy of persuasion.

Against this background, we have to ask ourselves how to evaluate Guzmán's *conversio* at the end of the novel. The pícaro's sincerity has been defended by critics again and again. Cavillac has even pleaded for a triple conversion, which is religious, political and poetical at the same time. What makes his reasoning particularly original is the idea that the pícaro's commitment to Christianity correlates with the internalization of a Tacitean-mercantilist individualist ethic (cf. Cavillac 2007: 67-133). Ehrlicher does not generally put into question the pícaro's conversion, but he points to the fact that the 'good deeds' necessary in Catholicism are not put to practice any more. The concrete consequences of the conversion are only announced with a "genuine narrative cliffhanger" (Ehrlicher 2010: 230-231; my translation).

That the *conversio* represents an ambiguous matter is confirmed on the semantic level. At first glance, Guzmán's statement "halléme otro" (Alemán 2010: 506), central in this context, is unquestionably a commitment to Christianity. But on the other side of the coin, the pícaro is insofar 'the other' as he is excluded from the Christian order for being a sodomite. That is why the homosocial space of the galley is not "a space on the margins of the cycle of sin" (Cavillac 2007: 78; my translation), as Cavillac puts it, but a marginal space where the cycle of sin reaches its climax.

The reason for the continual play-on-words is that Guzmán tries to euphemize his lifetime confession in order to gain the goodwill of the King of Spain, whom he secretly addresses, similar to the subjects who sent *relaciones de méritos y servicios* to him (cf. Folger 2009). He hopes that the monarch, in his function as *vicarious Dei*, will make use of his *derecho de gracia* in order to free him from the galley. These considerations can explain Guzmán's sudden conversion. However, since grace is denied to him until further notice, he has no other choice but to follow the example of Circe by enchanting the reader of his apparently epic life story.

Bibliography

Alemán, Mateo. *Guzmán de Alfarache I*. Ed. José María Micó. Madrid 2012.
Alemán, Mateo. *Guzmán de Alfarache II*. Ed. José María Micó. Madrid 2010.
Cavillac, Michel. "Le discours atalayiste au Siècle d'Or." Ed. Michel Cavillac. *Atalayisme et picaresque. La vérité proscrite*. Bordeaux 2007. 39–65.
Cavillac, Michel. "Les trois conversions du Guzmán de Alfarache." Ed. Michel Cavillac. *Atalayisme et picaresque. La vérité proscrite*. Bordeaux 2007. 67–133.
Covarrubias Horozco, Sebastián de. *Tesoro de la lengua castellana*. Ed. Ignacio Arellano and Rafael Zafra. Madrid, Frankfurt/Main 2006.
Dällenbach, Lucien. *Le récit spéculaire. Essai sur la mise en abyme*. Paris 1977.
Dunn, Peter N. *Spanish Picaresque Fiction. A New Literary History*. Ithaca 1993.
Ehrlicher, Hanno. *Zwischen Karneval und Konversion. Pilger und Pícaros in der spanischen Literatur der frühen Neuzeit*. Munich 2010.
Ferrer-Chivite, Manuel. "Lazarillo de Tormes y sus zapatos. Una interpretación del tratado IV a través de la literatura y el folklore." Ed. José Luis Alonso Hernández. *Literatura y folklore. Problemas de intertextualidad*. Salamanca 1983. 243–269.
Folger, Robert. *Picaresque and Bureaucracy. Lazarillo de Tormes*. Newark 2009.
Foucault, Michel. *Histoire de la folie à l'âge classique*. Paris 1972.
Geisler, Eberhard. *El dinero en la obra de Quevedo. La crisis de identidad en la sociedad feudal española a principios del siglo XVII*. Tr. Elvira Gómez Hernández. Kassel 2013.
Homer. *Odyssee*. Tr. Roland Hampe. Stuttgart 2010.
Kamen, Henry. *The Spanish Inquisition. A Historical Revision*. New Haven, London 2014.
Kruger, Kathryn Sullivan. *Weaving the Word. The Metaphorics of Weaving and Female Text Production*. Selinsgrove/London 2001.
Leopold, Stephan. "Aeneas in Kastilien. Zur Typologie von Natur und Politik in Garcilasos II. Ekloge." Ed. Wolfgang Matzat and Gerhard Poppenberg. *Begriff und Darstellung der Natur in der spanischen Literatur der Frühen Neuzeit*. Munich 2012.
Molho, Maurice. "El pícaro de nuevo." *Modern Language Notes* 100.2 (1985): 199–222.
Molina, Tirso de. *Don Gil de las calzas verdes*. Ed. Enrique García Santo-Tomás. Madrid 2009.

Rabaté, Philippe. "El discurso agustiniano de Mateo Alemán. De la herencia adánica a la 'reformación' individual en el *Guzmán de Alfarache*." *Criticón* 107 (2009): 104–135.

Redondo, Álvaro. "Folklore y literatura en el *Lazarillo de Tormes*. Un planteamiento nuevo (El 'caso' de los tres primeros tratados)." Ed. Aurora Egido. *Mitos, folklore y literatura*. Zaragoza 1987. 79–110.

Rojas, Fernando de. *La Celestina. Comedia o tragicomedia de Calisto y Melibea*. Ed. Peter E. Russell. Madrid 2004.

Ruhstorfer, Karlheinz. "Sola Gratia: Der Streit um die Gnade im 16. Jahrhundert, seine Auswirkungen für die Neuzeit und seine Virulenz in der Gegenwart." *Zeitschrift für Katholische Theologie* 126 (2004): 257–268.

Vasvari, Louise. "La semiología de la connotación. Lectura polisémica de 'Cruz cruzada panadera.'" *Nueva Revista de Filología Hispánica* 32.2 (1983): 293–324.

Vélez de Guevara, Luis. *El diablo cojuelo*. Ed. Francisco Rodríguez Marín. Madrid 1941.

Vila, Juan Diego. "'Tanto se desmedra más, cuanto yo más lo acaricio'. La ruta equívoca de Guzmán en el laberinto homosocial de las galeras." Ed. Michèle Guillemont and Juan Diego Vila. *Para leer el Guzmán de Alfarache y otros textos de Mateo Alemán*. Buenos Aires 2015. 251–274.

Warning, Rainer. "Formen narrativer Identitätskonstitutionen im höfischen Roman." Ed. Hans Robert Jauss and Erich Köhler. *Grundriß der romanischen Literaturen des Mittelalters. Vol. IV. Le roman jusqu'à la fin du XIIIe siècle*. Heidelberg 1978. 25–59.

Gender Trouble Without Subversion
Libro de entretenimiento de la Pícara Justina[1]

HANNO EHRLICHER

Libro de entretenimiento de la Pícara Justina, a text published in 1605 by someone calling himself "licenciado Francisco de Úbeda, natural de Toledo", lends itself well to a gendered reading. This is particularly the case because for the first time in the history of the then-young picaresque genre, a novel, the *Pícara Justina*, is centered on a female protagonist. A focus on biological and/or social gender is not in itself groundbreaking, but the approach that I will take in this essay goes beyond this level of analysis. I will not focus on the protagonist as an agent but rather will look beyond her, towards the genre logic at work in the novel. I will show that one of the novel's most innovative features is to expose and parody the genre's logic by biologising the picaresque genre as a real family based on sexual reproduction. The author of *La Pícara Justina* thus inverts the *pícaro*'s ambitions of moral change into the 'watchtower' (*atalaya*) that Mateo Alemán's *Guzmán de Alfarache* (1599 and 1604) first brought into play.[2] The attempted moralization of the *novela picaresca* is carnivalized and thus rejected by creating a female counterpart to the male narrative.

---

1 I have to thank Dr. Anthony Santoro for his valuable assistance in the preparation of this English version of the text and to Dr. Judith Rideout for a final critical reading.
2 The imagery of the watchtower was introduced only with the titling of the second part of the text, *Segunda parte de la vida de Guzmán de Alfarache, Atalaya de la vida humana*. For modifications and variations of titling see José María Micó's commentary in Alemán (2003: 64).

The space for interpretation that Mateo Alemán had expressly left open to his readers in the second part of his novel *Guzmán de Alfarache*[3], enables the hermeneutical collaboration of 'discreet' readers (*discretos*) willing to fix the moral sense of the story, a moral that the author intended to be unambiguous but which is expressed ambivalently in the narrative. However, this freedom of interpretation could also be used for an 'indiscreet' continuation of the newly developing paradigm of picaresque storytelling. One such adaptation is the *Libro de entretenimiento*. In 1969, Marcel Bataillon argued for Francisco López de Úbeda, a Toledan doctor, being the book's author; we can verify that Úbeda lived during this time and, according to Bataillon (1982), moonlighted as a *buffo*, entertaining the nobles at the court of Rodrigo Calderón, to whom the first edition of the work is dedicated. Bataillon's thesis, which soon became the dominant interpretation, was later to come under more critical consideration. In 2004 a counter-thesis was advanced based on the discovery of a purchase contract, which suggests that a Dominican friar named Bartolomé Navarrete authored the text (Rojo Vega 2004, 2005).[4] This new thesis not only renders Bataillon's authorship thesis implausible,[5] but also undermines his interpretation of the novel as a personal satire that shows real events from the court of Philipp III during his travels to the city of León in 1602, a novel therefore intended for a small primary audience able to understand this picaresque masquerade. Even before the new document had been discovered, Thomas Bodenmüller rightly pointed out that reducing the text to mere satire cannot explain how it found a wide audience far outside the

---

3   The preface to the reader in the first part announces a space for individual moralization ("En el discurso podrás moralizar según se te ofreciere: larga margen te queda"; Alemán 2003: 112), and this space is really left open in the subsequent text, which produces a much more ambivalent moral message than has been recognized by orthodox interpretations of the novel as strictly counter-reformational moral writing. For more on this moral ambivalence, see Ehrlicher (2010: 200-237) and Ehrlicher (2016).

4   This refers to the discovery of a contract covering the resale of printing rights for a "libro intitulado la pícara" from a bookseller named Diego Pérez of Medina del Campo, who had purchased it from "fray Baltasar Navarrete de la orden de señor santo domingo", to a second bookseller named Gerónimo Obregón. The document is dated 18th April, 1605, after the publication of the *editio princeps*, whose *privilegio* is dated 22nd August, 1604, and was probably on the market in early 1605. We can thus assume that the sale of the rights took place following the publication of the first edition.

5   Rojo Vega's new authorship hypothesis has not gone unchallenged. See Torres (2009a and 2009b), who explicitly positions himself against it. For the current status of the discussion on the book's authorship, see Mañero Lozano (2012: 30–53).

tight circle of the court. The pirated Barcelona edition, the later Brussels edition, and subsequent translations into other European languages[6] all point to this being a major novel of its time. If, on the one hand, Bataillon comes up short with his determination that the novel's satirical function is a farce based on real historical events, then Bodenmüller may go too far when he does not accord the satire any relation to social reality but rather reads it only as a "discourse parody," a novel that discusses the conditions of language itself and ultimately the epistemological basis of knowledge (Bodenmüller 2001: 171-172). Bodenmüller's own analysis of the impact of the Spanish text in Italy shows, however, that the structural function of the text as a carnivalization of the governing discourses is accessible only to the modern critic who, trained in Foucauldian discourse analysis, understands how to recover the structure of an analogic worldview from the thinking of the early modern era and how to objectify it. It's hardly surprising that Barezzo Barezzi, a renowned expert of the picaresque genre, allegedly did not recognize "the expressed criticism in the *conceptismo picaresco* of the epistemological bases of an analogical understanding of language [...]", as Bodenmüller writes (271), given that Barezzi was himself a participant in the analogical discourse formation and unable to interpret this structure consciously.

While Bataillon's description of the text as a reference to very specific historical events, renders the text potentially unreadable to the modern reader, Bodenmüller's reading as a parody of discourses presumes the break with the early modern way of thinking and can thus fit only with the modern reader. Both approaches, however, tend to ignore perhaps the most obvious object of satire: the hypotext of *La pícara Justina*, namely, *Guzmán de Alfarache*. After all, the pícara calls Alemán's hero, with whom she wants to wed in what will be her third marriage, "señor" on multiple occasions.[7] In addition, she freely refers to

---

6   The earliest translation into Italian was done by Barezzo Barezzi, probably between 1615 and 1619. The 1626 German translation is based on Barezzi's Italian translation and was followed by the French translation (Paris, 1635), and finally the English by John Stevens (London, 1707). To learn more about Barezzi's and Stevens's translations, see Bodenmüller (2001: 175–331).

7   López de Úbeda (2012: 191): "Yo, mi señor don Pícaro, soy la melindrosa escribana, la honrosa pelona, la manchega al uso, la engulle fisgas, la que contrafisgo, la fisguera, la festiva, la de aires bola, la mesonera astuta [...] la novia de mi señor don Pícaro Guzmán de Alfarache, a quien ofrezco cabrahigar su picardía para que dure los años de mi deseo." For other mentions of Guzmán as "señor," cf. 690 and 969.

herself as "Guzamana de Alfarache."[8] Despite all of their methodological differences, Bodenmüller agrees with Bataillon in determining that the satirical function of the text cannot be seen in this apparent intertextual reference to the 'genre' of the picaresque. The already-established 'conventions' of the picaresque genre would only be instrumentally used toward a different end.[9] In doing so, the copper title frontispiece of the *Pícara Justina* (fig. 1) becomes the main point in a logical circular argument defending the claim that the 'genre' became the convention that supposedly predates the hypertext but that can only be understood with its help.

Fig. 1: Frontispiece of López de Úbeda's La Pícara Justina, Medina del Campo 1605.

8 López de Úbeda (2012: 646): "Yo, la licenciada Justina Díez, llamada por otro nombre la Guzmana de Alfarache." Luc Torres (2005) discusses the current status of the research into the intertextual relationship between these two texts. Despite the claim made in his title, he offers less of a systematic approach to the current research on the topic and more of a resume of his own approach, which does not really engage with the generic question and interprets the *Pícara Justina* sociologically as a product of a specific festival culture.

9 Bodenmüller (2001) specifically uses Bataillon's premise that "López de Úbeda has made a purely instrumental use of the genre conventions" (35); he also writes that the "features of the picaresque genre are being parodied" but that "they have a subordinate meaning in the total conception of the novel" (40).

The fact that the copper frontispiece is still interpreted very differently by the experts, however, is a significant sign that "a clearly defined characteristic of the genre" (30) is still not at all consensual, to say nothing of what would have been the case in 1605, when the new genre was emerging. To defend his argument, Bodenmüller criticizes Parker, who interprets the fact that the figure of Lazarillo is pictured in his own boat as a proof of the exclusion of the *Lazarillo* from the picaresque genre. For Bodenmüller, the distance between the *nave picaresca* and Lazarillo's rowboat signifies only an internal differentiation within the *novela picaresca*. But the generic relationship is even more controversial than either interpreter realized: while the little boat is connected to the larger sailboat by a rope and therefore forms a little fleet,[10] Lazarillo (obviously in vain) rows windward as the wind pushes the sailboat in the opposite direction. The alleged 'progenitor' of the genre thus becomes an antagonist who strives in a different direction but whom one can assume will still be pulled in the same direction as the larger boat. Contrary to Lazarillo's will, the boat of the picaresque heads not toward the harbour of luck but rather drifts straight towards the *puerto del engaño*. The image, however, does not itself correspond with any established genre convention that the etcher, Juan Baptista Morales y Fe, could have depicted. The *Pícara Justina*'s frontispiece is by no means conventional but very original and surely had surprised contemporary readers. The frontispiece shows a ship's crew that links together two different literary traditions which were hitherto separated; on one hand connecting the *pícaros* Lazarillo and Guzmán and on the other, joining them to a tradition of satires with female protagonists initiated by "Madre Celestina". The etcher has created the picture of a new genre that, before his own work, did not exist as such but came to be performative through the act of picturing it. None of the elements used in the picture are new but the conscious confusion of two lines of affiliation: the instantiated *de facto* connection between *Guzmán* and *Lazarillo* by the editors in the marketplace and the substantially older genealogy of the satirical in the guise of female deception.

Iconographically, the *nave picaresca* might hint not only towards the tradition of the ship of fools in general (see fig. 2),[11] but more specifically also to-

---

10 The combination of a small rowboat with a larger sailboat is not in itself unusual, as can be seen in the late Middle Age ship of fools-iconography, which the etcher references (see, as an example, the etching in Brant's *Ship of Fools*, shown in fig. 2).
11 Regarding the illustration's relation to Brant's *Ship of Fools* within the emblematic tradition, see Homann (1971: 13–23).

wards the frontispiece of *Retrato de la Lozana Andaluza*, first published anonymously in Venice in 1528 (fig. 3).[12]

Fig. 2: Frontispiece of Sebastian Brant's Das Narrenschiff, Basel 1494.

---

12 Surtz (1992: 180-181) offers an interpretation of the picture that is used early in *Mamotreto* XXIV. Both the Morales y Fe's frontispiece and the portrait of *La Lozana* differ from the ship of fools tradition in showing a mixed-sex crew in the *nave picaresca*. Manuel da Costa Fontes (1998), drawing on folkloric tradition, interprets the ship motif in the *Lozana Andaluza* as a metaphor for sexual intercourse, an intercourse that in the end leads to perdition, as is shown by the allegory of the 'death' of the city of Rome as well as the presence on the boat of the monkey, who is emblematically connected to the devil. Furthermore, the *nave picaresca*, which is driven by "gusto," also bears the mark of mortality via the presence of the allegoric figure of time, which eventually leads to death.

Fig. 3: Frontispiece of Francisco Delicado's Retrato de la Lozana Andaluza, *Venice 1528.*

Francisco de Úbeda created a heroine redolent of the one in Francisco Delicado's novel.[13] Among the parallels between the two heroines is their common sickness: syphilis. Both books treat the disease not as a minor detail but rather as a stigmatizing sign of prostitution and of unbridled female sexuality. The stigmatized female body is used for explicit moral judgment of a freely circulating 'in-heat' female libido,[14] but it also offers the possibility of enjoying a linguistic freedom that goes along with such an immoral life style, which is why López de

---

13 Francisco Delicado's authorship is undisputed, since he claimed credit for his work. For a biography of the author, cf. Damiani (1974).

14 *Lozana Andaluza* contains a moral interpretation of history in the form of an added letter of the author *(Epístola del autor)*, which describes the sacking of Rome and interprets this 'sacco' as punishment for sin (Delicado 1994: 489-492). The *Pícara Justina* also ends with a formal submission to the "Santa Iglesia romana y de la Santa Inquisicón" and, in its final *Aprovechamiento*, insists on a moral value of its autobiography (López de Úbeda 2012: 970-971).

Úbeda was able to present his book first and foremost as a "libro de entretenimiento". What the author offers via the Celestina tradition, which was also already explicitly evoked in Delicado's text by the subtitle of the frontispiece[15], is a transformation of sexuality into discourse by means of witty use of language and aims at a morally legitimate pleasure. This conceptual fusion of sex and language, a characteristic of the female line of the picaresque, can be seen in the fact that Celestina can only fulfil her role as procuress and handmaid to a love that transcends class and social differentiations because she is a seamstress ("labrandera"). The strings she pulls can be read on many levels, not only as metonyms for the weaving of the 'tangled web' of her intrigues[16] but also as the elementary material to produce textiles. Celestina's use of stiches is thus a symbol for the principle of a desublimated narration that stresses the physical, material side of language and collapses the symbolic character of language with a concrete and sensually experienceable material world. This is seen in *Lozana Andaluza* with the fact that the syphilis-ridden body of the heroine becomes a concrete visual object for studying Rome's fall into sin. The symbolic coincidence of *roma* and *amor* produced textually by the palindromic character of a symbolic chain is likewise embodied in the main protagonist of *Lozana*, or more precisely, by her face, which is stigmatized by the near-complete loss of her nose.[17] Lozana thus is shown both as a "ramera romana" in Rome and as someone who physiologically has become "roma" (flat-nosed).[18]

The *Pícara Justina* displays this tendency to corporalize language less radically than does Delicado's book, which is very drastic in its desublimation of

---

15 "El qual Retrato demuestra loque en Roma passaua y contiene munchas [sic!] mas cosas que la Celestina." – "This *Retrato* shows what happend in Rome and contains much more things than *La Celestina*" (see fig. 3).

16 One of Celestina's six occupations is "maestra de hazer afeytes y de hazer virgos" (Fernando de Rojas 2005: 110), in which capacity she procures artificial substitutes for ruptured hymens, using ox bladders or simply stitching together the remains of the hymen, as Pármeno tells his master (112). Jannine Montauban (2003: 75sq.), drawing heavily on Mary S. Gossy's work (1989: 50sq.), sees this as proof of a successful subversion of a patriarchal economy.

17 "y por esto es bueno fuir romano por Roma que, voltadas las letras, dice amor, y entendamos dejar lo que nos ha de dejar" (Delicado 1994: 480).

18 Lozana's missing nose is first clearly mentioned in *Mamotreto* VII, when the heroine, full of envy for the "nariz como asa de cántaro" of a Mercedarian Monk, announces her wish to bite off said organ (Delicado 1994: 195). On the "Roma/roma" wordplay, see Allaigres's commentary (Delicado 1994: 127-130).

language. Delicado goes so far as to allow his audience to participate in the multiple orgasms of his heroine[19]; already his choice to title his chapters "Mamotretos" is a kind of dissemination which not only generates multiple significations but is also aimed directly at the sex drive.[20] The centrality of syphilis, the physical symptoms of which are here moved from the loss of the nose to hair loss,[21] shows that the "licenciado" aims essentially in the same direction. He also uses a particularly permissive language related to the sexual female body. The motto, *El ajuar de la vida picaresca*, which is written around the frontispiece, works towards a materialization and embodiment of language. The wordplay here that formally conducts this materialization of language is an intertextual relation to the later "ajuar de Viejas,"[22] which also describes infertility. It is possibly also an intertextual reference to the sexually connoted "ajuar cosido y sorzido" in the *Lozana Andaluza* (Delicado 1994: 179).[23] The materialized language dissects the

---

19 See *Mamotreto* XIV, which transforms not only sexuality into discourse but rather the sexual act itself, as Luis Beltrán (1996) has shown.

20 See also Allaigre's argument, which shows that Delicado's "mamotreto" functions not only as a formal structuring strategy and indicates a didactical use of the content, but also refers to the "paroxismo erótico" as a "objeto principal del libro" (Delicado 1994: 26–45).

21 Hair loss as well as the disfigured nose has been considered as main symptoms of syphilis as can be seen alyready in Pietro Aretino's *Sei giornate*. On this use, see Folke Gernert's study (1999: 146–161).

22 See López de Úbeda (297), where the heroine reacts to Perlícaro's malicious mentioning of her age and insists on her right to disguise this societally stigmatized flaw.

23 See also Claude Allaigre's comprehensive explanation of the semantics of this passage in his introduction (97). This coincidence in double entendres is not necessarily evidence of a direct intertextual relationship between the two books as we can also find the sexual connotations in the general corpus of Golden Age erotic poetry (see the examples in Alzieu, Jammes and Lissorgues 1975). But the hypothesis of intertextuality between *Pícara Justina* and *La Lozana Andaluza* could explain not only the usage of the 'ajuar' metaphor but also the author's pseudonym. Francisco is also Delicado's first name, and 'Úbeda', alluding to the proverbial 'cerro de Úbeda', is connected in the *La Lozana Andaluza* prologue to the missing "vergüenza y conciencia" of the female protagonist (see Delicado 1994: 168 sq. and Allaigre's accompanying commentary). The author's name would thus be a pseudonym fed by the author's principal source of inspiration, while the strongly erotic and even obscene character of this source would explain why it had to be kept a secret, contrary to the many other

linguistic symbolic chain into its elementary components, i.e. the single letters, and associates these with concrete objects from the pleasure-oriented hedonistic picaresque world of living; to make sense out of these components, the reader has to perform the act of reading in a very concrete and sensual way, going through a sequence of perceptions during which first meaningless signs composed of pictures and letters have to be collected and picked up in order to synthesize them and give them a meaning within a final total statement. This kind of wordplay frames the *vida picaresca* as a mobile and ever-unstable life aimed at an accumulation of objects that can be repeated again and again, in an ongoing round, endlessly recasting the framing square that has also become a field within which to play with language. This kind of repetitive movement corresponds with the logic of reproduction implied in the word *ajuar* – the dowry given for marriage, which was at that time generally contracted in order to reproduce. But it stands in tension with the morally directed movement of the emblematic *nave de la vida picaresca*, which sees the *desengaño* of death as its goal. Contrary to the potentially unlimited duration of the genre, we have the limited duration of the genre's representatives, who (in contrast to the actively moving *Lazarillo*), steer idly and passively, driven towards a location that they do not know themselves yet. They stand in direct contrast to the observer, who is able to look past these figures and can see the destination, which is also helpfully in the *subscriptio* written in a small font at the foot of the frontispiece.

It would be to completely misunderstand the complex generic staging found in the emblematic frontispiece of the *Pícara Justina* to reduce it simply to the female protagonist being a descendant of 'mother' Celestina. The text is more than just part of a gendered line of tradition which could be understood as an alternative to the dominant male pícaros. As the composition of the crew of the *nave* so ostentatiously demonstrates, the text's generic sense does not reside in the substitution of one alleged 'origin' for another[24] but lies rather in the fact that the novel gave birth to a new genre by uniting hitherto separate lines of affiliation. The new genre is performed as the foundation of a new family based on marriage and sexual intercourse.

The main goal of the foundation of this new picaresque family is parody, focused on Alemán's male hero. Guzmán's claim to be an exemplary individual is

---

sources that are mentioned in the *Prólogo summario* but which were probably only partial influences.

24 It is for this reason that I argue that all approaches that seek to determine the actual 'origin' of the picaresque in *Celestina* or *La Lozana Andaluza* fall short. For two examples of this, see John B. Hughes (1979) and Bruno M. Damiani (1994).

rendered implausible when he is contaminated by the materialistic logic of his sexually driven female counterpart. His intentions of self-betterment and moral conversion are rendered ludicrous when he once again becomes part of the realm of the senses typical of the picaresque life. The life of the protagonist described in *Pícara Justina* complements the incomplete biography of Guzmán and continues the narration where it had been left open by Alemán, who had abandoned his hero at the point of a hoped-for liberation from the galley. The announcement of the marriage of the two pícaros, which would be the third marriage for each,[25] makes it clear that the pretended moral conversion of the male pícaro to an *Atalaya* was never effective. Despite multiple bad experiences that generated a misogynistic outlook, he nevertheless begins again with another woman who in all likelihood will not bring him luck, who will not be able to bear him any offspring due to her advanced age, and whose special dowry is first and foremost a venereal disease. Despite critical feminist claims that the *Pícara Justina* serves as an affirmation of an 'autonomous' female subjectivity,[26] the fact that it does not actually do so should come as no surprise when viewed in light of its generic purpose. In her letters to her future husband, the pícara offers herself more as a submissive subject whose long string of identity roles taken in her life to that point culminate in the role of "novia de mi señor don Pícaro Guzmán," a role in which she promises to increase the male *picardía*, from which she in turn hopes to derive some advantage and pleasure ("a quien ofrezco cabrahigar su picardía para que dure los años de mi deseo"). Unlike the *Lozana Andaluza*, the *Pícara Justina* does not permit an enjoyment of unbridled female sexuality via language but rather serves as a means to contaminate the given life story of another person. The operative genre logic in Francisco de Úbeda's novel also explains why the progression of the pícara's autobiography is at best a secondary goal; the fe-

---

25 The fourth and final book, *De la Pícara Novia*, mentions all three of Justina's husbands: Lozano, Santolaja, and Guzmán, respectively. Guzmán's marriage to, and divorce from, his first wife are told in the *Segunda Parte*, third book, chapters 2 and 3 (Alemán 2005: 354-401). His second marriage follows shortly thereafter (chapter 4, 402-431); Gracia, his second wife, ultimately leaves him for an Italian. Both marriage episodes are used for long, misogynistic, moralistic digressions concerning the nature of women, who, according to the 'insights' that Guzmán will pass on to his master in the galley, will only bring men bad luck (cf. Alemán 2005: 512).

26 See Montauban (2003: 82–88). Anne J. Cruz reaches the same result from a different methodological perspective: the use of the female body in the *novelas picarescas* does not lead to female subjectivity but is rather only used in the service of the patriarchal order (1999: 159).

male narrator never moves beyond the beginnings of her autobiography, always relegating the remainder to sequels that had to be written in the future. The "estatua de libertad" the textually immanent author claims to have erected with his story does not have to be completed or finished. It has already become an effective counterweight to Alemán's moral watchtower, which had promised a perspective beyond the sinful life (López de Úbeda 2012: 971). This parodic purpose can best be shown in an address to the reader in which Justina directly picks up the conversion claims made by Guzmán and mockingly repeats them:

> No predico ni tal uso, como sabes; sólo repaso mi vida y digo que tengo esperanza de ser buena algún día y aun alguna noche, ca, pues me acerco a la sombra del árbol de la virtud, algún día comeré fruta, y si Dios me da salud, verás lo que pasa en el último tomo, en que diré mi conversión. Basta de seso, pues. Quédese aquí; voy a mi cuento (698).

This passage is clear evidence for the author of the *Pícara Justina* having read both parts of Alemán's novel (and Juan Martí's sequel). It also renders apparent the parodic intention. Justina copies an element that possessed vital significance in Guzmán's life and that was important for the credibility of his moral claim, incorporates it into her own discourse and 'humiliates' it, since in the logic of her sexually and materialistically coined discourse it takes on an entirely different meaning. Contrary to Guzmán's case, Justina's conversion does not have its basis in a radical change of consciousness and introspection but rather is grounded in a 'virtue' for which she had to pay with her body and the preservation of which she has claimed again and again in her "larga historia de mi virginal estado" (969), a state of grace which at this point she obviously no longer embodies, having been marked by her several marriages and her syphilis ("pelona francesa", 204). The female pícara counteracts Guzmán's conversion logic materialistically and sexually by referring to the completely different 'change' in her own sexually determined body, a change that directly concerns the male pícaro as her future husband. Distinct from Guzmán's moral conversion, Justina's physical conversion does not need any narrative verification in or by the autobiography, since this has already been made quite vivid before the start of the autobiographical part, in the *Introducción general*, where the act of writing itself is the center of a very complex and emblematic parody.[27]

---

[27] Guzmán's conversion claim is parodied alongside his confessional character when the pícara confesses her hair loss to "señora Pluma" and, by using the polysemy of the "confesar" and "confesa", turns the urge to confess into evidence that shows the stigma of the *converso*: "Confiésoos de plano, señora pluma, que, con solo un pelo que se

Justina already appears here as "melindrosa escribana" prior to her role as narrator, and exercises an ingeniously funny interpretation of the materials that form the basic elements of the writing process. This process is depicted as handwriting ("escrita de mano de Justina"), which permits a metaphoric fusion between body and writing process – 'bios' and 'graph'. This nexus unfolds on three levels on which Justina's body and the utensils that she uses for writing are conceptually connected:

In *número primero*, there is a fusion between the quill (*pluma*) and Justina's hair (*pelo*) into "pelo de la pluma." Also, while the protagonist interprets, with some imagination, this hair quill in an allegorical way, in a more realistic interpretation it hints at the symptoms of Justina's syphilis, one of which is hair loss.

Número segundo moves from the writing instrument to the medium that makes it possible to fix the writing and becomes the exegesis of the "mancha," the ink stain that comes into existence when she tries to blow the disruptive hair away from the quill. It is also a sign of her sinful 'flaw', which adheres doubly to Justina's sexualised female body according to the standards of the post-Tridentine morality, because she is not only a daughter of Eve, cursed with a sinful nature, but she also lacks the physical 'undamagedness' that would have been necessary for her social *honra*.

Número tercero dedicates itself to the last material medium that, along with the quill and the ink, forms the foundation of any handwriting process: the paper, which bears a watermark in the form of a snake. This is also a symbol that Justina interprets allegorically, and her pseudo-scholarly interpretations give rise to ambiguity. These interpretations appear to be designed to distract from the most evident interpretation, which derives from the biblical role of the serpent, that being the temptation to sin.

Taken as a whole, the tripartite allegory of the writing material is evidently a parody of the biblical allegory that is not oriented towards materiality but towards the immaterial spirit of the holy book. Humor is created both by this fundamentally materialistic misunderstanding of the function of the allegory as well as (and especially) through the concrete parodic use of the emblematic tradition on which the pícara freely draws. Alongside other moralistic, scholastic discourse forms, like fables and mythologies, the reference to *jeroglíficos* is one of the most prominent characteristics of the whole novel. It thus has been widely discussed in the scholarly literature (cf. Jones 1963, Oltra Tomás 1999, Hazas

---

os ha pegado a los puntos, me lleváis conoscida ventaja; y confieso, si ya por tanto confesar no me llaman confesa, que los pelos que de ordinario traigo sobre mí, andan más sobre su palabra que sobre mi cabeza [...]" (205-206).

2001, and Torres 2002). The fact that Justina exploits these traditions comically and carnivalizes them does not imply, however, that the genre logic of the picaresque is only used as a pretext in the *Pícara Justina* (as claimed by Torres 2002: 552). Nor does it compel the conclusion that the explicit connection to *Guzmán de Alfarache* should only be seen as a "feint to steer reception" supposed to trick thean "uncritical reader who tends to generic automatism" (Bodenmüller 2001: 38). Rather, the parodic discourses in the text analyzed by Bodenmüller and Torres truly gain their meaning by locating the *Pícara Justina* within the genre context, a genre which within the text itself is metaphorically declared to be a biological lineage. Although the 'carnival' of language that is clearly taking place in this work can be interpreted as the signature of a whole epoch, when one tries to lead it back to a general epistemological structure, such universalizing arguments also lose the concrete goal of the parody and thus the motif of the specific gendering of the protagonist.[28] Had the heroine really only been used as a "purely functional mouthpiece to stage multivalent discourse" (Bodenmüller 2001: 77), then her ostentatiously depicted sexual body would be meaningless and even dysfunctional. As pícara, she reverses the forms of the didactic scholarly discourse in general, but especially the use of these discourses in the narration of her male predecessor. This becomes especially clear in Justina's clever interpretation of the "culebra," which has become a firmly established basic emblem of her material writing process due to the paper she uses. Although Justina interprets the snake ambivalently and connects it with generally positive qualities like "desengañadora elocuencia" and the "prudencia, astucia y sabiduría" (López de Úbeda 2012: 252-253),[29] despite the predominant usage of the emblem as a negative symbol, this does not necessarily speak for the general carnivalesque conversion of a "pre-established zoological knowledge into the opposite" (Bodenmüller 2001: 126-127). Rather, it offers itself plausibly and concretely as an ironic continuation of the emblematic usage of the snake as previously made by Mateo Alemán. What is here inverted is less the emblematic tradition as a whole but rather Alemán's very individual and innovative use of the snake and the spider in his emblematic self-portrait.[30] By appropriating this distinctive symbol for

---

28 One can see carnivalesque elements, narrowly defined, in the 'bigornia' episode in particular. This episode is a 'climax' of the *Pícara Romera*. On this, see Bodenmüller (2001: 61-75); Bodenmüller uses Bakhtin's carnival theory, as does Torres (2001).

29 For possible sources of the allegorical interpretation, see Oltra Tomás (1999: 64-65).

30 For an interpretation of the emblematic portrait of Alemán in the *Guzmán de Alfarache* see Christian Bouzy (1992), Pedro M. Piñero Ramírez (2014) and Ehrlicher (2016).

her own purposes, the pícara not only counteracts the intentions of the author of *Guzmán* but also subverts the battle fought by the narrator in the name of serpentine wisdom with and against the deceit of the reader. It is easy to understand Justina's interest in using the snake as a positive emblem for herself: she desires to use scholasticism to veil her own sinful female nature, a deceit to which Guzmán will fall victim as did Justina's two previous husbands. The target of this carnivalesque inversion is thus not the clerical scholarly culture itself, a culture that made the emblematic popular in Counter-Reformation Spain and tried to use it as a medium of knowledge transfer, but rather Alemán's attempt to utilize it for his own purposes.

It is no coincidence that the interpretation of the snake's 'nature' is followed by a fight between Justina and Perlícaro through which the principle of the male picaresque, as given through Guzmán's narrative, meets its female counterpart. Scholarly attempts to give Perlícaro a more exact identity have so far proved futile. Nevertheless, the dispute about the historical identity behind Perlícaro remains unresolved. This shows that the persona may not have been modeled according to any concrete person, but represents a generic function, which is to bind the pícara with a male counterpart so that both figure as representatives of a genre, rather than as individuals. They thus embody the principle of satirical reversibility of the perspective of interpretation inherent in the picaresque novel in general (Bauer 1994: 105), here rendered as a concrete fight between the sexes. If we suspend for a moment the much debated question of to whom in real life Perlícaro might refer, his name can first of all be read as a linguistic defamiliarization of the word *pícaro*. When Perlícarlo appears in the novel, soon he gets involved in a duel with Justina about the meaning of his name. While Perlícaro explains it etymologically as a combination of the words *perla* and *Icaro*, Justina counterposes her own alternative explanation:

Mejor me parece a mí que fuera denominarle Perlícaro de que, en ser murmurador de ventaja, era perro ladrador (que el perro símbolo fue de la murmuración por el ladrar, como de la lisonja por el lamer), y en el trato era pícaro, y de uno y otro se venía a hacer la quimera de un Perlícaro (López de Úbeda 2012: 272-273).

The claimed value of the proper name is devalued from the mythic, even precious, down to something that is animal-like or connoting vice. Justina humiliates Perlícaro and, as Allaigre and Cortrait (1979) have shown, sexualizes him. The dialectic of the subsequent *fisgas* exposes both pícaros and shows the reader their 'true natures': Perlícaro exposes Justina by maliciously pointing out her age and thus her infertility, which is not only a grave social stigma, but will also devalue her as a bride. Perlícaro also exposes himself, however, because his dishonorable mention of Justina's stigma reveals that his own pretension to be an 'elevated' and exemplary individual leaves much to be desired, and that there is merit in Justina's claim that he behaves more like a gossipy "perro" and an "asnal mancebo" has some merit. Justina's stigma also afflicts her rival, who wants to denounce her, because in doing so he makes himself her equal. Within the logic of the picaresque as a genre, discovering the identity of the 'author' behind Perlícaro is less important than is the agonal coupling of Perlícaro and Justina that disavows the moral, almost theological claim of the *novela picaresca* as it was used in different forms by both Mateo Alemán and Juan Martí. The verbal coupling of pícaro and pícara in this fight corresponds with a sexual coupling that in the end is only discretely hinted at with the impending "noche de bodas" and which does not have to be explicit in order to be effective.[31]

The generic function of the *Pícara Justina* does not preclude other functions within the parody, but it does severely limit the subversive potential of the carnivalesque reversal of the moralistic. As a carnival within the framework of a genre, the linguistic transgressions remain in a comical enclave and become elements of a 'lower' novel that doesn't make any claim to higher education and knowledge. Justina may, according to the words of her male creator, be built like a 'statue of liberty', but by no means is she a monument of the modern era. She neither assists in the revolution against the existing gender order nor does she assist in making a decisive change in the order of things we have come to call modernity.

Bibliography

Alemán, Mateo. *Guzmán de Alfarache* I [1599]. Ed. José María Micó. Madrid 2003.
Alemán, Mateo. *Guzmán de Alfarache* II [1604]. Ed. José María Micó. 5th edition. Madrid 2005.
Allaigre, Claude and Cortrait, René. "'La escribana fisgada'. Estratos de significación en un pasaje de la *Pícara Justina.*" *Hommage des hispanistes français à Noël Salomon.* Barcelona 1979. 27–47.

---

31 "Soy recién casada. Es noche de boda. A buenas noches" (López de Úbeda 2012: 970) – these are the final words of the picaresque narrator before the author's salvation clause, wherein he once again explicitly subordinates himself to the moral authority of the church.

Alzieu, Pierre; Jammes, Robert and Lissorgues, Yvan. (Eds.): *Floresta de poesías eróticas del Siglo de Oro.* Toulouse 1975.

Bataillon, Marcel. *Pícaros y Picaresca. La Pícara Justina* [1969]. Madrid 1982.

Bauer, Matthias. *Der Schelmenroman.* Stuttgart, Weimar 1994.

Beltrán, Luis. "The Author's Author, Typography, and Sex: The Fourteenth Mamotreto of *La Lozana andaluza.*" Ed. Giancarlo Maiorino. *The Picaresque. Tradition and Displacement.* Minneapolis, London 1996. 86–136.

Bodenmüller, Thomas. *Literaturtransfer in der frühen Neuzeit. Francisco López de Úbedas* La Pícara Justina *und ihre italienische und englische Bearbeitung von Barezzo Barezzi und Captain John Stevens.* Tübingen 2001.

Bouzy, Christian. "'Ab insidiis non est prudentia' ou le bal emblématique du serpent et de l'araignée". Ed. Marie Roig Miranda. *De la Péninsule Ibérique à l'Amérique Latine. Mélanges en l'honneur de Jean Subirats.* Nancy 1992. 59–70.

da Costa Fontes, Manuel. "The Art of 'Sailing' in *La Lozana andaluza.*" *Hispanic Review* 66.4 (1998): 433–445.

Cruz, Anne J. *Discourses of Poverty. Social Reform and the Picaresque Novel in Early Modern Spain.* Toronto u.a. 1999.

Damiani, Bruno Mario. *Francisco Delicado.* New York 1974.

Damiani, Bruno Mario. "La *Lozana andaluza* as Precursor to the Spanish Picaresque." Ed Carmen Benito-Vessls. *The Picaresque. A symposium on the rogue's tale.* Newark 1994. 57–68.

Delicado, Francisco. *Retrato de la Lozana Andaluza* [1592]. Ed. Claude Allaigre. Madrid 1994.

Ehrlicher, Hanno. *Zwischen Karneval und Konversion. Pilger und Pícaros in der spanischen Literatur der Frühen Neuzeit.* München 2010.

Ehrlicher, Hanno. "Ambivalencia emblemática: autorrepresentación y moral en Mateo Alemán." *eHumanista. Journal of Iberian Studies* 34 (2016), forthcoming.

Gernert, Folke. *Francisco Delicados Retrato de la Lozana Andaluza und Pietro Aretinos Sei giornate. Zum literarischen Diskurs über die käufliche Liebe im frühen Cinquecento.* Geneve 1999.

Gossy, Mary S. *The Untold Story. Women and Theory in Golden Age Texts.* Ann Arbor 1989.

Homann, Holger. *Studien zur Emblematik des 16. Jhdt. Sebastian Brant, Andrea Alciati, Johannes Sambucus, Mathias Holtzwart, Nicolaus Taurellus.* Utrecht 1971.

Hughes, John B. "Origenes de la novela picaresca. *La Celestina* y *La lozana andaluza.*" Ed. Criado del Val, Manuel. *La Picaresca. Origenes, textos y estructuras.* Madrid 1979. 327–334.

Jones, Joseph R. "'Hieroglyphics' in *La Pícara Justina*." Ed Josep M. Solà-Solé et al. *Estudios literarios de hispanistas norteamericanos dedicados a Helmut Hatzfeld con motivo de su 80 aniversario.* Barcelona 1963. 415–429.

López de Úbeda, Franciso. *Libro de entretenimiento de la pícara Justina* [1605]. Ed. David Mañero Lozano. Madrid 2012.

Mañero Lozano, David. "Introducción." Francisco López de Úbeda. *Libro de entretenimiento de la pícara Justina.* Ed. David Mañero Lozano. Madrid 2012. 111–159.

Montauban, Jannine. *El ajuar de la vida picaresca. Reproducción, genealogía y sexualidad en la novela picaresca española.* Madrid 2003.

Oltra Tomás, José Miguel. „Los emblemas en *La Pícara Justina.* El caso de la 'Introducción general'." *Voz y Letra. Revista de Filología* 10.1 (1999): 51–70.

Piñero Ramírez, Pedro M. "Los retratos de Mateo Alemán." *Mateo Alemán. La obra complete.* Ed. Pedro M. Piñero Ramírez and Katharina Niemeyer. Vol. 1. *Obra varia*, Madrid, Frankfurt a.M. 2014. XXI–CX.

Rojas, Fernando de. *La Celestina.* Ed. Dorothy S. Severin [1499]. Madrid 2005.

Rey Hazas, Antonio. "El bestiario emblemático de *La Pícara Justina.*" *Edad de Oro* 20 (2011): 119–145.

Rojo Vega, Anastasio. "Propuesta de nuevo autor para *La pícara Justina.* Fray Bartolomé Navarrete O.P. (1560-1640)." *Dicenda. Cuadernos de Filología Hispánica* 22 (2004): 201–228.

Rojo Vega, Anastasio. *El autor de 'La pícara Justina'.* Burgos 2005.

Surtz, Ronald E. "Texto e imagen en el Retrato de la Lozana Andaluza." *Nueva Revista de Filolgía Hispánica* 40.1 (1992): 169–185.

Torres, Luc: *Discours festif et parodie dans 'La pícara Justina' de Francisco López de Úbeda.* Paris 2001.

Torres, Luc. "La Pícara Justina, espejo de feria de la emblemática hispana." Ed. Antonio Bernat Vistarini and John T. Cull. *Los días del Alción. Emblemas, Literatura y Arte del Siglo de Oro.* Barcelona 2002. 547–558.

Torres, Luc. "La 'Guzmana de Alfarache'. Huellas del Libro del pícaro en *La Pícara Justina*: estado de la cuestión." Ed. Carlos Mata Induráin and Miguel Zugasti. *Actas del Congreso "El Siglo de Oro en el Nuevo Milenio".* Vol. II. Pamplona 2005. 1645–1654.

Torres, Luc. "A vueltas con la autoría del *Libro de entretenimiento de la Pícara Justina* (siguiendo las huellas del médico toledano Francisco López de Úbeda)." *Voz y Letra* 20.1 (2009a): 23–42.

Torres, Luc. "Addenda a 'A vueltas con la autoría del *Libro de entretenimiento de la Pícara Justina'.*" *Voz y Letra* 20.2 (2009b): 3–5.

Genealogy, Gender, and Genre in Alonso de Castillo Solórzano's *La Garduña de Sevilla* (1642)

FRANK ESTELMANN

By providing a new discourse, gender theories helped to create a better understanding of the semantics and the historical context in which picaresque Spanish literature evolved. They notably casted a new light on post-tridentinian Spanish discussions and legislation on pauperism and welfare, charity, and *honra*, and to the *converso* 'problem' that favoured the emergence of the picaresque genre (Castro 1976; Maravall 1987; Bataillon 1969). Anne J. Cruz extended her interest in the debates on the secularization of charity by relating Lazarillo's "discourse of poverty" to gendered readings of the classical texts (1996; 1997; 1999; 2010). Rosa Navarro identified *Vuestra merced* as the possibly female narratee of the *Lazarillo de Tormes*. Both approaches provide evidence of how traditional topics of the picaresque have been supplemented by gendered ones during the past few decades (Durán 2006: 15-20). Another factor was the new popularity of the pícara books. Since the 1980s, texts like Francisco López de Úbeda's *Libro de entretenimiento de la Pícara Justina* (1605) or Alonso Jerónimo de Salas Barbadillo's *La hija de Celestina o la ingeniosa Elena* (1612) came to the forefront of critical attention.[1] While most of the older studies diminished in their importance, these books continue to "expand our notion of the genre and enrich our understanding of early modern gender" (Cruz 2010: 14). The pivotal problem is their staging of a female heroine at a time when subaltern figures such as the pícara represented potentially subversive cultural agents in Spanish society in

---

1 Antonio Rey Hazas' edition of *La hija de Celestina* and *Teresa de Manzanares* and its elaborate introduction illustrate the lively interest for the *pícara* books that originated in the 1980s (1986).

social and economic decomposition (Cruz 1999; Hazas 1983). Substantial analysis of the female picaresque novel as "literatura de reacción" (Coll-Tellechea 2005: 20-23) to this situation started to appear around the same time as their first critical editions.

The novels of Alonso de Castillo Solórzano (1584–1647?) were soon included among the most relevant titles in the corpus of the female picaresque. Castillo Solórzano was a prolific writer during the reign of Philip IV of Spain, "un portavoz de esa 'nobleza media', urbanizada que no se inscribía ni en la nobleza de los grandes títulos ni mucho menos en la incipiente burguesía mercantil sospechosa de conversa" (Mansilla 2012: 32). For reasons yet to be established, the following paper will primarily be dedicated to his *La Garduña de Sevilla y anzuelo de las bolsas* (1642). This is the last volume of his picaresque 'trilogy' that is composed in addition to *La niña de los embustes, Teresa de Manzanares, natural de Madrid* (1632) and *Aventuras del bachiller Trapaza* (1637).[2] But in fact, the story of Rufina, the 'marten of Sevilla' and "la última pícara del siglo XVII" (Arredondo 1993: 22), is quite peculiar when compared to its more conventional predecessors that are generally preferred by literary critics and that are a better guide of when to explore the general impact gender studies had in the field of picaresque scholarship. The first paragraphs of this article will hence be dedicated to *Teresa de Manzanares* before turning to *La Garduña de Sevilla* for further and detailed elaboration.

TERESA DE MANZANARES AND *LA GARDUÑA DE SEVILLA*, NOW AND THEN

Blanco Aguinaga's remarks on *Teresa de Manzanares* are a perfect example of how well and early the abovementioned gendered and contextual factors interlocked. As a literary historian whose studies on *Cervantes and the picaresque* (1957) are widely regarded as the starting point of contemporary picaresque studies, he was not considered a specialist on gendered roles in literary texts when he declared in 1983 that this novel should not be reduced to "anomalies to an otherwise well structured picaresque narrative" (60-61). Abandoning a formalist

---

2 The label 'trilogy' is convenient, but purely conventional. There is no evidence that Castillo Solórzano thought of his three independently published novels as a trilogy. Abbreviations will be used to give the page references in the running text: TM (for *La niña de los embustes, Teresa de Manzanares*), BT (for *Aventuras del bachiller Trapaza*) and GS (for *La Garduña de Sevilla y anzuelo de las bolsas*).

approach popular at that time, he claimed that *Teresa de Manzanares* points to the changing role of women in the transition from the feudal system to capitalism in Spanish history. For him, this period of transition favoured the emergence of female literary agents like Teresa. As Teresa succeeds through the "cash nexus", as he calls it, through the instrumental use of marriage as business or of prostitution, Blanco Aguinaga regards her as a symptom of her era (1983: 64). According to him, the author of the novel is dedicated to the fabrication of Teresa's first hand account of her life and tells a deeply contemporary story. Its literary function is to control a potentially subversive energy manifested in a female figure by presenting her in a casual and comical form of entertainment to his courtly and urban public.

One might very well compare this reading to a recent one, that of Reyes Coll-Tellechea, to observe important continuities and discontinuities between now and then. Coll-Tellechea implicitly agrees on most of Blanco Aguinaga's conclusions. But in her analysis, she goes one step further towards the recognition of female agency: "La vida de Teresa gira en torno a tres ejes que se cruzan: el trabajo manual remunerado, la explotación libre de la sexualidad y la instrumentalización del matrimonio" (2005: 55). She claims that in an early capitalist society like hers, Teresa does not need to sell her body and soul to marriage or prostitution. Unlike Justina in López de Úbeda's *La Pícara Justina* or Elena in Salas Barbadillo's *La hija de Celestina* a few decades earlier, Teresa as a *mujer libre* utilizes a socially recognized way to achieve personal freedom: manual labor. Teresa, in fact, acquired manufacturing skills to braid and craft wigs that turn out to be fashionable amongst the ladies at the Spanish court (TM 230-231). Even though she seems to reject the manufacturing sphere of (re)production by leaving Madrid, her childhood, youth and early adult life, it remains an alternative to her future career as a pícara. While Blanco Aguinaga and Coll-Tellechea share basic methodological assumptions – they both interpret Teresa as an indicator of social change in early modern Spain – they disagree on the degree of symbolical menace to the social order Teresa represents as a literary figure.

It is tempting to extend that preliminary look to a few more studies, especially to those of the editors Antonio Rey Hazas and Fernando Rodríguez Mansilla that both provide a synthesis of the respective states of research between now and then.[3] Rodríguez Mansilla's recent introduction should be emphasized. He analyzes Teresa's braiding as an allegory of her future capacity to manipulate through discourse (2012: 75-101; cf. Gossy 1989). It is, in fact, a mark that dis-

---

3 For a detailed discussion of the older reception of Castillo Solórzano's *pícara* novels, see Karoline J. Manny (1995: 12-27).

tinguishes her socially. In this light, Teresa de Manzanares's core principle is personal autonomy, especially her business acumen demonstrated by putting her money in financial shares with the Fuggers, in case she gets mugged during her travels through Spain (TM 265) or her refusal to be prostituted by one of her husbands (TM 342). Through one of the four profitable marriages, she also manages to acquire a nobility title and calls herself "doña Teresa de Manzanedo". Unfortunately, this is a privilege she loses again when marrying her fourth husband. Throughout the novel, masculine domination seems to be unquestioned, but in Rodríguez Mansilla's perspective, it is not unaffected by the pícara's subversive strategies.

Interpretations like his tend to take into account a detail often omitted in older studies. At the end of her 'autobiography' Teresa alludes to a potential autobiographic sequel of her story: "[…] y así convido al señor letor para el en mi segunda parte, diciéndole que del mercader tuve tres hijos y una hija. Todos salieron al padre en las costumbres, sola la hija imitó las mías. Para la segunda parte remito contar las vidas de todos […]" (TM, 420). The announcement of a sequel is one of the picaresque genre's most notorious characteristics. In order to identify it in the genre's history one can consider the two sequels of the *Lazarillo de Tormes*, the *Guzmán de Alfarache* or *El Buscón* (cf. Hinrichs 2011). This case, however, is truly remarkable. It indicates that Teresa is not being punished for her misdeeds.[4] Further still, it has a proleptic reference to the pícara's future children who will create her legacy. Castillo Solórzano has not published the promised sequel that would have exploited all four histories of the three sons and one daughter. The protagonist of the last volume of his trilogy, Rufina, is not Teresa's daughter but Hernando Trapaza's, the male protagonist of the second volume *El bachiller Trapaza*. But the announcement of a sequel at the end of his first picaresque novel is an emblem for generic evolution anyway. It helps Castillo Solórzano represent the evolution of the picaresque trilogy in a genealogical family portrait.[5]

What should be considered is that Teresa is "probably the best drawn out of all Spanish *pícaras*" for a very specific reason (Rodríguez-Luis 1979: 37). She is an extreme case for the staging of women in Golden Age Spanish prose literature. When she narrates her own story the female-gendered voice of Teresa's

---

4   Unlike Elena, for example, who is executed by the royal authorities at the end of Salas Barbadillo's *La hija de Celestina*.
5   Valbuena Prat has concluded that the author's trilogy is structured by "la ley biólogica de la herencia" (1986: 82).

"autobiografía tutelada" (Cabo Aseguinolaza 1992: 53)[6] is always threatening to escape from the principal narrator's control and domination. That is what makes this text so attractive to scholars willing to combine the methodological renewal offered by gender studies, the interest in the corpus of pícara books, and the preference for female agency as a normative principle.

Although gender studies offer further studies into the picaresque novel, they also add new exclusionary implications. This is proven by the critical reception of *La Garduña de Sevilla*. Until Fernando Rodríguez Mansilla's edition of the text in 2012 and a reedition of *Teresa de Manzanares* (Mansilla 2012), Rufina's story was controversially analyzed. One reason why it was neglected in the literary history of the picaresque genre until then was that it was not only written by a man, but also narrated by an extradiegetic and conventionally male narrator.[7] His absolute control over the text can easily frustrate studies that try to focus on picaresque polyphony and the staging of the pícaro's or the pícara's autobiography as connected phenomena. Hence, Rufina as a 'non-agent' (of and in her story) is said to lack the freedom of action *and* discourse most of her predecessors utilized. This is precisely why her book had always seemed less alluring. For our purpose it is sufficient to point out Cabo Aseguinolaza's postulation that we should prefer "la vinculación esencial del narrador a lo narrado" in texts like *Teresa de Manzanares* over "el divorcio entre el que cuenta y el mundo contado" in *La Garduña de Sevilla* (Aseguinolaza 1992: 52).[8] Unfortunately, this view is widely accepted today.[9] As a consequence, *La Garduña de Sevilla* seems to pre-

---

6 For the Pícara novels as first-person narratives in this context see Juan Antonio Garrido Ardila (2009: 92-100).

7 María de Zayas was the exception to the rule of male authorship of picaresque fictions. See her short novel "El castigo de la miseria" published in the *Novelas amorosas y ejemplares* (1637). For the convention to read zero focalized novels as being generated by a male narrator, see Ansgar Nünning (1994).

8 I also refer to the influential conceptualization of the so-called 'epigones' that degraded and ruined the genre's properties (cf. Rico 1976: 129–141). Rico's judgement is re-echoed in most contemporary studies on the Spanish literature of early modern Spain.

9 In most studies, the (pseudo)autobiographical mode of narration is regarded as primordial in the definition of picaresque poetics; see for example Klaus Meyer-Minnemann (2008). What characterizes the picaresque genre in this author's perspective is "la trayectoria de la vida del pícaro y su presentación narrativa autobiográfica" (22). A less dogmatic conception can be found in Ardila (2008: 221–237). It stands out because it acknowledges "una variedad de voces narradoras" (229) in picaresque

sent no real complexity concerning rules about how the narrative information is selected or restricted to most scholars. After all, Castillo Solórzano's last novel has thus been excluded by a factor of two: as the pure product of male manipulation and as deviant from most taxonomies or poetics of the picaresque genre, both observations being intrinsically linked to each other.[10]

An additional point can be mentioned. Rodríguez Mansilla chooses the ambiguous term of "una 'dama apícarada'" to describe Rufina. He alludes to her as "la amada ideal, propia del universo de la novela cortesana" (2012: 37, 115; Arredono 2006). To him, her novel represents "la despicarazación de la picaresca" not only narratologically but also thematically (Mansilla 2012: 119). Its plot and protagonist manifest the strong influence of the short courtly novels popular in Spain and especially in the literary works examined. Castillo Solórzano was a best-selling author known for publishing ten collections of *novelas cortesanas* in addition to his three picaresque novels and various comedies (Kindelán 1983: 10). He even included three of them in the novel. For Rodríguez Mansilla their presence destabilizes the picaresque composition; most scholars would deduce that it should be seen as representative of the genre's decline in Spain's literary history, an assumption, however, that has yet to be verified.

La Garduña de Sevilla's formal and thematic characteristics do not suit the normative core in contemporary designs of gender and the picaresque. As a matter of course, this is the reason why we should be interested in it. From *La Garduña de Sevilla* emerges a (meta) literary analysis a lot of modern scholars have refused to perform with the same indispensable clarity. Lastly, it reflects genealogy and (re)examines the literary evolution that lead to it. By doing so, it helps us to verify the descriptive norms and sometimes unintentionally prescriptive norms that guide our understanding of picaresque Spanish literature's origin and its evolution during the first half of the 17th century.

As we generalize its effect, this novel also confronts us with a certain paradoxical frame of mind. Generic evolution should not be reduced to an architextual poetics, since it is equivalent with the "continuous modification of the genre" (Mañero-Lozano 2009: 18). Castillo Solórzano not only projects the picaresque legacy in the realm of genealogy and seriality, but he also hybridizes it with other modes of discourse like the *novela cortesana*. Among other things, this results in more flexible and experimental gender configurations as those

---

fictions. Garrido Ardila mentions Castillo Solórzano's *La Garduña de Sevilla* in this context.

10 See for example Coll-Tellechea (2005: 53), and Rey Hazas' comment on the *Picaresca femenina* (1986: 85-91), cf. note 4.

provided by the picaresque tradition itself. It thereby sheds a light on the interplay between generic evolution and gender most helpful in transcending the limitations of a thematic comprehension of historic configurations of gender. Further evidence that *La Garduña de Sevilla* should be a vital ingredient to our understanding of the picaresque genre emerges from its European success. Through its translations into English, French, and German it was one of the most read, edited, and thus influential picaresque Spanish books outside of Spain – unlike the other volumes of Castillo Solórzano's trilogy. To anyone who believes that discussions of translations provide an important clue to the comparative approach in picaresque studies,[11] *La Garduña de Sevilla* can illustrate the remodelizations that were necessary to successfully import a Spanish picaresque novel in other literary polysystems. Each of the three consecutive points – dynamic generic transformation, remodeling of gender through generic hybridization and translation (or literary transfer) – will now be subject to a differentiated analysis of *La Garduña de Sevilla*. The last topic will only be revisited shortly in the conclusion of this article.

DYNAMIC GENERIC TRANSFORMATION IN *LA GARDUÑA DE SEVILLA*

By a lot of standards, *La Garduña de Sevilla* is indeed the most distant from the picaresque tradition, even though one of its translators John Davies compared it to Mateo Alemán's *Guzmán de Alfarache*. But today it is agreed that the intertextual relation that binds it to *Guzmán*, the founding text of the picaresque genre, is as loose and incoherent as its manifestation of a picaresque poetics. Peter Dunn has suggested, for example, that it bears "only the most shadowy resemblance to *Guzmán*" (Dunn 1993: 107)[12]. This observation is hardly surprising. For all the criteria one might employ in such judgment *La Garduña de Sevilla* is a heterogeneous text, a 'composite' ("compuesto") of different styles to restate the concept Castillo Solórzano himself proposed in the preface to *Teresa de*

---

11 By referring to referential, formal, and comparative approaches to picaresque literature, I think of the pertinent repartition of picaresque studies established by Fernando Cabo (1992). A recent comparative study is in Ardila (2009). Literary transfer as a concept is discussed by Werner and Zimmermann (2002).

12 Other authors have alternatively tried to link the novel to López de Úbeda's *La Pícara Justina* with about the same result. See Lucas Torres (2002).

Manzanares.[13] Its *ad hoc* poetics of variation leaves no space for a solid picaresque framing (cf. Eco 1989). The lack of a pseudo-autobiographical narrator has already been mentioned. That *La Garduña de Sevilla* concludes with a happy ending is also troubling. In contrast to any other picaresque novel – and notably to his own *Teresa de Manzanares* – Castillo Solórzano takes his vicious heroine to an unexpected denouement: everything is fine in the end. Rufina successfully climbs the social ladder and is finally set up in a retail trade in Zaragoza with her beloved husband Jaime who she had met shortly before: "Siguió su parecer el mancebo y así, dejando a Madrid, se fueron a Aragón, donde en su metrópoli la insigne ciudad de Zaragoza, tomaron casa y en ella pusieron tienda de mercaderías de seda, ocupándose algún tiempo en esto" (GS 644). Quite aside from its implication of an immoral and yet successful life proven in a picaresque novel,[14] this ending has a disturbing function from a narratological point of view as well. It does not coherently contextualize the episodes, but rather ends strangely (Hazas 1986: 101). Rodríguez Mansilla is among those who insist that the novel's conclusion does not live up to expectations:

> El final feliz del libro descansa, precisamente, en que la protagonista deja de ser pícara. Esta es la mayor innovación de Castillo Solórzano y representa una ruptura en la pequeña tradición de la picaresca femenina. Desde el inicio, el personaje de la pícara (Justina, Elena, Teresa) se orienta a usurpar el papel de la dama, pero solía acabar mal, malcasada o cruelmente ajusticiada. Rufina, en cambio, sí lo logra (Mansilla 2012: 121).

To put it into different terms, *Teresa de Manzanares*' genealogical promise is not completely renewed in *La Garduña de Sevilla*. Rufina has not given birth, neither will she in the future, but Castillo Solórzano introduces a new idea in genre evolution: Without having committed to a different life she has herself ceased to be a pícara and was rewarded with happiness.

A picaresque loophole at the end of *La Garduña de Sevilla* may survive. The narrator promises another sequel: "Donde los dejaremos, remitiendo a segunda

---

13 "Teresa de Manzanares, hija nacida de las verdes riberas de aquel cortesano río, se presenta con sus embustes a los ojos de todos. Su travesura dará escarmientos para huir de las que siguen su profesión; y esto sea disculpa de haber sacado a luz su vida, formada de los sucesos de muchas que han servido de hacer aquí un compuesto" (TM 180, "Prólogo al lector").

14 Rey Hazas states that the conclusion of *La Garduña de Sevilla* is synonymous with "una descalificación global de la sociedad barroca española, una considerable crítica social, quizá sin que su autor hubiera reparado en ello" (1986: 110; cf. note 4).

parte el salir de aquí, en la cual ofrezco más sazonadas burlas in ingeniosas estafas por la señora garduña de Sevilla y anzuelo de las bolsas" (GS 644). We can tell by this sentence that the next book – one Castillo Solórzano never published – is exclusively meant to exploit the comical and satirical modes of writing. It will not depend on a picaresque predetermined genealogy. This can only mean that the function of picaresque story-telling has shifted towards literary entertainment. This does not imply a complete dismissal of its traditional entertaining *and* moralizing function. Both the book's author and censor take care to assign a moralistic purpose to the narration (GS 425–426). Their conventional claim covers the artist's obligation to society as a norm for literary productivity; it does not, however, represent Rufina's story as a comical agent.

Quite a few other elements in *La Garduña de Sevilla* seem to feature characteristics of the picaresque genre while representing a multifaceted break with its tradition. Among which is Rufina's low birth, her desire of social rising, and her inclination for mocking and robbery. These elements do not necessarily relate to picaresque poetics by accepting a rhetorically fixed narrative model. Instead they testify to a literary experiment via the medium of the metaliterary and parodistic use of both genre expectations and intertextual references. This is why we are obliged to redirect our attention to a picaresque reading of the novel and why we need to work through the dilemmas of such a reading at the same time.

A good way to support the variety of full meanings of *La Garduña de Sevilla* is to follow Castillo Solórzano's gradual abandoning of his initial indebtedness to Quevedo's *El Buscón*. Clearly, this indebtedness goes back to *Teresa de Manzanares* and *El bachiller Trapaza*. If the modern editor called the latter novel "a putrid intertextual potage", we may expect that its basic ingredient was Quevedo's picarism (Joset 1986: 35). Its hero Hernando Trapaza is created according to Pablos' model. The technique is patently obvious if we consider that we are told the story of yet another another "Icaro segoviano" (BT 80). The concepts of honor and blue-blooded ancestry (*honra, limpieza de sangre*) are strikingly present as well as the desire for social advancement of a subaltern figure. The foreword of *El bachiller Trapaza* calls for the discourse of the rotten life of an arrant liar: "el discurso sobre la rota vida de un embustero" (BT 58). It thereby presents what Juan Antonio Garrido Ardila has called a "tesis dogmática" (Ardila 2008: 233) that in this case goes back to *El Buscón*. Almost everything from beginning to end can be read through Quevedo's pattern of action. Just like Pablos, Trapaza is a comical hero ("heroe jocoso", BT 59), trickster, and a "picarón" (BT 241) whose futile efforts to climb the social ladder are retraced in the novel. He repeatedly experiences public dishonour and shame in scenes (f.e. BT 86) that mimic Quevedo's "rey de gallos"-episode. Trapaza is finally sentenced to five years of forced labour on the royal galleys. His former mistress Estefanía had denounced his crimes to the authorities after having discovered that he is a complete fraud (Dunn 1952: 39). A similar disenchantment occurs in *El Buscón* when Pablos' fraud is uncovered by the family of his future wife. In this brief moment Pablos sees an end to his social rise. Similarly, Trapaza re-starts genealogical causality as much as he repeats as a "pícaro en las costumbres de mentir, engañar y ser fuller" (BT 278) the circular movement of social determinism within the picaresque tradition, especially the tradition Quevedo had initiated a few decades earlier.

What makes Trapaza unique is that he doesn't die childless as Pablos and most prior pícaros had. Estefanía finds herself pregnant when he leaves for the galleys. Their daughter is Rufina. The novel dedicated to her is the sequel to the one Castillo Solórzano had written about her father. This genealogical relation between *El bachiller Trapaza* and *La Garduña de Sevilla* has already been stated. In addition, an interlocking intertextual effect can be observed. The first chapter of *La Garduña de Sevilla* includes the last episode in Trapaza's life and thereby binds this text directly to *El bachiller Trapaza*. From Estefanía's success liberating her daughter's father, Trapaza, from forced labor and marrying him at the beginning of *La Garduña de Sevilla* something can be learned. One must bear in mind what a great disappointment Trapaza is to his wife: Estefanía becomes strikingly aware of her husbands 'uncorrectable' nature, his "mala inclinación" to gambling and his predisposition to otiosity ("ociosidad") (GS 435). There is an intertextual reprise, of course, that goes back to López de Úbeda's *La Pícara Justina* and to what a disappointment the gambler Lozano had been to its protagonist, but Trapaza's delight, gambling and leisure, entails more than his neglecting his wife. It also results in both parents' blatant disregard for their daughter Rufina. Left for many years without any considerable paternal and maternal control or education the adolescent Rufina starts to make the most of her independency and above all of her sexual appeal. Her stellar picaresque career starts with her first marriage to the much older merchant Lorenzo de Sarabia soon after the death of her mother.

As can be seen by such an opening, Castillo Solorzano initially relies on a typical picaresque setting already used in *Teresa de Manzanares*. Rufina's initial situation is the same as her parents' had been. The text is, in fact, explicit about Rufina's natural 'inclination' to crime, the 'depraved customs' she grew up in and the fatal resemblance to her parents that conditioned her life:

El asumpto deste libro es llamar a una mujer *garduña* por haber nacido con la inclinación deste animal de quien hemos tratado. Fue moza libre y liviana, hija de padres que, cuando le faltaran a su crianza, eran de tales costumbres que no enmendaran las depravadas que su hija tenía. Salió muy conforme a sus progenitores, con inclinación traviesa, con libertad demasiada y con despejo atrevido (GS 429).

However, Castillo Solózano mirrored the life of the sequel's protagonists in the sequel's narrative structure, namely by repetition and expansion. Therefore his innovative choice was to transform the picaresque heritage into the story of the second Pablos (Trapaza), who founds a legacy with Rufina's, his daughter's story as narrated in a sequel. Within Castillo Solórzano's 'trilogy' the function assigned to *El bachiller Trapaza* is to make obvious its underlying intertextual relation to *El Buscón* which prepares the ground for a sequel that finally results in a parodistic reversal. This reversal will be retraced step by step. Its outcome, however, is clear: Rufina and the novel dedicated to her escape from genealogical (parental) and generic (picaresque) predetermination. Hence, *La Garduña de Sevilla* proves extremely rich when subjected to the operation of a genealogical and generic reading that are both faced with a dilemma and with ultimate failure.

One word describes Rufina, i.e. "hermosura" (GS 437) – from the beginning of the novel, her beauty inevitably attracts pretenders willing to reward female submission with a legal status and a secure existence ("comodidades", GS 442). It is Trapaza who arranges Rufina's first marriage in Madrid. Her following adulterous life is explicitly defended by the narrator (GS 442) who advises against marrying young women to old men (GS 442). When Rufina's first husband dies he leaves "su adúltera esposa" (GS 447) with nothing but her pretty face (GS 451). But instead of *mudar de vida*, a change of lifestyle that the moralistic sermon of Mateo Alemán's *Guzmán de Alfarache* would have called for at this point, Rufina deliberately choses to "mudar de habitación" (GS 451). She moves to a different Sevillan neighborhood. This reminder of the well-known sentence against horizontal mobility at the end of *El Buscón* (Randall 1964: 101-108) is not so much re-enacted but parodistically reversed in a reply to Quevedo's novel. Instead of causing more problems by providing new stages for the same behavior, Rufina's horizontal mobility effectively protects her from further difficulties. Her crucial role as a literary agent fighting against excessive "codicia" (greed) cannot be overemphasized, especially because the motif goes back to the first experiences of Lazarillo de Tormes. To begin with, the whole city of Seville applauds Rufina mugging Marquina, a rich and avaricious colonist who hides all his treasures (GS 452-453). After impersonating the daughter of one of the oldest aristocratic families of the Empire, Rufina is able to provoke Marquina's compassion before stealing his gold: "[…] en Sevilla fue celebrado el hurto holgándose muchos de que fuese así castigado quien tan pocas amistades sabía hacer con lo que le sobraba" (GS 477). On the journey to Madrid, in Carmona, and with the help of her companion Garay, she outwits a Genovese, Otavio, stunned by her appearance. The rich Italian turns out to be a passionate alchemist and an easy prey for the witty pícara's next confidence trick – in an episode reminiscent of *Marcos de Obregón* (1618) and Quevedo's satires of the alchemists. There is, again, no reason to object to her theft of Otavio's gold from a moral point of view as it is the man's immorality that is punished by Rufina. Similar to many of his contemporaries Castillo Solórzano draws a sharp line between the Genovese's pretentious "codicia" (GS 523) and the noble values of responsibility, generosity, and honesty of true nobility. These values are ironically encouraged by a minority of 'low-borns' like Rufina seeking for their own material benefit. Traveling to Málaga, Rufina then plays a decisive role in discovering the hermit Crispin's real identity as a thief in the third book of *La Garduña de Sevilla*, its fourth book being reserved for her success in outplaying Crispin's revenge in Toledo. Unlike Pablos in *El Buscón* or her own father, Rufina has by now become a valuable social instrument and thus, she successfully enforces social norms. Her picaresque repertoire combining *estafas* (GS 452), *burlas* (GS 453) and theft has become instrumental to the author's satire of contemporary Spain.

It has become obvious that the initial picaresque setting of *La Garduña de Sevilla* is abandoned at the very moment the intertextual reference to Quevedo's *El Buscón* starts to grasp at nothing. There is a growing contrast between Rufina pretending to be noble, by playing the harp and entertaining her lovers and the group of thieves around Crispín who abandon themselves to "esa pícara y peligrosa vida" (GS 549) that will lead them straight to the galleys at the end of the second book. Both worlds have fallen apart before the conclusion of the novel. When he finally allows Rufina to escape from replicating her parents' unfortunate misdeeds, the narrator has conceivably, to at least some degree, abandoned the deterministic idea of the social and biological inheritance of depraved behavior. Such a reversal could only have been achieved if he had been able to call our attention to the undramatized and yet purely comical crimes of a female figure.

The last turning point of the narration does nothing more but to codify Rufina's post-picaresque life. Rufina marries Jaime who is a devious thief ("gran bellaco socarrón", GS 587). He had initially been sent by Rufina's enemy, Crispin, to seduce and to play a prank on her. Jaime gets in Rufina's door and bed by pretending to be noble, inversing the conventional role by using a pícara's strategy against her. Rufina immediately falls in love with Jaime ("de solo ver a este hombre se le incline", GS 589) and gets deceived by him: "Ella vivía engañada, porque se pensaba que su huésped era el que se había pintado en la relación

[...]" (GS 598). Surprisingly, however, during one of their "colloquios amorosos" (GS 595) – both lovers pretend to be "fino amantes" (GS 599) – Jaime lays aside his mask. He uncovers his true identity and his feelings for her: "Yo no soy el que mi relación os ha dicho, si bien soy nacido en Valencia, pero de padres humildes, gente honrada y limpia. [...] Yo os he descubierto mi pecho, ahora disponed de mí lo que fuéredes servida [...]" (GS 626). Rufina is now willing to opt for authenticity as well: "Esto de haberse declarado en decir quién era, dando por fabulosa la relación que la había hecho, la obligó para declararse también con él" (GS 626). After managing to declare their mutual attachment Jaime denounces Crispín's whereabouts to the authorities before he and Rufina happily get married in Madrid where they mug an author of comedies. Finally, Rufina and Jaime decide to move to Zaragoza (GS 644) where they establish the business that provides income and may secure their future luck.

Focusing on the pícara's economic motivation one can, of course, "be assured that the two worlds (of romance by birthright and romance by fraud) are not really interchangeable when the couple is set themselves up in the retail trade", as Peter Dunn has suggested before he concludes:

So the bourgeois happy ending contains an unresolved ambivalence that would be felt differently by different publics: crime (ingenious fraud, not brutality) does pay; but blue-blooded reader looking down from their comfortable height could view the successful accommodation with amused disdain. Those readers who had made it into the urban respectable middle class or low aristocracy might feel less comfortable in their disdain. To those who were sliding into poverty, clinging heroically or pathetically to their *hidalguía* and their *honra*, such fictions were very possibly a too vivid representation of what their world was coming to (Dunn 1993: 246).

Rufina lives in a society where money and 'self-marketing' start to overtake social prestige and social determinism. Eventually, the achievement-oriented ideology of capitalism that is the hidden side of her successful accommodation and compromise with Jaime interrupts the picaresque 'cyclical morphology.' Interesting to notice, in this sense, is that one of the older critics that analyzed all three picaresque novels of Castillo Solórzano, Alberto del Monte, recognized the urbanization and commercialization among their most prominent features (1971: 147-149). As pointed out by Nieves Romero-Díaz (2002), Castillo Solórzano integrates Rufina as an ancient pícara in an urban setting that connects her with his growing urban 'middle class' reading public.

REMODELING GENDER THROUGH GENERIC HYBRIDIZATION

The mixture of different modes of discourse in *La Garduña de Sevilla* is impressive. As readers, we are confronted along the main plot with different poems (satiric poems, *décimas*, *romances*) written and presented by different characters, with letters exchanged and notes between them and even with comedic plays like the *Entremés* composed by Rufina's lover Jaime. The different discourse modes are all relevant to the plot. Jaime's one act-play is meant to deceive an author of comedies from his real intention to rob him. Several *romances* of her own invention are artfully sung to Marquina (GS 465-466) and to the Genovese alchemist (GS 519-520), who fulfills a similar function. Meanwhile, Garay's "versos satíricos" (GS 537) on Otavio's ridiculous attachment to alchemy are meant to tell the Italian that he has been deceived. Special cases, however, are the aforementioned three short stories. They are told by three different narrators. The first one, "Quién todo lo quiere, todo lo pierde", is read by a cleric from an anthology of *novelas* to entertain a group of travelers on their way to Madrid. Rufina is among them. Moralistic in tone and content it forces a lover's choice between honor and love and a deceitful woman who works her charms on her lovers to control them. In the second one, "El conde de las legumbres", we are confronted with a noble warrior in service of the Spanish king in Flanders. This warrior acts like a crazy fool and calls himself 'the Earl of Legumes' in order to win over the heart of a German princess. His story is told on the superordinate diegetic level by Garcerán who is a member of Crispín's gang of thieves. The third and last short story, "A lo que obliga el honor", is performed by Jaime. In this story doña Vitoria is dishonored and abandoned by don Pedro to whom she had faithfully admitted to her house. She then successfully fights for her honor by offering her services as a maid to her lover's future wife.

All of these short stories are of considerable length and address typical courtly values such as confidence, promise, freedom and duty, the woman's self determination and family honor (cf. Kindelán 1983; Manny 1995). They function as entertainment for the characters during moments of inaction – between stations during their travels, in sleepless nights or simply between dinner and nighttime. In other words, they are artful and entertaining "ellipsis que sacan al lector de la acción principal" (Mansilla 2012: 27). Their primary function is fundamentally different than the one provided by the various 'mediums' of poem, play, letter etc. As micro representations of an idealized courtly world mainly concerned with the intrigues of love, they seem to represent, at first, a sharp contrast to the life of the book's protagonists (Manny 1995: 158). In a generic perspective, they confront the picaresque narration with courtly *novelas cortesanas*. After a while though, the contrast between the content and the genres fades as 'doña' Rufina and her false gentleman 'don' Jaime marry, thus interweaving the short courtly novel and the picaresque.

It is useful to delve into this topic because it has important repercussions on the gendered construction of identities. In general terms, it is one of the characteristics of Castillo Solórzano's picaresque novels that their protagonists, male or female, are well educated and literary competent. Teresa has learned to read and write 'in perfection' with her first two old *maestras* that took the young orphan at the age of ten (see TM 210). Trapaza has been taught to read and write as well (see BT 67). The one-time student in Salamanca composes quite a few of the satiric verses included in his novel. It is not surprising then that Rufina not only uses handwritten notes to manipulate other characters, but she is also able to discuss her enthusiasm for the genre of short stories when listening to "A lo que oblige el honor" during her travels:

Rufina, que era amiga de tales libros y cuantos deste género salían los había de leer, diole deseo de ver el estilo con que escribía el licenciado Monsalve y así le rogó mucho que, si no le era de enfado sacar el libro, estimaría oír dél una novela, porque se prometía que de su buen ingenio sería muy pensada y mejor escrita (GS 481).

Considering her literary competence displayed throughout the novel, the fact that she does not tell her own story in a fictional autobiography is purely coincidental. Abandoning the autobiographical voice of the pícara's results, by no means, in an impersonal and single dimensional narration.

More importantly, Rufina uses her remarkable literary skills to overcome her social disadvantage of being a woman in a world dominated by men. In many senses she is the most accomplished early modern pícara because she is the best-educated *dama* among them. In the text's general perspective, Castillo Solórzano's recognition of female self-determination and authorship is too obvious to be omitted. It suffices to point to the laudatory references to his personal friend María de Zayas and her 'felicitous genius' ("el ingenio de doña María de Zayas y Sotomayor, que con justo título ha merecido el nombre de Sibila de Madrid, adquirido por sus admirables versos, por su felice ingenio y gran prudencia"; GS 482) and to another female writer that had come into prominence, Ana

Caro de Mallén.[15] Zayas had also publicly claimed "la pureza de los ingenios" by publishing her *Novelas amorosas y ejemplares* (1637; 2007: 159). Castillo Solórzano's laudatory poem to that book had already confirmed his compliance with her claim. When literally evoking Zayas' "ingenio" in *La Garduña de Sevilla* he repeats this compliance. But does it also extend to Rufina's literary competence as a manipulative character?

Rufina's derision, mockery, and robbery clearly depend on costumes, words, and actions that allow her to impersonate seductive aristocratic ladies. She successfully pretends to be a direct descendent of an old aristocratic family from Burgos as far as Marquina is concerned (GS 458). She also convincingly performs a similar identity in order to impress Crispín: "Yo soy natural de Almería, nacida de padres nobles [...]" (GS 544). Her 'natural' appearance of femininity is much needed for usurpations of identities. When she seduces the avaricious Genovese by pretending to be ill and needing to recover in his *Quinta*, his mistake is not to see through her carefully chosen disguise. He cannot see the pícara behind the beautiful damsel in distress: "[...] pues el conocer que su hermosura no tenía nada de mentirosa, sino toda natural y verdadera, que es para el hombre el mayor incentivo de amor" (GS 514). Teresa's beauty is regarded as natural and true, but her disguise is not. After all, Rufina's mastery of writing, singing and playing instruments goes with her simulation of an aristocratic identity. There may be something awkward about her ability to communicate through writing and to use poetic verses and literary 'academias' for her goals. The reader does not know why she is able to sing a *romance* in all due form and accompany herself with a guitar in order to please and later mug Marquina (GS 465-466). But all things considered, these unlikely elements vouch for the transgression of social norms by the instrumental use of gender difference. They provide a conventionally gendered façade to subaltern empowerment and social privilege. It seems as though Rufina's desire to advance, her struggle for recognition and material benefit requires the representation of an inconspicuous and uncontroversial aristocratic femininity that includes literacy and a literary competence. What is needed then is, in other words, her ability to perform like a heroine of a courtly short novel.

Rufina's case is important if you want to reconsider the picaresque genre's history regarding categories of gender. On a first reading these books defend what Cruz has called the "dimorphic disjunction" by referring to Mateo Ale-

---

15 Castillo met Zayas "a quién compuso unas décimas y un soneto que figuran en la primera edición de *Novelas amorosas y ejemplares* (1637)" in Zaragoza where he served the viceroy de Aragón Pedro Fajardo. For details see Patrizia Campana (1992: IX).

mán's *Guzmán de Alfarache* that states: "Sea la mujer, mujer, y el hombre, hombre" (2005: 2/393).[16] If the baroque aesthetics approved of and even encouraged stylistic and generic variation or hybridization, then the heteronormative gender norms called for strict compliance. There is no easy stance against these norms particularly in the female picaresque novels where they are part of confidence tricks and are thus required for effective seduction, manipulation, and deceit. Getting deeper into the topic, however, the claim of a reproduction of heteronormative repertoire in the picaresque genre may entail a multi-faceted argument that has several and partly refractory implications. Three of them can be isolated. Their description can then lead to the conclusion.

The first argument concerns the complexity that persists and the exceptions that are made within the normative framework. If novels like *La Garduña de Sevilla* permit only limited transgressions of gender norms, they display those norms rather univocally. What is meaningful in Rufina's case, for example, is her depiction as a marten (the grammatical gender of "garduña" is female) inclined to steal. In this metaphor the origin of female picarism is traced back to the 'animalistic' nature of women driven by their insatiable appetite. This characterization involves a misogynistic repertoire. Meanwhile, the novel shows an increased awareness of its own gendering of identities. When Rufina, for example, answers the false eremite's advances with faked modesty and reservation the reader focusses on her 'feminine' behaviour:

Aunque yo no me incluya en el número de las que pueden con su beldad inquietar a los hombres, le confieso, hermano Crispín, que me conformo con su opinión, que es tan poderosa la fuerza de la hermosura que *a mí, con ser mujer*, me lleva y deja suspensa cuando tengo algún bello objeto adelante de mis ojos; y así no me admira que los hombres hagan estremos estando enamorados (GS 547-548; emphasis added).

A case could be made on how misogynistic declarations like this translate a preoccupation with, fear of, and imaginary defense against the emancipation of women in social reality, as investigated by Eugenia Saínz González:

El éxito de la pícara, impensable en el siglo XVII, refleja el temor de la colectividad masculina al ascenso e independencia de la mujer. La pícara no es solo el esperpento moldea-

---

16 According to Cruz (2010: 11), this statement of principles "belies the fluctuating status of gender in the early modern period, where the 'other' – whether Jews, Arabs, Italians, or new world indigenous – easily shifted into the category of woman".

do por la mirada misógina del autor; es también la encarnación literaria de la mujer fatal del Barroco" (Saínz González 1999: 45).

But as readers we know that Rufina imitates the role of a lady. If you include femininity as an integral part of her performance, it depends not so much on nature than on acting or performance. The acculturalization or performativity of gender in the literary practice can almost imperceptibly undermine the ideological or theoretical core assumption of its naturalization.

Secondly, not all characters in a picaresque novel are under the same heteronormative control and supervision. Peter Dunn has called for the investigation of the "minor types" such as the unfaithful maidservants that appear quite regularly in Castillo Solórzano's *novelas cortesanas* (1952: 55). There is, in fact, a good reason to extend that proposal to his picaresque novels. One of the few examples of cross-dressing in the history of the picaresque genre can be found in *El bachiller Trapaza*. In order to make money Trapaza and his coadjutor Pernia decide that the latter should disguise as "la Monja alférez, una señora que, inclinada a lo bélico, pospuesto el hábito mujeril, hizo en las Indias cosas notables por la Guerra" (BT 173). *La Monja Alférez* was a historic battlesome nun who, after leaving her family, fought in the Spanish colonies dressed as a man before returning home to tell her story in an autobiography that served as testimony of her exploits.[17] Pernia is effective in reenacting her role. Significantly it is not the Pícaro Trapaza himself who changes his appearance. The crossdressing is suggested to a random character who disappears soon after. As Trapaza puts it: "[…] podemos fingir que sois la Monja alférez; […] fingiré que vais a los galeones de la Carrera de Indias, y, deseando que os entren a ver, pondremos precio a la entrada y ganaremos dinero" (BT 173) Why Trapaza prefers the role of a guardsman to that of a 'masculine woman' is blatantly clear: gender confusion is not acceptable in a picaresque protagonist without further ado. The exceptions to the rule are all born of necessity. Guzmán de Alfarache for example shaves and wears women's clothes to pass unrecognized when he escapes from prison: "[…] ya tenía prevenido un vestido de mujer" (2005: 488).[18] The motif resurfaces in *La Garduña de Sevilla* when Crispín wears women's clothes for the same reason (GS 584). A Pícaro is compelled to regard cross-dressing as the last resort. In

---

17 A modern edition of this famous autobiography is the *Historia de la Monja Alférez, Catalina de Erauso, escrita por ella misma* (2015). For an elaboration on the representation of cross-dressing in this text see Sonia Pérez Villanueva (2013), and Christopher Kark (2012).

18 After being caught he states: "Pensé huir del peligro y di en la muerte" (ibid).

general, he should be exempted from any symptom of effeminacy. It is in fact relatively easy to verify this hypothesis. There is a presumably effeminized man for example who falls victim to Teresa's mockery (TM 301-303). Teresa promises him that his beard will start to grow and hands him an elixir. However, this elixir brutally burns and deforms his face. In the end, the whole city of Córdoba laughs about the mutilated fool that wanted so hard to become a real man. Teresa's companion Jerónimo even uses the practical joke – one of the biggest 'mockeries' ever offered by a woman ("mayores embustes que ha trazado mujer", TM 322) – as a theme for a satirical one-act play (*entremés*) reproduced in the novel. Controlled by the male narrator, female protagonists like Teresa usually represent and even promote heteronormative standards. But this is not equally true for the secondary characters like Pernia in *El bachiller Trapaza* who may serve to celebrate gender trouble. The corresponding discursive energy that permits a fluctuating status to gendered representations in a picaresque novel is henceforth being relegated to a sideline after having been banned from the center. Within picaresque narratives, gender trouble may be forced to remain an exception. But it remains within the scope of the picaresque. There is a difference between the fluctuating gender status attributed to a male character like Pernia (or the beardless gentleman) on one hand and the discourses of enclosure that define the Pícara as a woman on the other. But Castillo Solórzano's theories are not disproportionate in principle. Rufina is playing the role of a woman just as Pernia performs *la Monja Alférez*.

The third consequence appeals to common notions of genre specificity and liminal representation of gender confusion, but it extends the object of investigation to narrative discourse and its generic complexity. As demonstrated, Castillo Solórzano's last picaresque novel displays the "progressive infiltration" of idealistic genres into the picaresque narrative (cf. Hazaz 1986: 102). The most prominent tools used for this infiltration and "la imposición de lo cortesano sobre lo picaresco" (Mansilla 2012: 102) are the three courtly short stories included in the novel. Now, their gendered conventions are different from those displayed in the picaresque main plot. It is again Dunn who has observed that Castillo Solórzano in his short stories "often gives the woman the initiative in the amorous chase" which finds its "most complete expression" in *Los efectos que hace amor* (a *novela cortesana* included in his anthology *Los alivios de Casandra*, published in 1640) "when the lady even goes so far as to have her lover kidnapped" (Dunn 1952: 55). A similar kind of observation can be made related to the interpolated short stories in *La Garduña de Sevilla*. The story of the noble warrior in service of the Spanish king in Flanders who acts like a crazy fool in "El conde de las legumbres" reinforces the suggestion. His "fingirse loco" and "vestirse [...] de un hábito ridículo" (GS 555) represent a complex play of gender norms, all the more since they are related to the fictional autobiography in which the 'Earl of Legumes', son of an old Galician king, fell into the river Sil where he was raised by nymphs. Such an 'effeminized' behavior would not be found in a pícaro unless on the verge of despair. In a courtly setting and in a courtly genre, however, it is a legitimate strategy to declare one's love to a lady, especially when it is performed by a successful military commander who as an ideal male lover is prepared to humiliate himself in order to win over the heart of a princess (Del Monte 1972: 147). The king approves of the actions at the end of the story (GS 579).

Vitoria's example in "A lo que obliga el honor" is similar: Taking her destiny into her own hands, this desperately disappointed lady lowers herself to serve her lover's future wife in order to prevent his arranged marriage and in order to marry Pedro herself. The male and paternal authority of the fiancée's father is, of course, necessary to untie the promise that was given to Pedro by Brianda's family. But it is the lady's own courage, invention, and 'walk of shame,' in which she leaves her home deliberately to pretend to be a simple servant, that results in a happy ending for everybody involved. She acts without male authorization and takes over that was regarded as the man's responsibility.

Courtly short stories like the one aforementioned involve more fluctuating and playful gendered patterns than in a traditional picaresque setting, plot, or character. From a gender perspective, they are more than narrative digressions. They destabilize the picaresque narrative and tie it, in this case, to an idealistic love scheme that will finally be imitated by the picaresque protagonists when they start to act like courtly lovers. One may argue that Rey Hazas's intuition about the introduction of female protagonists made it necessary to enrich the picaresque tradition with courtly elements may be proven accurate (1986: 97). But this only strengthens the validity of the general observation: With the help of generic hybridization, the dissolution of the generic identity of the picaresque books and the focus not on generic identity but on generic and stylistic diversity and parodistic discontinuation, literary change becomes quite obvious and visible. Castillo Solórzano lacerated the margins of picaresque storytelling so that dissident elements of this tradition could enter picaresque narration with the intermediary of secondary characters and within-narratives so to expand into the diegetic center and recode it. In a palpable way, *La Garduña de Sevilla* is narrated from a perspective where problematic gender meets problematic genre.

LITERARY TRANSFER

It was the playful spirit and the composite form of *La Garduña de Sevilla* that inspired Antoine le Metel d'Ouville to turn to *La Garduña de Sevilla*. Ouville was the most important Spanish to French translator of his time and an author who had translated, amongst others, María de Zayas's *Novelas amorosas y ejemplares*. His version of Castillo Solórzano's novel was published in French as *La Fouyne de Seville*. What makes it so appealing is that Ouville had no problem transforming Rufina into a French libertine courtesan. Within the genetic relation that binds translations to their original texts, he transformed her into "une femme coquette & friponne", as stated in the "Avis au lecteur" of the first edition published by two different Parisian editors in 1661.[19] By moving to a "target-oriented type of equivalence" (van Gorp 1985: 139; Greifelt 1936: Chevrel 1995), Ouville gave the Spanish pícara another form. From the start, he set her in an environment of depraved "grand libertinage" (La Fovyne de Seville 1661: 2) that perfectly suited the French literary field at the time. 1661, when the translation was published, marked an important step in French political, cultural and literary history with the ascension to the throne of Louis XIV, the consolidation of French classical culture and literature, and the widespread assumption of French superiority in these fields. In its own context, it is quite comprehensible why this text was so appealing to a French audience, so popular that the French editor called it "un agréable ouurage" (La Fovyne de Seville 1661: 2). It not only represents an evolution within French comical novels – and the French translations of Spanish picaresque novels – shifting towards the amorous adventures of the protagonists,[20] but it also provides the burlesque denouement of a happy ending to a picaresque novel, a technique that had already been used by another French author and translator Paul Scarron in his adaptation of *La hija de Celestina* a few years earlier (cf. Estelmann 2016). Ouville's translation did not have to manipulate, however, the structure of the Spanish novel. Rather it imitates Castillo Solórzano's own transformation of the traditional pícara into a capitalist entrepreneur able to impersonate a lady and his fusion of the Spanish picaresque heritage and the *novela cortesana* of Italian origin. Elegant in tone and style, according to the general orientation of classicist translations in France, but general-

---

19 One edition is: La Fovyne de Seville, ov l'hameçon des bovrses. Traduit de l'Espagnol de D. Alonço de Castillo Souorçano. Paris, Lovys Bilaine, 1661. The other edition is: Paris, Avgvstin Covrbe, 1661.
20 As can be seen for example in the French version of Quevedo's *Buscón*; see van Gorp (1985: 141-142).

ly loyal in content, Ouville's task was to add a polygenetic and transcultural dimension to an already polygenetic and transcultural text. The "crucial role" played by the French translations acting as "an intermediary between Spain and countries like England, Germany and the Low Countries" (van Gorp 1985: 138) has repeatedly been pointed out. Ouville's text became so popular and influential that it prompted other translators to get involved. Rufina's novel was translated for a second time to French 60 years later in 1721, followed by a German translation in 1732.[21] It contributed substantially to the national literatures in question. Notwithstanding their lack of attention, Castillo Solórzano's "bastard picaresque fictions" as Maurice Molho once labelled them (Molho in: Ardila 2008: 42), were by no means a "dead end" (Rico (1976: 139) to an otherwise productive picaresque Spanish literary tradition. In fact, a novel like *La Garduña de Sevilla* reached into other literatures and served as one of the bridges to and from the picaresque Spanish tradition. In this respect, it marked an important step in the triumphant circulation of picaresque novels in late 17th and early 18th century European literatures.

BIBLIOGRAPHY

Alemán, Mateo. *Guzmán de Alfarache*. Ed. José María Micó. Madrid 2005.
Arredondo, María Soledad. "'Pícaras': Mujeres de mal vivir en la narrativa del Siglo de Oro." *Dicenda* 11 (1993): 11–33.
Arredondo, María Soledad. "Castillo Solórzano y la mixtura barroca: poesía, narrativa y teatro en La niña de los embustes, Teresa de Manzanares." Ed. Odette Grosse and Frédéric Serralta. *El Siglo de Oro en escena. Homenaje a Marc Vitse*. Toulouse 2006. 35–51.
Bataillon, Marcel. *Pícaros y picaresca*. Madrid 1969.
Blanco Aguinaga, Carlos. "Cervantes y la picaresca: notas sobre dos tipos de realismo." *Nueva Revista de Filología Hispánica* 11 (1957): 314–342.
Blanco Aguinaga, Carlos. "Picaresca española, picaresca inglesa: sobre las determinaciones del género." *Edad de oro* 2 (1983): 49–65.
Cabo Aseguinolaza, Fernando. *El concepto de género y la literatura picaresca*. Santiago de Compostela 1992.

---

21 This version (*Leben und seltsame Begebenheiten der Dona Ruifina einer beruffenen Spanischen Courtisane*) is based on the French one. Alberto Martino (2005) analyzes the impressive influence this translation had on the German book market.

Campana, Patrizia. "Introducción." Alonso de Castillo Solórzano. *Tardes entretenidas* Ed. Patrizia Campana. Barcelona 1992. VII–XLI.

Castillo Solórzano, Alonso de. *Aventuras del bachiller Trapaza*. Ed. Jacques Joset. Madrid 1986.

Castillo Solórzano, Alonso de. *Picaresca femenina de Alonso de Castillo Solórzano. Teresa de Manzanares y La garduña de Sevilla*. Ed. Fernando Rodríguez Mansilla. Madrid 2012.

Castro, Américo. *De la edad conflictiva. Crisis de la cultura española en el siglo XVII*. Madrid 1976.

Chevrel, Yves. "La réception des littératures étrangères." *Revista de Filología Francesa* 7 (1995): 83–100.

Coll-Tellechea, Reyes. *Contra las normas. Las pícaras españolas (1605–1632)*. Madrid 2005.

Cruz, Anne J. "Sonnes of the Rogue: Picaresque relations in England and Spain." Ed. Giancarlo Maiorino. *The picaresque. Tradition and displacement*. Minneapolis 1996. 248–272.

Cruz, Anne J. "The abjected feminine in the Lazarillo de Tormes." *Crítica Hispánica* 19 (1997): 99–109.

Cruz, Anne J. *Discourses of poverty. Social reform and the picaresque novel in early modern Spain*. Toronto 1999.

Cruz, Anne J. "Figuring gender in the picaresque novels: from Lazarillo to Zayas." *Romance Notes* 1 (2010): 7-20.

Del Monte, Alberto. *Itinerario de la novela picaresca española*. Barcelona 1971.

Dunn, Peter N. *Castillo Solórzano and the decline of the Spanish novel*. Oxford 1952.

Dunn, Peter N. *Spanish picaresque fiction. A new literary history*. Ithaca 1993.

Eco, Umberto: *The Open Work*. Tr. Anna Cancogni. Cambridge 1989.

Erauso, Catalina de. *Historia de la Monja Alférez, Catalina de Erauso, escrita por ella misma*. Ed. Ángel Esteban. Madrid 2015.

Estelmann, Frank. "Alonso de Salas Barbadillos La Hija de Celestina (1612), Paul Scarrons Les Hypocrites (1657) und die Verbreitung pikaresker Bücher über transnationale Formen der Intertextualität." Ed. Jan Mohr, Carolin Struwe and Michael Waltenberger. *Pikarische Erzählverfahren. Zum Roman des 17. und 18. Jahrhunderts*. Berlin et. al. 2016. 131–158.

Garrido Ardila, Juan Antonio. *El género picaresco en la crítica literaria*. Madrid 2008.

Garrido Ardila, Juan Antonio. *La novela picaresca en Europa, 1554–1753*. Madrid 2009.

Gossy, Mary S. *The Untold Story. Women and Theory in Golden Age Texts*. Ann Arbor 1989.

Greifelt, Rolf: "Die Übersetzungen des spanischen Schelmenromans in Frankreich im 17. Jahrhundert." *Romanische Forschungen* 1 (1936): 51-84.

Hinrichs, William H. *The invention of the sequel. Expanding prose fiction in early modern Spain*. Woodbridge 2011.

Joset, Jacques. "Introducción." Alonso de Castillo Solórzano: *Aventuras del bachiller Trapaza*. Ed. Jacques Joset. Madrid 1986. 9–43.

Kark, Christopher. "Latent Selfhood and the Problem of Genre in Catalina de Erauso's Historia de la Monja Alférez." *Revista de estudios hispánicos* 3 (2012): 527–546.

La Fovyne de Seville, ov l'hameçon des bovrses. *Traduit de l'Espagnol de D. Alonço de Castillo Souorçano*. Paris 1661.

Mañero-Lozano, David. "Towards a picaresque novel review. Creation, parody and evolution of a narrative genre." *South Carolina Modern Language Review* 1 (2009): 17–35.

Manny, Karoline J. *Trickster women and the lessons they teach. The moral as the unifying factor in the picaresque novels of Alonso de Castillo Solórzano*. Ann Arbor 1995.

Maravall, José Antonio. *La literatura picaresca desde la historia social (siglos XVI y XVII)*. Madrid 1987.

Martino, Alberto. "Die erste deutsche Übersetzung der Garduña de Sevilla. Ein spanischer Beitrag zur Produktion von 'Konsumliteratur' in den 30er Jahren des 18. Jahrhunderts." Ed. Monika Estermann et. al. *Buch-Kulturen. Beiträge zur Geschichte der Literaturvermittlung. Festschrift für Reinhard Wittmann*. Wiesbaden 2005. 93–188.

Meyer-Minnemann, Klaus. "El género de la novela picaresca." Ed. Klaus Meyer-Minnemann and Sabine Schlickers. *La novela picaresca. Concepto genérico y evolución del género (siglos XVI y XVII)*. Madrid 2008. 13–40.

Navarro Durán, Rosa. "Introducción." In: Alfonso de Valdés: La vida de Lazarillo de Tormes, y de sus fortunas y de sus adversidades. Introducción de Rosa Navarro Durán, ed. by. Milagros Rodríguez Cáceres 2d ed., Barcelona, Octaedro 2006, 7–84.

Nünning, Ansgar. "Gender and Narratology." *Zeitschrift für Anglistik und Amerikanistik* 2 (1994): 102–121.

Pérez Villanueva, Sonia. "Crossing boundaries: authority, knowledge, and experience in the autobiography Vida y sucesos de la monja Alférez." *Auto/Biography Studies* 2 (2013): 296–316.

Randall, Dale B.J. "The classical ending of Quevedo's Buscón." *Hispanic Review* 32 (1964): 101–108.

Rey Hazas, Antonio. "La compleja faz de una pícara: Hacia una interpretación de La pícara Justina." *Revista de literatura* 45 (1983): 87–109.

Rico, Francisco. *La novela picaresca y el punto de vista*. Barcelona 1976.

Rodríguez Mansilla, Fernando. "Estudio preliminar." Alonso de Castillo Solórzano: *Picaresca femenina de Alonso de Castillo Solórzano. Teresa de Manzanares y La garduña de Sevilla*. Ed. Fernando Rodríguez Mansilla. Madrid 2012. 11–150.

Rodríguez-Luis, Julio: "Pícaras. The Modal Approach to the Picaresque." *Comparative Literature* 31 (1979): 32–46.

Romero Díaz, Nieves. *Nueva nobleza, nueva novela. Reescribiendo la cultura urbana del barroco*. Newark 2002.

Saínz González, Eugenia. "Misoginia o miedo en la picaresca femenina." *Verba hispánica* 8 (1999): 27–48.

Salas Barbadillo, Alonso Jerónimo de; Castillo Solórzano, Alonso de. *Picaresca femenina. La hija de Celestina – La niña de los embustes, Teresa de Manzanares*. Ed. Antonio Rey Hazas. Barcelona 1986.

Sieber, Harry. "Literary continuity, social order, and the invention of the picaresque." Ed. Marina Scordilis Brownlee and Hans Ulrich Gumbrecht. *Cultural authority in Golden Age Spain*. Baltimore, Md. 1995. 143–164.

Torres, Lucas. "Hijas e hijastras de Justina: venturas y desventuras de una herencia literaria." Ed. María-Luisa Lobato and Francisco Domínguez Matito. *Memoria de la palabra. Actas del VI congreso de la Asociación Internacional Siglo de Oro*; Burgos – La Rioja 15–19 de julio 2002. Madrid 2002, 1763–1771.

Valbuena Prat, Ángel. *La novela picaresca española*. Madrid 1986.

Van Gorp, Hendrik. "Translation and literary genre. The European picaresque novel in the 17th and 18th centuries." Ed. Theo Hermans. *The manipulation of literature. Studies in literary translation*. London, Sidney 1985. 136-148.

Velasco Kindelán, Magdalena. *La novela cortesana y picaresca de Castillo Solórzano*. Valladolid 1983.

Werner, Michael and Bénédicte Zimmermann. "Vergleich, Transfer, Verflechtung. Ansatz der *histoire croisée* und die Herausforderung des Transnationalen." *Geschichte und Gesellschaft* 28 (2002): 607–636.

Zayas y Sotomayor, María de: *Novelas amorosas y ejemplares*. Ed. Julián Olivares. Madrid 2007.

Body and Gender in *Till Eulenspiegel*
Inversions of Masculinity in the 16th century

HANS RUDOLF VELTEN

THE EULENSPIEGEL CHAPBOOK OF 1515

Till Eulenspiegel is the hero of the chapbook published in 1515 by the Strasbourg printer Johann Grieninger titled *Ein kurtzweilig lesen von Dil Ulenspiegel*, one of the most popular jest novels ("Schwankromane") of the 16th century. The book, probably first issued in 1510, was reprinted in 23 German editions by 1600 (Tenberg 1996: 42), and numerous adaptations appeared, the best known of which are certainly Hans Sachs's dramatizations and Johann Fischart's grotesque satire *Eulenspiegel reimensweis* in 1572. The popularity of *Ein kurtzweilig lesen von Dil Ulenspiegel* is also shown by its translation into various European languages: Flemish, English, French, Latin, Danish, and Polish. Even before 1520 Jan van Doesborchs, a publisher in Antwerp, printed a selection of the episodes in English; it was presumably successful, since multifarious reprints and new printings followed in Antwerp and London, for instance by William Copland (Hill-Zenk 2010: 2-9). Despite this remarkable demand, many contemporaries objected to the publication of Eulenspiegel's pranks. Martin Luther spoke of "useless blabbering and ridiculous buffoonery"; at times the Catholic Inquisition placed the work on the Index, denouncing Eulenspiegel's "coarse, indecent, swinish, shameful and dissolute follies, pranks, and indecencies" ("grobe[n] unflätige[n] säwische[n], scham- und zuchtlose[n] narrentheidunge[n], Bossen und unflätereye[n]"), according to Lazarus Sandrub as late as 1608 (Röcke 1978: 114).[1]

---

1 I thank Cathy Waegner for helping me with the translation of this text. She translated all citations of early modern German, except the original text of the Eulenspiegel

The success of the book and the popularity of the main character cannot be attributed only to the typographical presentation of text and illustration (Melters 2004: 72-104), but also to the genre conventions of the jest novel: the cohesion of the prankster episodes in terms of subject matter, their variable order, the consistency and superiority of the prankster hero (Fischer 1957/58: 291-299). The syntagmatic pattern of biography encourages the series of prank episodes to be read in the mode of a life's journey; thus Eulenspiegel can be considered a distant relative of Lazarillo de Tormes and Guzmán de Alfarache, as well as the great-grandfather of Simplicius (cf. Röcke 1987: 141-144). However, the interconnections to the picaresque novel are complex. My argument is divided into four parts. First I will attempt to explain why a jest novel such as Ulenspiegel can have a legitimate place in a volume devoted to the picaresque novel. In doing so I will expand on several structural connections between the two genres. Then I will discuss possible forms and functions of the enactment of masculinity in Ulenspiegel with regard to the figure of Till, his sexuality, and his relationship to both genders. In two concluding steps I will inquire into not only the coherences between gender and body but also the reasons for the specific gender representations in the text, particularly the gesture of the fecal.

JEST NOVEL AND PICARESQUE NOVEL: INTERCONNECTED GENRES

It is astonishing only at first glance that the two genres – jest novel and picaresque novel – have been dominated for some time by similarly based discussion of structure, revolving around the tension between paradigmatic and syntagmatic narrative structures, in short between episodicity and syntagma within the large and long genre history of the early modern novel. Surely this tension changed as the novel developed, with the early open episodic structure of the jest novel hardening into a stronger syntagmatic homogeneity (Kipf 2010: 151). This discussion of structure, which in detail proceeded differently regarding the two respective genres, on the whole made clear that the German jest novel is one of the genre precursors of the European picaresque novel (Emmelius 2014; Mohr and Waltenberger 2014; Kipf 2014). A further point speaks in favor of this view: The consistency of the protagonist in the jest novel, in contrast to collections of farcical tales or novellas, creates an affinity to the picaresque tradition. It is this sin-

---

chapbook *Ein kurtzweilig lesen*, of which I used the translation of Paul Oppenheimer 1991.

gle protagonist who offers possibilities to syntagmatic linkage, even when the jest novel employs this linkage to a limited extent by only weakly profiling the life story of the hero. For example, of the 95 chapters, only 15, eight at the beginning and seven at the end, support the biographical schema.

Analogies can be found in the typological configuration of the hero-figure in the two genres. Comparison of the Lazarillo and Eulenspiegel figures, for instance, reveals both as, according to Röcke (1987: 272), "unfeste Helden" ("unstable heroes") of low birth who, as outsiders, confront an array of figures integrated into social and class structure. The fictional life path of the unsteady protagonists moves topographically from place to place and socially from master to master. Further similarities include repeated motifs such as hunger and physical violence, largely unpunished trickster heroes, as well as structural elements such as the prankster schema based on craftiness and deceit. This is accompanied both by body staging of grotesque hyperbole and by flippant language on the part of the narrative voice, as with the ambivalent and ironic narration as early as in *Der Pfaffe Amis* (cf. Velten 2016), questioning the truth of fraudulent rhetoric, or even admitting the lie (Waltenberger 2014: 246). Naturally there are significant differences. For the first time, in picaresque novels overarching questions relating to the immanence of life are touched on: war, physical violence, criminality, blows of fate – all of this is missing in the jest novel. Eulenspiegel, for example, undergoes no striking development despite the biographical schema; no retrospective confession of a lifetime of trickery is present; in fact the autobiographical perspective that can lend the protagonist as narrator compelling depth is completely absent (Bollenbeck 1985: 145-48).

The Eulenspiegel book appeared at what can be considered the peak of the jest novel, as reflected in its form. It draws on the material of its predecessors, notably the roguish cleric Amis – a genre-founding verse narrative written by "Der Stricker" in approximately 1240 – and the verse tales collected by Philip Frankfurter and published under the title of *geschicht und histori des Pfaffen vom Kalenberg* in 1473. In contrast to these works, *Ein kurtzweilig lesen* was the first jest novel not composed in verse but rather in early modern German prose. Subsequent specimens of the genre do not adopt the prose model, although they tie in with the structure and content of the 'fool biography' that Kalenberger and Eulenspiegel prescribe. The defiant heroes of the jest novel were popular until the end of the 16th century, the 1597 *Lalebuch* even presenting an entire group of self-proclaimed fools who attempt to rebel against the world that is growing ever more rational. The popularity of the genre ends, as it were, at the very moment the picaresque novel gains prominence. It is hardly surprising that all heroes of the jest novel, even those I have not mentioned, are *male*. The two clerics Amis and Kalenberger are male, as are the parasite Markolf, Eulenspiegel, and the fools Peter Leu, Claus Narr, and Hans Clawert. But *how masculine* are they actually? Is there an enactment of their masculinity in relation to other men and women in the text, and how does this masculinity relate to the dominant symbolic gender differences of the time?

WEAKLY MARKED MASCULINITY?

In the following I will pursue these questions with focus on the Eulenspiegel figure. It is a literary figure, even if Dyl Ulenspiegel is historically supposed to have lived in the 14th century. However, since Walter Erhart's study (1995) we know that gender questions typical for an epoch are processed in literary texts and can be extracted, since gender features and relations are discursively organized and frequently manifest themselves in narrative structures. This can be valid even for medieval texts, as the editors of the volume *Aventiuren des Geschlechts* emphasize: As early as in this era semiotic systems of masculinity are encoded in plot, figures, and narrative patterns (Baisch et al. 2003: 14-15). The Eulenspiegel figure does not distinguish itself through a multiplicity of gender-specific characteristics.[2] From the very beginning it is clear that Eulenspiegel is male, since the preface calls him "a peasant's son" and in the second tale he is characterized not only as a "deceiver and mocker" but also "a rogue" and "mischievous" ("Bub und Lecker"; "Schalck"; "schalckhafftig"; 2, 12-13), a continually repeated characterization. With this, however, his specific masculinity is not yet delineated. Only in episode 34, when during a pilgrimage to Rome he stops at an inn, does the narrator become more exact when reporting the female host's reaction: "She said that Eulenspiegel was a handsome man and asked him where he was from" ("Da sach sie, das Ulenspiegel ein schön Man was, und fragt ihn, wa er her wär"; 34, 102). This description of his physical appearance, which by the way does not end in an erotic encounter, but rather in a farcical competition with the landlady, remains the only line which offers a concrete gender-specific characterization. A further, oft-cited quotation from the episode 35 reveals a great deal about Eulenspiegel's attitude toward regular professional work, but hardly about his masculinity, except that he does not fit into the male gender norm and heteronormative schema of early modern times (this will be discussed in more detail below): "I'm a lazy, strong rogue, who doesn't like to work" ("ich

---

[2] I quote from Lindow (1515/1978); after the quotation comes the chapter number, followed by the page number.

bin auch ein fauler starcker Schelm, der nit gern werckt"; 35, 105). Episode 21, which contains relatively much information about the hero's identity and character, offers no additional details relevant for his masculinity:

Eulenspiegel was always cheerful in company, but as long as he lived, there were three sorts of things he avoided. First, he never rode a gray horse, but always a reddish-gray horse, for the sake of a clownish appearance. Second, he never enjoyed staying wherever there might be children because people worried more about their needs than his. Third, he disliked staying where there was an old, generous innkeeper. For an old, generous innkeeper did not take proper care of his possessions and was usually a fool (Oppenheimer 1991:39).

Ulenspiegel, der was allezeit gern bei Gselschafft, und dieweil er lebt, da hatt er dreierlei Sach an ihm, die er flohe. Zum ersten reit er kein graw Pferd, sunder alweg ein val Pferd von Gespot wegen. Daz ande, er wolt nienen bleiben, wa Kinder waren, wann man acht der Kinder mer ihr Nötlichkeit dann sein. Die drit Sach waz, wa ein alter milter Wirt waz, bei dem waz er nit gern zu Herberg, wan ein alter milter Würt, der achtet seines Gutes nit und wer gewönlich ein Bott (21, 63-64).

The three items named say a great deal about social habits and characteristics of the hero. The dun horse (not reddish-grey, as Oppenheimer suggests) proverbially alludes to a guileful, roguish rider (Bässler 2003: 334-337). Children are rivals and dangerous observers, just as the drunkenness of the landlord can lead to unanticipated incidents, which could cross the wily calculations of the rapscallion protagonist. Only the comment about the children hints at his sexual abstinence: he is only reluctantly in their presence, and wastes no thoughts on procreation, neither as sexual act nor as lifetime goal. We learn nothing about any sexual activity, not even insinuations of such, and Eulenspiegel dies childless. This lack of sexuality means that the actual practices and rituals of wooing and emotional attachment to the female sex are absent; Eulenspiegel thus distinguishes himself with a "degree zero genital performance," as Schwarz frames it (2013: 344). However, it cannot be claimed that Eulenspiegel is not familiar with sexual discourse: His false confession in episode 38 that he slept five times with the housekeeper of his father confessor shows that the scamp is eminently well versed in sexual practices, their social normalization, and their social implications. He predicts that the priest will beat his housekeeper (whether from patriarchal strictness or from jealousy remains open), and Eulenspiegel can thus blackmail the man of God with the threat of reporting him for breaching the seal of confession.³

One could assume that this weakly marked masculinity of the Eulenspiegel figure could point to a veering from the heterosexual norm to homo- or transsexuality, to transvestism or the switching between gender roles – or even to a third gender in the form of androgyny or hermaphroditism, with the possible goal of presenting a medium to deconstruct male hegemony (cf. Breger/Döring 1998; Halberstam 1998). Unfortunately the text does not support such a hypothesis. Despite frequent disguising situations, which usually relate to professional roles, transgression of boundaries through cross-dressing never arises as is the case with Grimmelhausen's Courage In *Ulenspiegel* the processes of displacement, substitution, or gliding over from one to the other gender are not evident. Eulenspiegel's sexual one-dimensionality is accentuated precisely in comparison with Courage. Whereas the pícara masks, distorts, disguises her femininity, Eulenspiegel undertakes nothing to perform or to hide his masculinity (Strobel 1995: 87-89). It is enough for him to mislead his antagonists with false statements. He is indeed acquainted with the concept of masquerade; practices of disguise accompany nearly every episode. But they never relate to gender identity and at no time he peddles himself as a servant girl or female messenger. Male or female desire that could be hidden behind the masquerade is reduced with Eulenspiegel to the acquisition of food and money, in other words to subsistence.

However, the resulting detachment, one might even say asociality reflects the fragility of Eulenspiegel's gender position,[4] even beyond the sexual dimension. He seems to be a figure who only rudimentarily fulfills the predominant norms of masculinity: He is not loyal, does not tell the truth, he is rebellious rather than respectful of social hierarchies, he flees rather than show bravery, he escapes from punishment rather than stand by his deeds, he places no value on honor or good repute – on the contrary, his reputation is a negative trademark. He does not enter into marriage, which normalizes and regulates gender relations, and thus he does not establish a household with responsibility (he leaves his mother in poverty); he also does not join a monastery (only for amusement shortly before his death in episode 89). He does not exhibit any typical male vices: He does not thrash others – instead, he is thrashed himself; he does not drink or

---

3 Chapter 31, in which Eulenspiegel "proves" the women's chastity by means of a fraudulent relic, a skull, indicates that he knows what adultery is.

4 Kraß postulates that the heteronormative masculinity in patriarchal societies is also principally endangered, although a man who belies the expectations of the hegemonic masculine role can be stigmatized (Kraß 2009: 15).

gamble; he does not brag; he has no sex life. Eulenspiegel deconstructs masculinity as determined in the early modern, Christian-patriarchal social order by withdrawing from the duties and the responsibility of a provider and father of a family, and hence ignoring the norms of the gender difference in marriage, namely male power and authority, female obedience, and, since Luther, being on good terms with one's spouse (cf. Dinges 1998: 7-28; Becker-Cantarino 2005: 58-59).

GENDER RELATIONS

Eulenspiegel's barely marked masculinity develops in contour when contrasted with a strongly normalized conception of early modern masculinity of the Reformation era, as exemplified in the figure of Dr. Faustus in the eponymous prose novel (*Historia von D. Fausten*, 1587). Faust, like Eulenspiegel a peasant's son, takes a different path from Eulenspiegel, who wants to live without working; Faust is obsessed with the idea of investigating the world and conquering it intellectually – a proactive Renaissance character, who does not fear sealing a pact with the devil. He lives among men in a purely male world. For this reason he, like Eulenspiegel, rejects marriage his entire life, despite being driven by lust. Shortly before Faust's death he encounters seductive Helena, produced by Mephisto, and begets with her a son. After his death the woman and child disappear, as Faust's demise means their end too. Becker-Cantarino reads in this a warning of the Protestant author with regard to the other sex: "In a patriarchal marriage female fertility and sexuality are brought under male guardianship, whereas extra-marital sexuality is demonized" (5005: 60). Only marriage could save Faust, but he scorns it and fails.

The Eulenspiegel book exhibits neither strong sexually coded gender differences nor the distinct masculinity of the Faust figure. Nevertheless, Eulenspiegel interacts communicatively, socially, and cognitively with the many female figures in the book, beginning with his mother, his Godmother, and the neighbors, from young servants to older and elderly peasants, landladies, and wives of handworkers (females appear on the scene in a total of 42 episodes; cf. Aichmayr 2000). Looking at these encounters with the female sex, can there be made observations that are of relevance for the enactment of masculinity? I begin with the mother. She appears in the first six episodes, again in the ninth, and then toward the end of the book in the 90th episode. Eulenspiegel's relationship to her is first and foremost economically determined. In the sixth episode we find a focalized statement by the hero himself:

'Dear God, help me!' thought Eulenspiegel. 'How can I satisfy my mother? Where can I possibly find bread for her house?' Thus he went out of the village where his mother lived, toward the city of Stassfurt. There he noticed a rich baker's establishment... (Oppenheimer 1991: 11).

'Lieber Got hilf', gedacht Ulenspiegel, 'wie wil ich die Muter stillen. Wa sol ich Brot uberkumen in ihr Huß?' Und gierige uß dem Flecken, da sein Mum in wont, gen Stasfurt in die Stat und vermerckt eins reichen Brotbäckers Handlung... (6, 21).

This leads to his first deceitful prank which is psychologically motivated, based on economic necessity. After the ninth chapter his mother is no longer present and does not reappear until the end of the prankster series, when she visits him at his sickbed: "When she came to him now, she cried and spoke: 'Mine dear son, where are you ill?' – 'Dear Mother, here between the bed-box and the wall'" (Oppenheimer 1991: 183). ("Da sie nun zu ihm kam, ward sie weinen und sprach: 'Mein lieber Sun, wa bist du kranck?' – 'Liebe Muter, hie zwüschen der Kisten und der Wand'"; 90, 256-257). Her poverty has remained constant, however. When she asks him for money, he gives her a cryptic answer that obscures whether he can give her nothing or whether he does not wish to give her anything. Psychological interpretations of certain passages, claiming that Eulenspiegel wants to avenge himself on his mother for the strict way he was raised, are not, in my opinion, convincing, since a psychologically motivated syntagma cannot be presupposed. It is more productive to recognize in the episode of old age, like in the first chapters, that the social determination and economy of family bonds are characteristic for the 16th century. Simultaneously the mother represents the monogamous Christian housewife; in spite of her poverty she raises her son strictly but providently – for instance when she serves as a substitute for the fatherly superego by encouraging him to learn a trade (Runte 2013). Eulenspiegel counters with unsparing meanness. When she asks him for a "sweet word" ("süß Wort," 90, 257; Oppenheimer 1991: 183), trusting in daily language routines, he responds: "Honey, that's a sweet word." Later he tops this with a vulgar joke.

Eulenspiegel's treatment of his mother establishes a behavioral pattern for his dealings with all women. The females he encounters do not receive treatment based on gender but rather on social position.[5] Superiority in communication is important to him, providing linguistic and cognitive capital that can be converted

---

5   That this pattern can also be found in the picaresque novel is demonstrated by Cruz (1999: 144-163).

to food and money. Whether the women are under the control of men (servants, wives) or act on their own behalf (peasants, landladies), the gender relationship is always overgrown with production and power relations. Women and men are both rivals for Eulenspiegel; a difference in this socially based agon is hardly discernible. However, gender-specific aspects can be noticed in the women's behavior. A few times Eulenspiegel serves as the punishing instrument for hubris or fashion consciousness: in chapter 30 the female host is arrogant; the women whose furs Eulenspiegel washes can also be criticized for their addiction to fashion, the most widespread gender-specific satirical cliché of early modern times. Elderly women tend to be an exception to this pattern. They are more skeptical, although they are duped by Eulenspiegel not least because of their ugliness. During a performance of a village Easter play, for example, he has the pastor's housekeeper, who plays the angel, be addressed by one of the peasant actors as a "priest's old one-eyed whore" ("alt einäugig Pfaffenhur"; 15, 40; Oppenheimer 1991: 24) – the scandal does not stop short of a brawl. In episode 31 Eulenspiegel informs a landlady that she is cross-eyed, which no one has ever told her before, and in 91 he responds to the question posed by an old Beguine who is caring for him as to what he regrets in his life with an aggressive speech act: He only regrets that he has not "stitched up the arses of [...] old women" ("ärß geflickt," (91, 259; Oppenheimer 1991: 184), thus insulting them as useless creatures.

Once, however, Eulenspiegel must accept defeat in a confrontation with an elderly woman. After attending a peasant wedding, the protagonist performs some stunts on his horse for an old farmer's wife. While doing so, he loses his purse. Noticing this later, he immediately rides back and finds the woman at the same spot – but the purse is no longer there. When asked about the purse, the old woman answers:

Yes, friend. For my wedding I picked up a rough purse indeed. I still have it and am sitting on it. Is that the one?" "Ha," said Eulenspiegel. "If you've had it since your wedding, it must be quite a rusty purse by now. I've no need of your old purse." Thus was Eulenspiegel – roguish and cunning as he was – nonetheless tricked by an old farmer's wife and forced into losing his purse (Oppenheimer 1991: 140).

Ja, Fründ, in meiner Hochzeit uberkam ich ein ruhe Desch, die hab ich noch und sitz daruff, ist es die? – Oho, daz ist lang, sprach Ulenspiegel, da du nun ein Braut warest, das muß vonnöten nun ein alte rostige Desch sein. Ich beger deiner alten Deschen nit. Aber Ulenspiegel, wie schalckhafftiger und listig er was, so ward er dennoch von der alten Bürin geäfft und müst seiner Deschen entberen (67, 196).

Here Eulenspiegel is outwitted, tricked, beaten with his own weapons, one-upped. The woman refers to a second meaning of "purse," a thinly disguised sexual metaphor for the female sex organ ("rough purse") on which she is sitting. Eulenspiegel has no other choice than to acknowledge the sexual innuendo and reply in kind ("don't want your old purse"), yet must travel on without his money. This is the one and only obscene speech act in the text, and it is indicative that Eulenspiegel does not utter the initial words. Obscenity as the reverse of the sexual is as difficult to find in the Eulenspiegel book as sexuality.[6] Nevertheless, obscenity is here an unequivocal symptom of sexual relations; talk of the "rough purse" is more likely to appear in prankster tales written by and for men, but it is indeed used here disparagingly to describe the vulva of the older woman. This talk is typical for the male group culture of the early modern and provides evidence of misogynous and fearful attitudes toward the other sex. That this peasant woman operates with the obscene cliché herself proves that she is well-versed, quick-witted, and confidently in command of the situation. Eulenspiegel is forced to replicate, but emptily, because the retort merely confirms and intensifies her aggressive speech act ("old rusty purse"). Discursively he is repulsed, but he knows that the old woman has the upper hand and that his purse is lost to him. The two contenders come to a truce regarding gender role patterns on the level of the obscene and attempt to outstrip his/her opponent through mockery – this is, however, only a game that frames the real struggle for the wallet containing Eulenspiegel's money, actually the center of attention since only that money has practical value. The obscenity leads to Eulenspiegel's defeat in the facetious competition with an unlikely adversary, an elderly, rural woman. She temporarily takes over the role of Markolf here when he triumphs over Salomon by shifting the latter's responses into the vulgar and obscene, and thus can profanely infect Salomon's language (Curschmann 1487/1993: 151-179). The trickster Eulenspiegel has met his match: The verbal clash between his and the old female peasant can be read as a symptom of the battle of sexes carried out in the mode of derision, and the battle is tellingly fought with a representative who presents her gender quite negatively – not with her body, her seduction skills, her drives,

---

6   Rüdiger Schnell suspected that the author of the Eulenspiegel book avoids the sexual because the writer counted on women in his readership with whom "obscene portrayal [is] incompatible" (2008: 418). The early modern humanist Heinrich Steinhöwel apologized to his female readership for the translation of an offensively bawdy tale by Poggio. In this regard, Schnell underlines that the vernacular prankster tale collections reckoned with female readers, which had the consequence of a stark reduction of obscene details (420).

but rather with 'male' attributes such as the calculated appraisal of a situation, masterful self-control, and the employment of uncircumventable language registers.

SEXUALITY AND DEFECATION

In his study *Till Eulenspiegel: der dauerhafte Schwankheld* (1985), Georg Bollenbeck offered crucial insights concerning the Eulenspiegel figure. He ascertained that in the rich inventory of Eulenspiegel's comic jeering gestures and body enactments not a single phallic signal was to be found. Bakhtin's theory of the grotesque body (1995 [1965]) would thus not be appropriate in this case, since the phallus is *the* central sign of the grotesque body. In the Eulenspiegel book, however, Bollenbeck continues, nothing projects from the body into the world (1985: 139). This is different in other jest novels. The phallic comedy is present in *geschicht und histori des Pfaffen vom Kalenberg* (1473) when the duchess, who happens to be passing by while the protagonist is washing his trousers in the Danube River, is so fascinated by his exposed genitals that she pays him a visit. In Bartholomäus Krüger's *Hans Clawert* (1587/1882) the phallus is also involved in a comic corporeal performance. In order that his bride can stay seated on a horse with no saddle, the protagonist summarily lets her reach into the slit of his trousers, where she promptly finds something to grasp. The obscene detail reveals an early modern gender norm – the man turns the naivety and libido of the woman to his own advantage.

There is nothing of the like in the Eulenspiegel book. Why does it contain no phallic humor? Would this not seem particularly appropriate for Till as rough prankster? asks Bollenbeck. His answer is as follows:

In our opinion the vagabond's special mode of reproduction accounts for the striking exclusion of sexual organs. Eulenspiegel lives as a parasite, consuming only and contributing nothing to the overall reproduction in the society of his time. The concept of the grotesque body, based on barter economy, construes the penis as projecting into the world and creating new bodies for the continuation of life and world. It stands for fruitfulness – an especially important aspect in natural economies. With Eulenspiegel nothing points out beyond the body (Bollenbeck 1985: 139; translated from the German original).

As true as this formulation is, it overlooks the close relationship manifested between body and world through consumption and excretion, a relationship present with the grotesque body's ingesting and emptying. This is reflected chiefly in

Eulenspiegel's acts and gestures of defecation, which, in contrast to the sexual, are excessively present in the *Eulenspiegel* book. One could justify this presence by drawing on Sigmund Freud's theory of the comic based on the release of previously repressed inhibitions (human excretions were a source of embarrassment in the 15th century), although the significance of fecal comedy is hardly covered by this theory (Freud 1999: 163-169). I think that Bollenbeck made an incisive point with his socio-historical interpretation of parasitical survival and the individual self-preservation strategies of the hero, including the self-assertion through revenge to counter personally suffered social injustice,[7] yet this does not lead us farther in dealing with the issue of masculinity and gender relations. We should focus on the question of how Eulenspiegel's fecal actions and his lack of sexual markers are connected to his masculinity.

Approximately one fourth of all chapters of the Eulenspiegel book contain – illustrated by the woodcuts – fecal body acts and scatological language, which are nearly always centered in a multi-level comic conflict. Thereby Eulenspiegel uses his body, gestures, and language to obtain a desired object (food, money) or to harm other people. Using body language such as derisive gestures, like a child baring its behind to irritate the neighbors, is not meant here; rather, the purposeful instrumentalization of Eulenspiegel's own excrement in the throes of a conflict with employers or landlords, including defecating or farting in rooms (chapters 16, 52,69, 90), spoiling foodstuff or basic material with ordure (46, 51, 72, 88), eating or handling feces (24, 35, 92), and repeatedly the defilement of tavern inventory (79, 81, 85). Or he administers a laxative 'purge,' which causes others to soil beds and sheets unintentionally, as in the case of the Magdeburg doctor whom Eulenspiegel punishes for his arrogance (15). Generally these pranks are repulsively disgusting, as when Eulenspiegel fouls a piece of butter with his stool and uses it as gravy (72) or, in the next to the last chapter, when he lets the cleric, who should give him absolution, reach into the moneybox, in which only excrement is to be found.

Eulenspiegel's fecal humor has always been problematic for researchers, whose interpretations vary widely. Röcke sees in Eulenspiegel's obsession with human waste the sign of an agrarian economy serving as a signal of resistance to the rising division of labor and economization of all spheres of life (Röcke 1987:

---

[7] Bollenbeck draws here on Ernst Bloch, who saw the explanation for lack of sexuality in an orientation toward sustenance in the lower classes: "Hunger and worry leave the libido of the lower classes little space, and whoever's stomach constantly growls does not sweat from fear of castration," cited in Bollenbeck (132); translated from the German original.

248). In contrast, Bollenbeck opines that many of Eulenspiegel's excremental antics serve as revenge for discriminatory treatment, at least as far as they are typical of the rover's competitive behavior (1985: 131). On a symbolic level, human fecies stand, in the premodern period, for the evil; in folk mythology, the anus is identified with the devil's loophole, and an entrance gate for the demonic (Werner 2011: 122-125). If we consider Eulenspiegel a mostly negative figure, which aims to do evil, this interpretation seems convincing; but there is no space for humor. Psychoanalytically one could explain the acts with feces as an unresolved pre-Oedipal anal phase on the title hero's part, virtually as sexuality that has not developed beyond infantilism (Moshövel 2011: 11-13; Heinritz 2002: 23, 29). But this interpretation hardly exhausts the meanings of Eulenspiegel's instrumentalization of feces. Furthermore, strong textual evidence for such an interpretation is missing. An origin of the anal fixation in early childhood is not locatable, nor are the usual concomitant effects that Freud mentioned such as miserliness, pedantry, and exaggerated sense of order. Finally, the anal fixation has been explicated with Lacan's symbolism of the original desire structure of a child for its mother; Eulenspiegel is diagnosed with a neurosis ("névrose obsessionelle par rapport au surmoi"; Runte 2013: 58) that enfolds the need to present his mother with a product of his own. This interpretation also falls short because of the difficulty of grasping the contradictory, kaleidoscopically assembled prankster-rogue of the early modern using the means of developmental psychology.

Fecal capers seem to give Eulenspiegel just as much joy as his audience, although this displaced sensation of pleasure does not explicate them. Basically, it should be remembered that he uses his bodily excretions as means to an end. For he himself does not experience revulsion and embarrassment, as the episode of coprophagy in the court of the Polish king shows (chapter 24). Here Eulenspiegel must enter into a contest with the court jester, doing something which the opponent cannot imitate. The victor will be given a new outfit of clothing and twenty guilders ("nüw kleiden und [...] zwentzig Guldin darzu geben"; 24, 72). After a series of buffooneries, Eulenspiegel realizes that something special will be needed to win. One hears him say, "I shall thus do something that I otherwise find unpleasant" ("Ich will darumb thun, das ich sunst ungern that"). And he "shits a pile in the middle of the hall and took a spoon and divided the dung in half" ("scheiß einen Huffen mitten in den Sal und nam ein Löffel und teilet den Treck recht mitten entzwei"; 24, 72; Oppenheimer 1991: 46), devours one half, challenging the opponent to eat the other half. According to his own report, Eulenspiegel has to force himself to eat his own feces. His strategy has nothing to do with uninhibitedness or lack of self-consciousness, but rather with self-control and rational overcoming of repugnance and discomfiture in service of economic profit.[8] For Eulenspiegel's determining characteristic is a cognitive one: He draws on practical knowledge. He can comprehend a contingent situation and has a command of situational know-how, which makes success possible, as Hübner (2012: 18) emphasized.

If Eulenspiegel's excrementally marked enactments of his body demonstrate self-control and, with aplomb, estimation of the situation at hand, one could ask whether this know-how that generates masterly action is coded as masculine. Eulenspiegel's masculinity would reveal itself above all in practical cleverness, traditionally a male feature along with rationality and intellectual capabilities in general as they are shown in the Faust figure discussed above. But this hypothesis is not maintainable regarding the Eulenspiegel book, for, as we have seen in the episode with the peasant woman who sits on his purse, self-control and know-how belong to the domain of the old woman as well; in fact she is better versed in them than Eulenspiegel. This finding also correlates with the term "gevüegiu kündikeit" ("appropriate practical intelligence") which can be considered as ungendered, a term that the Stricker introduced to the genre of verse legends or "Märendichtung" as early as the 13th century (Ragotzky 1981).

It is striking, however, that in the Eulenspiegel book not a single woman masters the feces-centered trickery like Eulenspiegel, through neither flatulence nor defecation. Dealing with excretions is not ascribed to women. None of his opponents can vanquish him in this respect. Defecating is a weapon he utilizes in single combat with his rivals – thus the contest of the two jesters takes on the shape of a tournament joust with two knights – courtly spectators and royal reward included. Eulenspiegel triumphs on the basis of his superior judgment of the situation, but above all on the basis of his own, self-produced and re-incorporated weapon – his feces. He remains sovereign over that which he produces.

The following aspect of the production of excrement as masculine-coded act seems central to me: In scatological description, female procreativity is transformed carnivalistically into male ability to defecate. This is recognizable in another carnivalesque text genre, the Shrovetide plays ("Fastnachtspielen"). They center around farmer-peasants, who produce manure, deal with ordure, and use drastically coarse fecal language (cf. Bachtin 1965; Pastré 2009). A rural peasant is a topos for autonomous male fertility that rivals that of women, since he

---

[8] Bollenbeck, in contrast to Elias, already ascribed deportment of embarrassment to Eulenspiegel: He is not a creature of instinct, uninhibited scoundrel, but rather possesses a highly developed sense of discomfiture (Bollenbeck 1985: 141).

spreads feces and manure on the fields and with that contributes to the fruitfulness of both man and soil. In his ethnological research Claude Lévi-Strauss (1971) brought to light that the equalization of excrement, penis, and child possesses universal traits, demonstrated by the siring and trickster motifs of prehistoric American myths: the coyote of North American cultures, who forms his children out of his excrements, and the South American demiurges who impregnate themselves and thereby resemble the pregnant farmer, an ubiquitous figure in European Carnival events. Those figures imply the male fantasy of the fecally fertile man who can completely exist without women. Since homosexuality requires a partner, the dream scenario of male independence and omnipotence is fully realized only by defecation. This autonomy is symbolized in the excremental remains of the rogue. The mound as *hic fuit* ("he was here") serves not only to mark his territory but also to provide an organic emblem of superiority and independence in the male hierarchical system.

Eulenspiegel triumphs in the fight for survival with his feces and his excretions, not with sexuality. With his own physical eliminations he can smite otherwise superior opponents such as the learned doctor in the Magdeburg court or the clergyman, whom Eulenspiegel can prevail upon to defecate in the middle of the pastor's own church. Both are, like the Polish court jester, men and both are Eulenspiegel's opponents. The symbolic-mythic subtext of the fecal thus relates to a masculinity that furnishes a counter model to the gender norms of the time and their reversal, a model that deploys the body as a medium of mockery acts. Hence acting with social valence – it is about honor and disgrace – comes into play once more. This is a carnivalesque, inverted, archaic masculinity, a model in which no one can hold a candle to Eulenspiegel.

Resumé

In the *Eulenspiegel* book we can discern only very weak sexual marking of the protagonist but very strong fecal configuration. The former is reflected in the absence of gender-specific description and sexual activity, although numerous chapters inform the reader that Eulenspiegel is well acquainted with sexual practices and their impact. Self-preservation dominates in relations involving the female sex, beginning with his relationship to his mother. In general, erotic and sexual abstinence predominates, as well as competition for nutriments with the help of practical cleverness and know-how. Sexual metaphors appear only negatively in the picture of the old hag, by whom Eulenspiegel is rhetorically bested, showing the battle of the sexes in the form of mutual mockery. From a socio-historical perspective, the anal episodes in the Eulenspiegel book also focus on survival and self-preservation, and in the same vein the body comedy of those episodes presumably owes much to the release of previously repressed inhibitions as well as to Eulenspiegel's situational superiority over his competitors through practical acumen. From the gender-specific point of view they are nonetheless to be seen as special, indeed the central manifestation of his masculinity. Not the sexual makes Eulenspiegel manly, but rather the fecal. This specific gender variant differs in nearly all points from the hegemonic patriarchic-Christian masculinity of the beginning 16th century, as shown by the Faust figure. Eulenspiegel's subversive variant counters the dominant image of manliness and proffers a man who maintains his independence bodily and intellectually to a great extent with the help of his bowel discharges. It is subversive that his male antagonists (female ones too) embody the typical norm of masculinity and emerge from their contact with Eulenspiegel as ridiculous. The protagonist's masculinity is not a hybrid form of male and female components, which could be described with the terms of the third gender or masquerade. His masculinity is insofar not transgressive, since it does not move between the sexes, in fact it is barely sexually marked. Eulenspiegel is "all man" – he is the subversion of the sexually coded male into a fecally coded one.

BIBLIOGRAPHY

Aichmayr, Michael Joseph. "Eulenspiegel und die Frauen: eine Begegnung im Spätmittelalter." *Eulenspiegel-Jahrbuch* 40 (2000): 41–58.

Bachtin, Michail. *Rabelais und seine Welt. Volkskultur als Gegenkultur.* [1965] Frankfurt a.M. 1995.

Bässler, Andreas. *Sprichwortbild und Sprichwortschwank: Zum illustrativen und narrativen Potential von Metaphern in der deutschsprachigen Literatur um 1500.* Berlin/New York 2003.

Baisch, Martin et al. (Eds.). *Aventiuren des Geschlechts. Modelle von Männlichkeit in der Literatur des 13. Jahrhunderts.* Göttingen 2003.

Becker-Cantarino, Barbara. "Dr. Faustus und die Landstörzerin Courasche: Zum Geschlechter- und Ehediskurs in der deutschen Literatur der Frühen Neuzeit." Ed. Axel Walter. *Regionaler Kulturraum und intellektuelle Kommunikation vom Humanismus bis ins Zeitalter des Internet.* Amsterdam/New York 2005. 53–70.

Bollenbeck, Georg. *Till Eulenspiegel: der dauerhafte Schwankheld. Zum Verhältnis von Produktions- und Rezeptionsgeschichte.* Stuttgart 1985.

Breger, Claudia/Döring, Tobias (Eds.). *Figuren der, des Dritten. Erkundungen kultureller Zwischenräume.* Amsterdam et al. 1998.

Butler, Judith. *Gender Trouble: Feminism and the Subversion of Identity.* New York 1990.

Büttner, Wolfgang. *Von Claus Narren. Sechshundert / sieben vnd zwantzig Historien / Feine schimpfliche wort vnd Rede / die Erbare Ehrenleut Clau=sen abgemerckt / vnd nachgesagt haben / Zur Bürgerlichen und Christlichen Lere / wie an=dere Apologen / dienstlich vnd fürderlich.* [Franckfurt am Mayn, 1573] Reprint Hildesheim 2006.

Classen, Albrecht. "Transgression and Laughter, the Scatological and Epistemological. New Insights into the Pranks of 'Till Eulenspiegel'." Ed. Paul M. Clogan. *Beyond the literary ambit.* Lanham 2007. 41–62.

Cruz, Anne J. *Discourses of Poverty. Social Reform and the Picaresque Novel in Early Modern Spain.* Toronto 1999.

Curschmann, Michael. *Frag vnd antwort Salomonis vnd marcolfi* [Augsburg: Ayrer 1487]. Ed. Michael Curschmann. *Marcolfus deutsch. Mit einem Faksimile des Prosa-Drucks von M. Ayrer* [1487]. Ed. Walter Haug/Burghart Wachinger. *Kleinere Erzählformen des 15. und 16. Jahrhunderts.* Tübingen 1993. 151–255.

Dinges, Martin (Ed.). *Hausväter, Priester, Kastraten: Zur Konstruktion von Männlichkeit in Spätmittelalter und früher Neuzeit.* Göttingen 1998.

Ein kurtzweilig Lesen von Dil Ulenspiegel. [1515] Nach dem Druck von 1515. Mit 87 Holzschnitten. Ed. Wolfgang Lindow. Stuttgart 1978.

Emmelius, Caroline. "Das Ich und seine Geschichte(n). Paradigmatische und syntagmatische Erzählstrukturen in der Novellistik, der mittelalterlichen Ich-Erzählung und im deutschen ‚Lazaril von Tormes' [1614]." Ed. Jan Mohr /Michael Waltenberger. *Das Syntagma des Pikaresken.* Heidelberg 2014. 37–70.

Erhart, Walter. *Wann ist der Mann ein Mann? Zur Geschichte der Männlichkeit.* Stuttgart 1997.

Ertz, Stefan (Ed.). *Das Lalebuch.* [1597] Stuttgart 1995.

Frankfurter, Philipp. *Geschicht und histori des Pfaffen vom Kalenberg.* [1473] Ed. Viktor Dollmayr. Halle a/S. 1907.

Freud, Sigmund. *Der Witz und seine Beziehung zum Unbewußten.* [1940] *Gesammelte Werke Bd. 6.* Frankfurt a.M. 1999.

Grimmelshausen, Hans Jakob Christoffel. *Simplicissimus teutsch.* [1668] *Werke in drei Bänden.* Vol. I/1. Ed. Dieter Breuer. Frankfurt a.M. 1989.

Grimmelshausen, Hans Jakob Christoffel. *Courasche* [1670] / *Springinsfeld* / *Wunderbarliches Vogelnest I und II* / *Rathstübel Plutonis*. Ed. Dieter Breuer, Frankfurt a.M. 2007.

Halberstam, Judith. *Female Masculinity*. Durham/London 1998.

Heinritz, Reinhard. "Erde zu Erde. Fäkalmotivik im Dyl Ulenspiegel." *Eulenspiegel-Jahrbuch* 42 (2002). 17–33.

Hill-Zenk, Anja. *Der englische Eulenspiegel: die Eulenspiegel-Rezeption als Beispiel des englisch-kontinentalen Buchhandels im 16. Jahrhundert*. Berlin 2010.

Historia von D. Johann Fausten [1587]. Ed. Stephan Füssel/Hans Joachim Kreutzer. Stuttgart 2012.

Hübner, Gert. "Eulenspiegel und die historischen Sinnordnungen. Plädoyer für eine praxeologische Narratologie." *Literaturwissenschaftliches Jahrbuch* 53 (2012): 175–206.

Kipf, Johannes Klaus. "Schwankroman – Prosaroman – Versroman. Über den Beitrag einer nicht nur prosaischen Gattung zur Entstehung des frühneuzeitlichen Prosaromans." Ed Catherine Drittenbass/André Schnyder. *Eulenspiegel trifft Melusine*. Amsterdam/New York 2010. 145–162.

Kipf, Johannes Klaus. (2014): "Episodizität und narrative Makrostruktur. Überlegungen zur Struktur der ältesten deutschen Schelmenromane und einiger Schwankromane." Ed. Jan Mohr/Michael Waltenberger. *Das Syntagma des Pikaresken*. Heidelberg 2014. 71–102.

Kraß, Andreas. "Queer Studies in Deutschland." Ed. Andreas Kraß. *Queer Studies in Deutschland. Interdisziplinäre Beiträge zur kritischen Heteronormativitätsforschung*. Berlin 2009. 7–22.

Krüger, Bartholomäus. *Hans Clawerts werckliche Historien*. [1587] Halle 1882.

Lacan, Jacques. *Das Seminar. Buch 8: Die Übertragung* [1960 – 1961]. Ed. Peter Engelmann/Hans-Dieter Gondek. Wien/Berlin 2015.

Lévi-Strauss, Claude. *Mythologiques IV: L'homme nu*. Paris 1971. (German Edition. *Mythologica IV: Der nackte Mensch*. Frankfurt 1976.

Melters, Johannes. „*ein frölich gemüt zu machen in schweren zeiten...*'. *Der Schwankroman in Mittelalter und Früher Neuzeit*. Berlin 2004.

Mohr, Jan, Waltenberger, Michael (Eds.). *Das Syntagma des Pikaresken*. Heidelberg 2014.

Moshövel, Andrea. "Zwischen Dämonisierung, Satire und Komik – der skatologische Eulenspiegel und sein Sieg über die Furcht." *Perspicuitas. Internet-Periodicum für mediävistische Sprach-, Literatur- und Kulturwissenschaft* (2011) Feb. 2017; https://www.uni-due.de/imperia/md/content/perspicuitas/moshoevel.pdf.

Pastré, Jean-Marc. "Fastnachtspiele: Eine verkehrte Anschauung der Welt und der Literatur." Ed. Klaus Ridder. *Fastnachtspiele. Weltliches Schauspiel in literarischen und kulturellen Kontexten*. Tübingen 2009. 139–150.

Ragotzky, Hedda. *Gattungserneuerung und Laienunterweisung in Texten des Strickers*. Berlin 1981.

Röcke, Werner. *Ulenspiegel. Spätmittelalterliche Literatur im Übergang zur Neuzeit*. Düsseldorf 1978.

Röcke, Werner. *Die Freude am Bösen. Studien zu einer Poetik des deutschen Schwankromans im Spätmittelalter*. München 1987.

Runte, Annette. "Comment saisir les hors-la-loi? Théories sur la marginalité." Ed. Alexander Schwarz. *Till Eulenspiegel. Traduire l'original / Zurück zum Original*. Lausanne 2013. 39–71.

Schnell, Rüdiger. "Männer unter sich – Männer und Frauen im Gespräch." Ed. Rüdiger Schnell. *Konversationskultur in der Vormoderne. Geschlechter im geselligen Gespräch*. Köln/Weimar/Wien 2008. 387–440.

Schwarz, Alexander. "Körper, Gender, Eulenspiegel." *'Wenn sie das Wort Ich gebraucht'. Festschrift für Barbara Becker-Cantarino*. Amsterdam 2013. 325–349.

Der Stricker. *Der Pfaffe Amis*. [1240] Ed. Michael Schilling. Stuttgart 1994.

Strobel, Katja. "Die Courage der Courasche. Weiblichkeit als Maskerade und groteske Körperlichkeit in Grimmelshausens Pikara-Roman." Ed. Elfi Bettinger /Julika Funk. *Maskeraden. Geschlechterdifferenz in der literarischen Inszenierung*. Berlin 1995. 82–97.

Tenberg, Reinhard. *Die deutsche Till Eulenspiegel-Rezeption bis zum Ende des 16. Jahrhunderts*. Würzburg 1996.

Till Eulenspiegel. His Adventures. Tr. Paul Oppenheimer. New York 1991.

Velten, Hans Rudolf. "Schwankheld und Sympathie. Zu Strickers 'Der Pfaffe Amis' und Frankfurters 'Des pfaffen geschicht und histori vom Kalenberg'." Ed. Friedrich M. Dimpel/Hans R. Velten. *Techniken der Sympathiesteuerung in Erzähltexten der Vormoderne – Potentiale und Probleme*. Heidelberg 2016. 97–124.

Werner, Florian. *Dunkle Materie: Die Geschichte der Scheiße*. München 2011.

Subversion and Stabilization of the Sexes by Transgression in Grimmelshausen's *Courasche* (1669)

MAREN LICKHARDT

When confronting the picaresque universe with questions from gender studies, we are treading on relatively unexplored terrain. We have to look very closely at the texts and we need highly differentiated concepts of identity, sexuality, physicality, sex, and gender, if we are to zero in on the picaresque character from this angle. More precisely, this applies to the male picaresque figure, regardless of how masculinity in this context may be defined in general and picaresque masculinity in particular. For even if this universe is populated mostly by male pícaros, this does not mean that masculinity really stands out as a firm category. It remains rather fleeting (in typical picaresque fashion). The female picaresque figure represents the 'other' category, which as such has already received more research focus. Femininity seems to be contoured more clearly in the texts themselves (and this is more or less typical for femininity). In German literature, we have Grimmelshausen's novel *Courasche* (1669), a novel in which the narrator's femininity is focused very intensively so that scarcely any research article can get away without consulting the pertinent categories, in which case this at first seemingly self-evident femininity becomes progressively intangible the more we scrutinize it. Picaresque and gender, as transgressive phenomena between appearance and reality, form a relationship in the novel that is very dynamic and in which they mirror each other.

Right at *Courasche*'s start, the first-person narrator constructs a polarity of the sexes by addressing the reader adversatively as "[You] gentlemen" (Grimmelshausen 1965 [1669]: 31; Wicke 2000: 412) and links the inferred or rather anticipated pejorative moral judgements of her own person to her physical sex that conspicuously "lack[s] one thing and has too much of several, in particular two things" (Grimmelshausen 1965: 33). Thus, the tale is conditioned on men constituting a different and, what is more, judgmental entity and on the narrator having a particular physical shape that prompts the relevant appraisals. That does not mean that an indissoluble relationship between physical make-up and the judgment is being postulated, rather that the nexus remarkably appears as an attributive relationship. Addressing the reader moreover updates the picaresque formula of the apologia or the confession; or more specifically, Courage's more or less reliable retrospective account of her life takes for its starting point a heterotopic narrative situation that is typical of the German picaresque novel. But while Simplicius is depicted as a chastened island dweller, Courage has found another place beyond society among the 'gypsies'. As "queen" or "genteel ruler over all other gypsies," (Grimmelshausen 2007 [1669/70]: 179)[1] as she is described in *Springinsfeld*, she has no regrets whatsoever about her life. Instead, the story is designed to take revenge on Simplicius (Grimmelshausen 1965: 34 and many more), who described her in the *Simplicissimus* Sauerbrunnen episode as „more *mobilis* than *nobilis*" (Grimmelshausen 2005 [1668]: 468) and, in order to drag Simplicius through the mud on account of the company he used to keep, she parades all her sins in a particular truculent manner. While in the case of the German picaresque novel, we may be dealing with a modified variation of the genre (Meid 1984: 72), the character's lack of remorse does represent once again a subverting of the German picaresque tradition (Büchler 1971: 9; Streller 1986: 53; Wicke 2000: 405, 407; Solbach 2003: 181). Whether her rejection of remorse and repentance makes her more reliable and puts her in a positive light by showing the hypocrisy of the only ostensibly chastened other figures (Meid 2002: 21-22) or whether she personifies a particular bad exemplar in the framework of a negative didaxis remain as open questions. In any case, this in genre-poetological terms expanding or surpassing stance heightens the "very transgressiveness of the dystopian world of Grimmelshausen's novels" (Tatlock 2003: 272), which, in terms of narrative technique, already manifests itself as a male author donning a female narrator's mask (278; Strobel 1995: 84). Disguise, pretense, and masquerade play even a greater role in the fictional setting. "Playing with identities emerges as an integral element of the picaresque genre,"[2] (82) when it comes to constituting Courage. The fact that she is constantly changing and must adapt herself in ever new ways goes hand in hand with her semi-outsider status.[3] Hers is not a fixed position in society, she wanders through dif-

---

1   All quotes from Simplicissimus and Springsinsfeld are translated by M.L.
2   Translated by M.L.
3   On Aspects of the Picaresque in general see Lickhardt (2014: 10-19).

ferent levels and dodges the social order (Strobel 1995: 82). The pícara Courage at first does not differ in mimicry and outsiderdom from her male counterparts (Solbach 1991). She moves through the world as someone of uncertain origin. Certainly, her ups and downs (Wagener 1970) or her fall (Streller 1986: 53), her enormous mobility (Arnold 1997: 96) in terms of her whereabouts as well as the range of her activities are structured by her marriages and the loss of her husbands (Strobel 1995: 82).[4]

In perspective and theme, the picaresque worldview is tied to sexuality and the relationship of the sexes. Also, the examples that reflexively express her status have bodily-feminine connotations. Hence, her changes of conditions are described by "this skin so often compelled to change its color [with make-up]"[5] (Grimmelshausen 1965: 32), and so evinces an episode of sexual inactivity, when she lacks suitors because of not being good enough for some and too good for others, her incompatibility with the world around her (73). In addition, we can find *desengaño* experiences that are linked to the battle of the sexes. On the narrative level, *caso*, i.e. narrative motivation, and *desengaño* collapse into one. It is the matter of Simplicius exposing her that motivates the narration of the entire novel (Bauer 2009). Immanent in the novel as the initial humiliation is her first husband giving her the Courage name, her gender unmasking and renewed masking, and her externally-imposed dual status as gutsy fighter and hypersexualized woman (Wicke 2000: 426). Picaresque writing and picaresque (gender) identity in these passages and in many more are staged as ascription opposing self-ascription. This divergence between appearance and reality that can be comprehended both genre- and gender-theoretically forms the abstract denominator of all of Courage's *desengaños*. The character's (non- or double) identity, tied in an extreme way to sex and gender, as well as her related written relationship with the world are fundamentally and fatefully established in this episode.

Without any doubt, Courage is branded sexually in a special way. Let us put aside for now that the name is just as little unique as the character's constitution; for the reader starting out it is impossible to avoid picturing a female sinner who, without whining, also shows up the sins of the men around her. Consequently, a long academic debate has grown up around the question of how the figure (according to Grimmelshausen) is to be evaluated as a female character. Dieter Breuer gets to the heart of the controversy: "On the one hand, Grimmelshausen's novel is interpreted as a cautionary example of traditional misogyny, on the other

---

4 For a comprehensive look at Courage's marriages, see Hamidouche (2006).

5 The original German text uses the word ‚make-up' which has not been translated literally into English.

hand as an early attempt at portraying a woman trying to emancipate herself under conditions of war and prevalent misogyny" (Breuer 2002a: 11).[6] It does not avoid the issue to designate the text or the character formation in this regard as ultimately polyvalent (Arnold 1969: 524; Lefebvre 1980: 32; Hillen 1992: 857; Arnold 1997: 90; Heßelmann 2003: 38), as is done in more recent research. This does justice to the text very well so long as a lenticular structure is applied to the genre background: whether Courage now appears as victim (Battafarano 1995: 256-259; Battafarano 2002) or as culprit (Hillenbrand 1998: 185, 189/190; Hillenbrand 2002: 59), as allegory (Feldges 1969), as symbolic cause or effect of the gruesome events in the Thirty Years War, in the picaresque framework the depravity of character and world necessarily mutually reference each other and the value judgment perspective remains ambiguous (Solbach 2002). It goes in circles up to the extent that it is subject to an ever-reversible process in the retrospective life- and worldview, not just in reference to the relationship of the figure's perspective and world, but also in reference to what lies between *discours* and *histoire* (Bauer 1993: 17, 209; Bauer 1994: 13, 25, 31).

As it happens, said academic debate was not exclusively a judgmental one, but instead revealed various differentiated facets of the figure. As a purely evaluative debate, it would not have done the novel justice (Bunte 2009: 449), had it only reproduced what is already laid out in the novel. The fictional author of the text, namely Philarchus Grossus von Trommenheim, effects a first reception in his "Addendum by the Author" (Grimmelshausen 1965: 183), in which the character is evaluated negatively. In so doing, he consummates what Courage at the very beginning had already expected. The very fact that the author's epilogue, i. e. a first reaction to the tale within the novellistic arrangement, is even added to the novel, is irritating in the framework of a realistic reading, since the reader learns in *Springinsfeld* that Courage herself was the last to keep the manuscript and the one who turned it over to the printer, so that she would have been able to keep this evaluation to herself. By the author as implicit reader and exegete nonetheless being so visibly (and ultimately also explicitly) inserted into the novel, the text immunizes itself prophylactically against negative moralistic judgment. This manner of reading is almost 'a present' for the reader, seeing that the text itself prefigures this already with the Sauerbrunnen episode and is motivated by it, so that the narration already consistently scores points against a bad repute. That being so, John W. Jacobson's observation that the research had

---

6 Translated by M.L. A recapitulation of this debate is also found in Menhennet (1997: 119), Eilert (2001: 113-116). Mathias Feldges (1969) and John W. Jacobson (1968) assuredly take the most striking positions in the debate's early phase.

abused the character, just as much as the masculine figures did fictionally, no longer sounds too harsh (Jacobson 1968: 42). Rather, Jacobson's verdict on the negative appraisals of the figure is already implied in the text, because the text-immanent behaviour toward Courage – for example, defamation and rape – always appears already as a (mis)guided or at least too reflex-like and simple interpretation of the character (as female figure), and so mirrors the interpretation of the expected reader. Conversely, it is then no longer anachronistic (cf. Hillenbrand 2002: 47) to work out the character's emancipatory traits, because the text-immanent difference between the narrator's conduct and the reactions of the other figures allows the reader to make judgments that may not turn out to be favourable to Courage but also may not necessarily lead to her unpopularity. The chasm between Courage's self-perception and the perceptions of others is negotiated in the text in a way that must disconcert the reader. With didactic intent, the novel deconstructs the misogynistic ascriptions to the character, because it reveals them to be nothing more than ascriptions. It is not even necessary to believe Courage in order to at least note the difference and independently reflect on it. Still, as narrator of her own story, she has a privileged perspective (Kaminski 2002: 93); it is not without reason that she is chosen as speech mask and perception medium – it makes her the story's instrumental subject and not simply its (negative) exemplary object.[7]

This emerges with special clarity in the example of the figure's demonization as witch. There are no hints anywhere in the text that Courage practices or is versed in witchcraft. She mentions (in the subjunctive mood) that she would have learned witchcraft had she stayed longer with her landlady, but that this had not been the case (Grimmelshausen 1965: 56). And why would she absolve herself of this sin when she unburdens herself of all the others? Of course, there will also remain residual doubts about highly intentional and deliberate narrative that can leave things out (Bauer 1993; Bauer 1994). But, in the text, the accusations of witchery are disclosed as mischaracterizations of the figure or of the relationship of the figures to one another, or, more concretely, as slander and potential character assassination of the female character stemming from male resentment, because the reader can see that said accusation fill the room only when men feel they have been humiliated by her (Grimmelshausen: 66; Battafarano 1997: 62, 67; Feldman 1991: 79; Wicke 2000: 428). Being outed publicly as witch would be equivalent to a death sentence, which is why this interpretational reaction to the character is not different from manifest violence. Hence, the gang rape is to

---

7 However, Alan Menhennet maintains that this does not need to be a contradiction and that both can be realized simultaneously in the narration (Menhennet 1997: 121-123).

end in the attempt to get rid of Courage by denouncing her as a witch (Chapter 12). This does not ultimately happen, as men were loath to be tagged as having consorted with a witch. Sexuality in this instance leads to equivalency. The men in the passage are very much aware of this: if it is not just witchcraft that can be sexually transmitted like an infection, the men, by the way, may also be tarred with the character's other 'female' sins of lust and whoring. With regard to Simplicius, this mechanism is constitutive for the novel. Along with many other passages, we could understand this infection fantasy as a metafictional direction to transfer Courage's sins wholesale also to Simplicius, who knows who he was consorting with at the Sauerbrunnen. Courage's sexual generosity could not be regarded as anything but negative in her day (Teuscher 1984: 107), whereas rape was not necessarily a criminal offense (Dane 2009: 369). Nevertheless, even here the men's sinfulness is unmasked (Kaiser 2009: 197-203), while the narrator feels godforsaken and abased (Grimmelshausen 1965: 85). More important for the present exploration of gender relations, however, is the fact that damage to a man's image opens the episode. He thus is subject to judgment by public opinion, but is able to indirectly reject it and put it on the female character within the framework of the early modern hierarchy of the sexes – to begin with, through violence, while the final contemplated act of character assassination falls through by happenstance (Maurer 1999: 97). This escalation of gang rape to public denunciation/execution is remarkable in terms of the great relevance in the novel of the judgment culture, which depends on an appearance that does not always turn out to be reality however. It is therefore consistent that Courage as experiencing ego is sensitive to public opinion and does not react first as narrating ego to the account by Simplicius (Bauer 2009: 107, 196).

To furnish another example, she describes how the fracas with the Italian concerning the pants, denotative regarding the gender theme, brought her into worse repute than him, even though he started it and was the loser. In the long view, the man does not stand there as unreasonable and weak, rather Courage ought not to have fought and beaten him (Streller 1986: 59; Zeuch 2009: 151). While he sinks into oblivion, she is regarded as sinister now and "suffered longer because of it than he did when they hanged him" (Grimmelshausen 1965: 69). The figure making herself a showpiece through storytelling in the final analysis represents a self-empowerment and subjectivation that is not in first line based on the public judgment by Simplicius but takes many others for granted: Men are ashamed of her or even fear her strength and survival skills. Women hate her because of her beauty (70). In the novel, enormous feelings of powerlessness are laid bare in the face of images of Courage circulated by others and against which she is defenseless (Wicke 2000: 427). And constantly, the judgmental reactions to the female character base themselves on gender role types that are patriarchally imprinted and that aim to restore the patriarchal gender order (Feldman 1991: 79; Kaiser 2009: 205). So it is ultimately logical and simultaneously paradoxical that she should once again recapitulate her transgressions. This concurrently represents the gateway for – and immunization against – negative judgments; the text is, on the one hand, very open, but, on the other hand, effects a certain closure through reflexive negotiation of interpretations, judgments, verdicts, ascriptions, and acts of reception. The text as a whole shows that it is possible not to behave according to gender normalization but that it is impossible to be judged outside these frameworks. It is interesting how intensely this normative framework within the novel is anchored on Courage as a counter reaction and how clearly and systematically she, for her part, already scores points in reaction against it. In doing so, she, time and again, in her writing – read realistically – postulates the judgement of her person or – read metafictionally – presupposes the interpretation of herself as a character in a novel. Even if we do not give Courage seamless credence, the novel draws a distinction between the immanent perspectives and between own narrative and perceptions by others, which makes the reader realize that judgments do not necessarily have to be tied to gender but that factually this happens full well. The text therefore reveals in critical fashion that there can be no judgments or interpretations independent of gender.

The gendered patriarchal judgment culture that conditions the misogynistic 'readings' of the character is explicitly shown as irrelevant in the text, because the protagonist exhibits nothing that identifies her as 'woman' as such. Right after the initial installation of gender polarity in the judgement culture framework described earlier, the novel deconstructs the character's sex through her multiple name and identity changes that accompany the much-discussed cross- dressing: "Maid Libushka (hereafter called Courage) enters the war, calls herself Janco, and must for a time serve as valet-de-chambre" (Grimmelshausen 1965: 35). After the conquest of her hometown, Libushka's nurse tells her to cross-dress as a man to keep her virginity. Being a woman or, better said, being recognized as a woman, is so dangerous in war that the nurse "would not give a buckle off a chastity belt" (36) for her honor. Since being a woman inevitably leads to getting raped, the only way out is to escape into the other sex. For that Libushka has to "shear [her] head and put [herself] in men's clothes" (36). To be sure, not being a woman is no guarantee of safety at all in war. As a man, she could still be killed but saving her honor obviously is the nurse's main concern. So Libushka has to deal with two problems: like any creature caught in the turmoil of the war she must not only survive it, but she also has to preserve her maidenhead and honor as a woman. There are obviously no concerns about her physical and psychic integrity (Kaminski 2002: 85). Taking the nurse's advice, Libushka crossdresses as a man, and at first glance it seems to be remarkably easy to transcend, transgress or even transform the female body. It just so happens that not much more than cross-dressing is necessary to pass for a man and to fit in with a man's world of war:

> Well, I fitted quite nicely into my new role in this masquerade. [...] and because I also had a great liking for arms, I took care of his in such a manner that my master and his servants could rely on them, and therefore I soon got him to give me a sword and to dub me fit for military service by giving me a cuff on the ear. [...] Next, I tried my best to rid myself of all my feminine ways and to acquire masculine ones instead, I purposely learned to curse like a trooper and to drink like a tinker besides (Grimmelshausen 1965: 38).

The text conveys clichés of masculine behavior that the female character must adopt in order to pass as a man. This is the minimum called for beyond cross-dressing, but except for her vulnerable body, nowhere does the text project an essential female concept or femininity nor a male concept or masculinity (Battafarano 1995: 257; Zeuch 2009: 147). Sexes are deconstructed to genders. External features like haircuts, clothes and a register of superficial behaviours work as gender markers (Bühler 2012: 204). If she has to, Libushka obviously can curse and drink like a man without any problem. And she does not stop there. Throughout the novel, she fights like a man, is as cruel and as successful as some men and even more so than some others; she is powerful, self-determining, sexually active and so on. In quite an explicit way, the text shows that no role models, role registers, or role stereotypes need to be attached to the biological sex. There is no such thing as an inherent sexual identity (Strobel 1995: 91; Zeuch 2009: 154). Gender is created and staged performatively, is always and already a masquerade, which is particularly so in the case of the itinerant picaresque trickster (Strobel 1995: 82, 84). This is demonstrated not only by Courage having first to learn what it is required for 'masculinity' but explicitly also for 'femininity' (85/86). For example, she is described as learning women's work (Grimmelshausen 1965: 35). In addition, in front of the mirror she practices the typically female-associated coquetry register, such as laughing, crying, and sighing (50). She also performs well in this regard, because later she is a popular prostitute. Moreover, she openly tells of how she deploys fake tears in front of a man as a winning strategy (58, C 90; Tatlock 2003: 280). Conversely, she says of the man that she first falls in love with "if he had worn lady's dress not one in a thousand but would have taken him for anything but a beautiful maiden" (Grimmelshausen 1965: 39). Indeed, Courage seems to want him precisely because of his androgyny or his androgyny directly (Zeuch 2009: 146), for she portrays these aspects as the attractive ones while describing his traits with male connotations in a rather negative manner (Grimmelshausen 1965: C 40). The Italian personifies everything she wishes for herself. He is a man who does not have to disguise himself for his martial life style, although he is obviously no more masculine than Courage. But even in this context, the text would not be what it is if it gave the character an unambiguous pose. At times, *Springinsfeld* exhibits feminine traits, and he does not belong to the characters lusted after by Courage. She speaks about this figure in the language of betrayal, for she describes him at one point as pale "as if he had but recently had a baby" (103) and "he did not seem to [her] man enough to deceive Courage" (126).

Courage found her role after she had tried and learned both gender roles. She is a female soldier and "lusty and gay" (40) in war. But since she 'officially' cannot do this as a woman, she first wants to be a man (39) or, after she is outed as a woman, at least a hermaphrodite (67; Strobel 1995: 92; Haberkamp 2002; Bühler 2012: 205/206). She nevertheless reveals herself to the cavalry captain and characteristically is publicly presented in a dress on the occasion of her first marriage (Grimmelshausen 1965: 48). However, what she has to fight about with her later Italian husband (63) are the pants, and in the text the clothing symbols are more than just a metaphor for her wish to be a man, because eventually there are occasions when her longing is actually fulfilled in this staging (Arnold 1969: 532; Arnold 1997: 105; Bühler 2012: 204sq.). In practice, Courage after being outed as a woman, dresses in a mix of men's and women's clothes, by which she hopes to be able to cope with all roles and expectations.

> I did not ride in a lady's saddle like other officers' ladies, but instead in a man's saddle, and though I rode sidesaddle I still had pistols and a Turkish sabre under my thigh [...] and moreover I was dressed in breeches and a thin little taffeta skirt over them, so that in an instant I could sit astride and present the picture of a young trooper; for if there was an encounter with the enemy it was impossible for me to stay off to the sides and not take part. I often said that a lady who does not dare defend herself against a mounted man ought not to wear man's plumage [...] (Grimmelshausen 1965: 59sq.).

This scene combines both gender roles in one character (Strobel 1995: 89) and is coupled with a strong sexualization beyond the fact that the figure carries a phallus symbol under all her clothes (Haberkamm 2002: 136). This, in turn, leads to the conclusion about her prowess in war, for it is possible to say that the character 'has balls', whether she actually does or not. Courage would make the ideal heroine in a novel, because she is the bravest soldier (Grimmelshausen 1965:

66sq., 81) and the most beautiful woman (70); on the other hand, she would be the ideal anti-heroine in a novel because she uses both qualities solely for her own advantage (72; Zeuch 2009: 200). But neither of both apply to her, because her name happens to be Courage and she "had to put up with the name Courage" (Grimmelshausen 1965: 59). She got the name from the cavalry captain after having described her female sex organ this way: "Because he made a grab for my courage, which place no man's hands have touched" (40). For Courage and her cavalryman, the name connotes her female sex organ. For all the other characters, it alludes to the French military virtue of *courage* (Wicke 2000; Kaminski 2002: 89; Kaminski 2009: 230; Zeuch 2009: 147). This makes her appear "as paradoxical unity of male ideality and female physicality"[8] (Berns 1988: 312). It should actually provoke more curiosity in research than is the case as to why this name represents an insult for the character.[9] Although it stems from an ascription in the framework of a sexually-imprinted power constellation, it also designates the two components through which the character defines herself: sexual passion and power as well as battle readiness and being victorious. Someone who does not know how the name came about might jealously label her with it but would not in the act negate her bravery in any way.

Admittedly, trying to see a consummate performative game of the sexes in an early modern picaresque is stretching things slightly (cf. Strobel 1995: 87). The role play, after all, is an imposed one and in the picaresque framework can only be such, i.e., what is more clearly shown are the limitations on the part of society, the preformation of the roles as well as the normative reference to the roles as the liberating possibilities of a transgressive game. It is abundantly clear that the character evades the prevailing categories. However, by unveiling a sexual transgressivity, she is an irritant to society. So, the potential game in various respects quickly turns bitterly serious. It is particularly the picaresque that stages risky physicality, hunger, and violence, but barely lived libidinous sensuality. It invariably functions as critique, that is, in the novel the limitations are scarcely ever embraced precisely, because they are so clearly delineated; instead, in *Courasche* surely the sexist dual morality forms the target for this critique (cf.

---

8   Translated by M. L.
9   Certainly, the negative implications of the name and the naming are present (e. g. Zeuch 2009: 158), but this is also a matter of perspective, that is, it remains an open question why the character gives so much weight to the connotations from an outside perspective that relegate her to a marginal and inferior position – even though she could agree with the same connotations from her perspective but with different value judgments. The relevance of others' judgments emerges very clearly here.

Menhennet 1997: 132). Where sexuality contrary to a picaresque body discourse does play a role, i.e., is even thematized in the first place and depicts a positive body experience, it has, however, a thoroughly stabilizing function.

Being sexually unmarked or unidentified or in an intermediate hybrid state are exposed in the text as impossible possibilities. In this respect, the novel in fact unfolds a remarkably tricky dialectic and transgressivity, because these possibilities shine through among all the impossibilities. It shows in a very thought-out manner how the biological sex acts as a "social shackle [...]"[10] (Wicke 2000: 418) on the unfolding of the individual personality (419). Now, successful cross-dressing could harbor a great liberating potential; however, it turns out to be just another role prison for the character (Kaminski 2009: 228). To assert that this was due to every gender categorization exerting a discursive violence on the character could be an inference based on modern gender theory, yet it would aim right past the novel. Instead, the text places another stage in form of the character's body. For it is to her body that Courage ties her mental states, such as when she locates her anger in her gallbladder, and so introduces an antique, medieval and early modern fluids and temperament teaching (Grimmelshausen 1965: 33; Wicke 2000: 410). Courage also invokes her nature as the guiding thread of her way of life and thereby refers to a medical concept dating from antiquity (Breuer 2002b: 232). She is not only beholden to corporeality in the sense that we could say she does not constitute a transcendental figure; rather, in a special sense, she is imprisoned in her female corporeality by her strong sexual cupidity (Ermatinger 1928: 117; Bühler 2012: 202). Her sexual avidity grows with her breasts, hence depends on her body.

> In the meantime, the more time passed, the bigger my bosom grew and the more the shoe pinched me, in such a manner that I did not trust myself to conceal any longer either my bosom, which would soon show without, or the fire which was raging within it (Grimmelshausen 1965: 43).

Now it basically turns out to be a good thing for Courage that she gets into a scuffle with a soldier "during which work my adversary whisked his hand inside my trousers to seize me by that equipment which I, after all, did not possess." (43) The female body remains as a determining marker for Courage, one that she cannot get rid of. She can rid herself of all her feminine ways, of all the ways that are only ascribed to women (38). She can adopt all masculine ways, all ways that are only ascribed to men, yet wrongly as the text reveals. But she cannot

---

10 Translated by M. L.

discard her body. To keep her opponent from grabbing at nothing in that scuffle, she reacts over-aggressively to the point where bystanders must keep her from killing him. In the end, she is quite sure that he had caught on to her being a woman, but that he would never dare to reveal it because of shame at having been beaten by a woman. Not his or her small size but the sex is obviously very important for how the fight's outcome is regarded, revealing once again a sexist world. Being confronted by her master afterwards, the narrator explains: "Because he made a grab for my courage, which place no man's hands have touched." Then she confesses to him that she is a woman: "I bared my snow-white bosom and showed the captain of horse my firm, appealing breasts. 'Look, sir' I said, 'Here you see before you a maiden […].' (44) As noted previously, from then on, she is called Courage in allusion to the sex organ. The question remains why she reveals her womanhood – bearing in mind that there is no assurance that her opponent would have confessed to having been beaten by a woman (cf. Kaminski 2009: 229). She decides to expose herself quite willingly. And she does so because she *is* a woman (Van Ornam 1992: 34; Haberkamm 2002: 132sq.). She is a heterosexual woman, and this is determinative for her (Tatlock 2003). "To her great inconvenience, gender, in Courasche's case, cannot transcend sex" (Van Ornam 1992: 35). The character's biological sex appears to be something incapable of being deceived. Having fallen in love with her master, she is more interested in her sexual appetite than in preserving her virginity (46; Zeuch 2009: 147). Later, both her being set up as a prostitute as well as her marriages serve to secure Courage's financial situation and a certain social status, yet she stresses that frequently sexual desire is part of it and that she acts out her own physical needs (Solbach 1986: 72). Every transgression or every crossing of a border in a hybrid state are metaphors that the character grasps for when she fails (Haberkamm 2002: 133-135). Her frequent stylizations as woman (Bühler 2012: 207), her makeup, etc. correspond to a learned register that is not necessarily concatenated with her gender. But she is codified as a woman in the biological sense, not only by the detour of male expectation stances, but also by the fact that she desires men; in other words, she is distinguished by a marked sexual desire that unfolds a highly determinative power beyond all masquerades and that cannot be reshaped by mere clothing (Strobel 1995: 89). In the novel, a biologically grounded, heteronormative framework is assumed entirely without reflection and as self-evident (Wicke 2000: 427). Had she been sexually unmarked with reference to her libido, to begin with she could have continued to live as a man after all (Solbach 1991: 41). However, her body develops a life of its own in the course of her puberty which no longer allows her to carry on living dressed as a man. If the body determines the character to such a degree, the question remains whether, as a female body, concupiscence should not after all be misogynistically coded into it. However, following concept is interesting: a female character that, in the final analysis, wants to be a woman, and in the end, in a self-determined role, calls herself by her girl's name Libushka again, though not behaving or feeling like a stereotypical female in any way despite her heterosexual-feminine libidinous determination (Berns 1990: 420). This differentiated conception ultimately does liberate from some essentialist gender notions. Eventually, an enormous transgression also takes place via heterosexual sexuality. On one hand, through her sexuality Courage transgresses her own body in coupling with male bodies (Strobel 1995: 93), and possibly her sexual lust is also motivated precisely because she can attain a bisexual body through sexual union. On the other hand, her sexual zest represents the breaking of a norm and reversal of gender roles (Solbach 1991: 45), precisely because she does not comport herself in line with what is expected, given her overtly present biological sex. Considering that this causes her to come up against the severest defensive measures in no way, diminishes the fact that the novel shows the potential of crossing borders. In a certain sense, however, it is exactly the character's sexual appetite that serves to stabilize the sexes which only emerge in their polarity because of this appetite, while in every other respect they are dissolved. Is there not a possibility that sexuality in Grimmelshausen's novel has a calming, restorative function? When all is said and done, what does actually represent violation of norms: the overcoming of the sexual body, because then the woman can in fact be everything she wants to be; or being bound to the sexual body, for then the woman lives her passion as she wants? Here, too, the reflections end up going in circles, but then again that happens to be typical for picaresque texts.

BIBLIOGRAPHY

Arnold, Herbert A. "Moralisch-didaktische Elemente in Grimmelshausens Roman *Courasche*. Beitrag zu einer möglichen Interpretation." *Zeitschrift für deutsche Philologie* 88 (1969): 521–560.

Arnold, Herbert A. "Die Rollen der Courasche. Bemerkungen zur wirtschaftlichen und sozialen Stellung der Frau im siebzehnten Jahrhundert." Ed. Barbara Becker-Cantarino. *Die Frau von der Reformation zur Romantik. Die Situation der Frau vor dem Hintergrund der Literatur und Sozialgeschichte.* Bonn 1997. 86–111.

Bauer, Matthias. *Im Fuchsbau der Geschichten. Anatomie des Schelmenromans.* Stuttgart 1993.

Bauer, Matthias. *Der Schelmenroman*. Stuttgart 1994.

Bauer, Matthias. "Ausgleichende Gewalt? Der Kampf der Geschlechter und die Liebe zur Gerechtigkeit in Grimmelshausens *Simplicissimus, Courasche* und *Springinsfeld*." *Simpliciana* 31 (2009): 99–126.

Battafarano, Italo Michele. "Barocke Typologie femininer Negativität und ihre Kritik bei Spee, Grimmelshausen und Harsdörffer." Ed. Wilhelm Kühlmann. *Literatur und Kultur im deutschen Südwesten zwischen Renaissance und Aufklärung. Neue Studien*. Amsterdam 1995. 245–266.

Battafarano, Italo Michele. "Erzählte Dämonopathie in Grimmelshausens *Courasche*." *Simpliciana* 19 (1997): 55–89.

Battafarano, Italo Michele. "Courasches sich legitimierende Literarizität." *Simpliciana* 24 (2002): 187–212.

Berns, Jörg Jochen. "Die 'Zusammenfügung' der Simplicianischen Schriften. Bemerkungen zum Zyklus-Problem." *Simpliciana* 10 (1988): 301–325.

Berns, Jörg Jochen. "Libuschka und Courasche. Studien zu Grimmelshausens Frauenbild. Teil II: Darlegungen." *Simpliciana* 12 (1990): 417–442.

Breuer, Dieter. "Kontroversen um Grimmelshausens *Courasche*. Vorbemerkungen." *Simpliciana* 24 (2002a): 11–14.

Breuer, Dieter. "Courasches Unbußfertigkeit. Das religiöse Problem in Grimmelshausens Roman." *Simpliciana* 24 (2002b): 229–242.

Büchler, Hansjörg. *Studien zu Grimmelshausens Landstörtzerin Courasche*. Bern, Frankfurt a.M. 1971.

Bühler, Jill. "Anatomien der Lust in Grimmelshausens Courasche." *Simpliciana* 34 (2012): 197–213.

Bunte, Martin. "Grimmelshausens *Courasche* als Gegenbild der Lucretia. Vergewaltigung und Suizid im Spannungsfeld antiker Tugendbewertung und christlicher Sündenschuld." *Simpliciana* 31 (2009): 449–460.

Dane, Gesa. "Geraubt – Gefangen. Zu Grimmelshausens *Courasche* und Ziglers *Asiatische Banise*." *Simpliciana* 31 (2009): 363–375.

Eilert, Hildegard. "Mehr Demokratie mit der Landstörtzerin? Grimmelshausens Courasche-Editionen im 20. Jahrhundert." *Simpliciana* 23 (2001): 101–126.

Ermatinger, Emil. *Krisen und Probleme der neuen deutschen Dichtung*. Zürich 1928.

Feldges, Mathias. *Grimmelshausens Landstörtzerin Courasche. Eine Interpretation nach der Methode des vierfachen Schriftsinns*. Bern 1969.

Feldman, Linda Ellen. "The Rape of Frau Welt. Transgression, Allegory and the Grotesque Body in Grimmelshausen's *Courasche*." *Daphnis. Zeitschrift für mittlere deutsche Literatur* 20 (1991): 61–80.

Grimmelshausen, Hans Jacob Christoffel von. *The Runagate Courage*. Translated with an Introduction and Notes by L. Hiller und John G. Osborne. Lincoln 1965.

Grimmelshausen, Hans Jacob Christoffel von. *Der seltzame Springinsfeld*. Ed. Dieter Breuer. *Werke I.2*. Frankfurt a.M. 2007.

Grimmelshausen, Hans Jacob Christoffel von. *Der abentheuerliche Simplicissimus Teutsch*. Ed. Dieter Breuer *Werke I*. Frankfurt a.M. 2005.

Haberkamm, Klaus. "'Sebel unter dem Schenckel'. Zur Funktion des Hermaphroditischen in Grimmelshausens *Courasche*." *Simpliciana* 24 (2002): 123–140.

Hamidouche, Martina. "Courasches Ehen. Eine genderorientierte Untersuchung des Grimmelshausenromans." *Colloquia Germanica* 39 (2006): 231–242.

Heßelmann, Peter. "'Ein Spiegel böser Art?' Grimmelshausens *Courasche* in den Kommentaren der posthumen Gesamtausgaben." *Simpliciana* 24 (2003): 27–46.

Hillen, Gerd. "'Warumb das, Courasche?' Grimmelshausens Misogynie in Text, Kontext und Kritik." Eds. James Hardin and Jörg Jungmayr. *'Der Buchstab tödt – der Geist macht lebendig'*. Bd. 2. Bern 1992. 849–861.

Hillenbrand, Rainer. "Courasche als emanzipierte Frau. Einige erstaunliche Modernitäten bei Grimmelshausen." *Daphnis* 27 (1998): 185–199.

Hillenbrand, Rainer. "Courasche als negatives Exempel." *Simpliciana* 24 (2002): 47–66.

Jacobson, John W. "A Defense of Grimmelshausen's *Courasche*." *The German Quarterly* 41 (1968): 42–54.

Kaiser, Michael. "Gewaltspezialistin und Gewaltopfer. Historische Beobachtungen zu Grimmelshausens *Courasche*." *Simpliciana* 31 (2009): 183–206.

Kaminski, Nicola. "'Reine des Bohémiens.' Politische Utopie und 'zigeunernde Textur' in Grimmelshausens *Courasche*." *Simpliciana* 24 (2002): 79–121.

Kaminski, Nicola. "Gender-crossing: Narrative Versuchsanordnungen zwischen Eros und Krieg in Grimmelshausens *Courasche* und Lohensteins *Arminius*." *Simpliciana* 31 (2009): 227–244.

Lefebvre, Joël. "Didaktik und Spiel in Grimmelshausens *Courage*." *Simpliciana* 2 (1980): 31–36.

Lickhardt, Maren. "Zu Transformationen des Pikarischen." *LiLi* 44 (2014): 6–23.

Maurer, Michael. "Geschichte und gesellschaftliche Strukturen des 17. Jahrhunderts." Ed. Albert Meier. *Die Literatur des 17. Jahrhunderts. Hansers Sozialgeschichte der deutschen Literatur vom 16. Jahrhundert bis zur Gegenwart*. München 1999. 18-99.

Meid, Volker. *Grimmelshausen. Epoche, Werk, Wirkung*. München 1984.

Meid, Volker. "Von der Pícara Justina zu Grimmelshausens Courasche." *Simpliciana* 24 (2002): 15–26.
Menhennet, Alan. *Grimmelshausen, the Storyteller. A Study of the 'Simplician' Novels*. Columbia 1997.
Solbach, Andreas. "Macht und Sexualität der Hexenfigur in Grimmelshausens Courasche." *Simpliciana* 8 (1986): 71–87.
Solbach, Andreas. "Transgression als Verletzung des Decorum bei Christian Weise, J. J. Chr. v. Grimmelshausen und in Johann Beers *Narrenspital*." *Daphnis* 20 (1991): 33–60.
Solbach, Andreas. "Grimmelshausens Courasche als unzuverlässige Erzählerin." *Simpliciana* 24 (2002): 141–164.
Solbach, Andreas. "Männliche Frauen und weibliche Männer. Courasche im Gender-Kampf." Ed. Miroslawa Czarnecka. *Memoria Silesiae. Leben und Tod, Kriegserlebnis und Friedenssehnsucht in der literarischen Kultur des Barock*. Wrocław 2003. 177–189.
Streller, Siegfried. *Wortweltbilder. Studien zur deutschen Literatur*. Berlin 1986.
Strobel, Katja. "Die Courage der Courasche. Weiblichkeit als Maskerade und groteske Körperlichkeit in Grimmelshausens Pikara-Roman." Eds. Elfi Bettinger and Julika Funk. *Maskeraden. Geschlechterdifferenz in der literarischen Inszenierung*. Berlin 1995. 82–97.
Tatlock, Lynne. "Engendering Social Order. From Costume Autobiography to Conversation Games in Grimmelshausen's Simpliciana." Ed. Karl F. Otto. *A Companion to the Works of Grimmelshausen*. Rochester, NY 2003. 269–296.
Teuscher, Gerhart. "'Fromme tugenthaffte Frauen' oder 'arglistiges Weiber-Volck'? Das Frauenbild Grimmelshausens im Simplicianischen Zyklus." *Jahrbuch für internationale Germanistik* 16/1 (1984): 94–115.
Van Ornam, Vanessa. "No Time for Mothers. Courasche's Infertility as Grimmelshausen's Criticism of War." *Women in German Yearbook* 8 (1992): 21–45.
Wagener, Hans. "Simplicissimo zu Trutz! Zur Struktur von Grimmelshausens Courasche." *The German Quarterly* 43 (1970): 177–187.
Wicke, Andrea. "'Eine solche/ wie ihr wisset daß ich bin.' Strategien der Selbsterfindung im Simplicianischen Zyklus, untersucht am Beispiel der *Lebensbeschreibung der Landstörtzerin Courasche*." *Simpliciana* 22 (2000): 403–460.
Zeuch, Ulrike. "Verführung als die wahre Gewalt? Weibliche Macht und Ohnmacht in Grimmelshausens *Courasche* und *Simplicissimus*." *Simpliciana* 31 (2009): 143–160.

Role Switching and Gender Marking in the Picaresque Novel

MATTHIAS BAUER

According to Mary Louise Pratt, literature has a "display producing relevance" (Pratt 1977: 136). A novel, for example, does not only exhibit a more or less dramatic situation that causes some action, it also tests the frame of reference conventionally associated with the situation presented in the text. The story, therefore, turns into a kind of case study. By using the forms of perceiving and stimulating the reader's imagination, the author realizes the double meaning of 'display': to show and to exam, to set up and to run through. This idea of 'display' is already implicit in Aristotle's work, especially in his notion of the myth, since the myth offers insight into a specific course of events and thereby produces knowledge due to the category of logical consistency (Bauer 2005: 13-16). In this respect, the pragmatic maxim is relevant to literature: „Consider what effects, which might *conceivably* have practical bearings, you *conceive* the objects of your *conception* to have. Then, your *conception* of those effects is the whole of your *conception* of the object" (Peirce 1955: 290).

If the object of our imagination is the gender performance of the picaresque hero or the picaresque heroine, one might hesitate to apply this maxim, because it had been proposed by Charles Sanders Peirce (1839-1914) in the late 19th century. In fact, the maxim needs a slight revision to meet the requirements of cultural his-tory. However, with this slight revision, the maxim can be used as a heuristic tool. Even in the early modern times the novel had the task to juxtapose ideas and reality, concepts and experience, moral judgements and practical action. As Mikhail Bakhtin and others have argued convincingly, the Menippean Satire with its astonishing capacity to display the clash between concepts and experience was incorporated in the picaresque mode of narration (Bakhtin 1987). And if we follow Walter L. Reed's *Exemplary History of the Novel*, the constant interplay between the picaresque and the Cervantesque mode of narration was picked up and transformed by Fielding and Smollett, Sterne, Lennox and many other authors to confront ideas and reality (cf. Reed 1981).

I will come back to Lennox later, but my point of departure, not surprisingly, is Hans Jakob Christoffel von Grimmelshausen (1621-1676). A short comparison between some chapters in *Der abentheuerliche Simplicissimus Teutsch*, published in 1668, and *Trutz=Simplex*, published in 1670, might explain how the notion of the display function and my slight revision of the Pragmatic Maxim can help to understand the role switching and gender marking in the picaresque novel. Afterwards, I like to confront these findings with *The Female Quixote*. The third and fourth section of this paper, are then devoted to two novels written in the 20th century, an American and a German one. Both can be called hybrid works of art – first, because they merge the picaresque and the Cervantesque mode of narration, and secondly, because they reflect the bias in the gender concepts in contemporary societies.

GENDER TROUBLE IN WAR TIME

As German novelist Daniel Kehlmann has observed recently, Grimmelshausen did not depict the development of characters in such a way that we could speak of psychological consistency (Kehlmann 2015: 106). Rather, he presents stages of a journey through time and space that are separated by inconsistent behaviour. When Simplicius is converted into a kind of fool, he acts like a skilled jester though he never was trained or confronted with a role model in advance. It seems that he gains recourse to hidden forces by a cruel rite de passage. By accident he puts on a dress and is held to be a female, immediately. His queer performance begins as soon as he presents himself in this outfit to a group of soldiers of both sexes:

In diesem Auffzug gieng ich ueber die Gaß gegen etlichen Officiers-Weibern / und macht so enge Schrittlein / als etwan *Achilles* gethan / da ihn seine Mutter dem *Licomedi recommedi*rte / ich war aber kaum ausser Dach hervor kommen / da mich etliche Fouragierer sahen / und besser springen lernten / dann als sie schryen / Halt / halt / halt! lieffe ich nur desto staerker / und kam ehender als sie zu obgemeldeten Officiererin / vor denselben fiele ich auff die Knye nider / und bate umb aller Weiber Ehr und Tugend willen / sie wollten meine Jungfernschafft von diesen gailen Buben beschuetzen! (Grimmelshausen 2005: 206)

Accepted as a maid by one of the female soldiers, Simplicius gets into severe but funny gender trouble, because the husband of his protector, the husband's servant and the cavalry captain herself fall in love with the pretty 'maid':

Jch befand wol / daß mein Sach in die Laenge kein gut thun wuerde / dann die Rittmeisterin wurde je laenger je *importuner* mit ihren Reitzungen / der Rittmeister verwegener mit seinen Zumuthungen / und der Knecht verzweiffelter in seiner bestaendigen Liebe / ich wusste mir aber darumb nicht auß solchem Labyrinth zu helffen (Grimmelshausen 2005: 207).

Simplicius decides to let the servant know, but instead the guy only tries to kiss him. His master, witnessing this scene, puts the servant to flight, beats up the maid and hands her over to some nasty boys who finally reveal that the 'maid' is in fact a young male. Simplicius is arrested and interrogated as the officers suspect him to be a spy in disguise. Apparently, the farce becomes serious because the travesty takes place in the context of war. Dressed up as a civil maid, Simplicius is not only in a very weak position for he seems to be female, but also because a sharp distinction is drawn between friend and enemy. The hierarchy of gender positions and military ranks transforms the comical tale into an episode with a specific display function: The war lays bare what is a virtual practice in society – to regard a young, attractive woman as available for everybody who is strong enough to exert his will on her. It follows that there is no inviolable right of physical integrity; consequently, there is no chance to escape rape.

But there is another aspect worth mentioning. As easy as Simplicius could adapt himself to the role of the fool he is able to perform as a maid. What is more: he can provoke protection by presenting himself as a woman in danger of rape. Considered as a 'mock epic' the text hints at men's aggression but also parodies the stereotype of seduced innocence. If the comparison with Achilles belongs to the narrator's performance, the actor's performance consists of Simplicius' female outfit, his way of walking and his line of argument. This performance reflects the experience of the young protagonist who, so far, had learned only two concepts of female behaviour: the concept of virginity and the concept of coquettish flirt. And since the picaresque mode of narration always demands a sceptical reader aware of the hero's moral ambivalence (Bauer 1994: 25-31), this episode does not only display how gender trouble comes to happen in War Times. It also displays the rhetoric at work in the gender performance and its common topics, especially the stereotypes of male and female behaviour.

Trutz=Simplex is an even more advanced display of gender performance. To begin with, Grimmelshausen tells the story from a female point of view, making the narration appear to be an act of revenge. A woman reports how she became a warrior and a whore, how she was mistreated by men and how she herself mistreated men to survive but also to enjoy life among soldiers. Her immediate opponent is the male reader, reflected in some anonymous 'Herren' (masters) addressed in the text and, above all, Simplicius who humiliated her in his own account. *Trutz=Simplex* refers to this account by offering a kind of counter-plot. Logically, the female protagonist is involved in the war by pretending to be a male. When a siege was laid to her home town, 'Jungfrau Lebuschka' ('Maid Lebushka') was dressed up as a man and named 'Janco'. In this masquerade she is able to retain her virginity, but she is also trapped in her disguise when she falls in love with a cavalry captain. Interestingly, this captain is depicted as a man with no more beard than Janco himself who imagines the captain as another virgin, capable of wearing female clothes and attracting the male gaze: "[…] er hatte so viel Barts umbs Maul als ich / und wann er Frauenzimmer-Kleider angehabt haette / so haette ihn der Tausendste vor eine schoene Jungfrau gehalten; aber wo komm ich hin? Ich muß meine Histori erzehlen […]" (Grimmelshausen 2007, 27). Apparently, the trick is to stimulate the reader's imagination and to make him contemplate on the erotic potential inherent in the configuration. The narrator hints at an untold story. This story though hints at the psychological dilemma of the heroine. Fearing that she would not be accepted as a bride she hesitates to reveal her true compassion and to unmask herself. Rather she speaks of a 'war' in her own mind or soul, a war between temptation and role discipline: "Ob nun gleich dieser Krieg und Streit / den ich mit mir selber fuehrete / mich greulich quaelte / so war ich doch geil und ausgelassen darbey […]" (Grimmelshausen 2007, 28). Trying hard to dissimulate her feelings and the swollen bosom under her clothes, the servant is involved in a fight with a rough man who craps at 'his' penis, finds a vagina and is beaten nearly to death by the outraged protagonist. When the captain wants to know why Janco became so furious he learns that it had been the attack of the so called 'courage' that was too much to bear. In addition, to clear the situation, the heroine lays bare her bust. The captain is surprised but neither angry nor willing to let 'his' servant dress up like a wife. By promising to marry her someday he insists of a hidden affair, calls his lover 'Courage' and demands that she behaves and appears in public dressed like a male. It is only in the face of death that he finally keeps the promise so that Courage becomes his wife and widow in a minute. Similar to Simplicius, Courage is introduced into the world of war by a queer performance that displays both the inauthenticity of courtship and the social order of male-female relationship. But whereas the unreliable narrator in the first book presents himself as seduced innocence, his opponent reveals the strength of sexual desire. In accordance with the official moral of his times, Simplicius tries to convince the reader that he is a man of honour, whereas Courage never claims to be a gentlewoman. Instead she tries to discredit Simplicius by exhibiting her own bad reputation. The reader should infer that Simplicius is no better than Courage herself or even worse since he is a hypocrite.

In any case, the dialogic principle ruling the intertextual story telling is obvious – as obvious as the agonal design of gender marking and demarking. Determined to play roles in a world where honesty is fatal, the female narrator of *Trutz=Simplex* shows with much more accuracy than her forerunner the necessity but also the pitfall of dissimulation. Gender trouble, it seems, is unavoidable, since war and seduction are inextricably linked in the cultural practice of love. Therefore, gender performance – not only in times of war – affords the frequent crossing of the only theoretical divide between the masculinity, identified with aggression and femininity, commonly associated with peace. If Ovid in his famous *Ars amatoria* established and explored the metaphorical understanding of love as war, Grimmelshausen confronts this concept with the cruel reality he experienced himself in a time when every human being became a 'bestia'. Actually, he used the display function of the picaresque novel to question the dual nature of passion. To read his books today means to ask oneself, what effects, which apparently have practical bearings, are produced by the agonal conception of love and gender.

THE PITFALLS OF AFFECTION

It has often been remarked that Madame Bovary is a late descendant of Don Quixote because her mind is filled with romantic literature not compatible with *les mœurs de province*. Gustave Flaubert's novel appeared in 1857, more than 200 years after the first and second volume of Cervantes's major work. Half of the way, in 1752, a book was published under the title *The Female Quixote*, indicating a variation of theme, character and gender. Like in *Joseph Andrews* (1742) the focus is on affectation and hypocrisy, but unlike Henry Fielding, Charlotte Lennox chose a lady to ridicule the blind application of romantic concepts. Arabella has wrapped herself in the illusion that every young man must fall in love with her and has to suffer for this presumption. Even worse than her stubborn concept of courtship is her incapacity of empathy and her foolish behaviour towards cousin Glanville who, despite her ignorance and arrogance, loves her honestly. In fact, Arabella traps everybody, including herself, in a kind of double bind: If a man does not try to beguile her, he is impertinent; if he tries, his impertinence demands an even stronger repulse. Having suffered from such a repulse, Glanville (in Book I, Chapter XI) asks his cousin to explain why he was treated so harshly. This leads to the following dialogue:

You had the Boldness, said she, to talk to me of Love; and you well know that Persons of my Sex and Quality are not permitted to listen to such Discourses; and if, for that Offence, I banished you my Presence, I did no more than Decency required of me [...].
But, Madam, interrupted *Glanville*, if the Person who tells you he loves you, be of Rank not beneath you, I conceive you are not at all injured by the favourable Sentiments he feels for you; and, tho' you are not disposed to make any Returns to his Passion, yet you are certainly obliged to him for his good Opinion.
Since Love is not voluntary, replied *Arabella*, I am not obliged to any Person for loving me; for, questionless, if he could help it, he would.
If it is not a voluntary Favour, interrupted *Glanville*, it is not a voluntary Offence; and, if you do not think yourself obliged by the one, neither are you at Liberty to be offended with the other.
The Question, said *Arabella*, is not whether I ought to be offended at being loved, but whether it is not an Offence to be told I am so.
If there is nothing criminal in Passion itself, Madam, resumed *Glanville*, certainly there can be no Crime in declaring it.
However specious your Arguments may appear, interrupted *Arabella*, I am persuaded it is an unpardonable Crime to tell a Lady you love her; and, tho' I had nothing else to plead, yet the Authority of Custom is sufficient to prove it.
Custom, Lady *Bella*, said *Glanville*, smiling, is wholly on my Side; for the Ladies are so far from being displeased at the Addresses of their Lovers, that their chiefest Care is to gain them, and their greatest Triumph to hear them talk of their Passion: So, Madam, I hope you'll allow that Argument has no Force.
I don't know, answered *Arabella*, what Sort of Ladies there are who allow such unbecoming Liberties, but I am certain, that *Statira*, *Parisatis*, *Clelia*, *Mandana*, and all the illustrious Heroines of Antiquity, whom it is a Glory to resemble, would never admit of such Discourses.
[... *Glanville*:] But pray, Madam, if the illustrious Lover of *Clelia* had never discovered his Passion, how would the World have come to the Knowledge of it?
(Lennox 1998: 43-45)

Evidently, this is a meta-discourse on etiquette and highly significant for the style of Lennox' book. *The Adventures of Arabella* mainly consists of comic dialogues as the one quoted above. The heroine acts according to a script that forbids spontaneous exchange of feelings. She demands a role playing that makes it nearly impossible to reach the aim that the discourse of courtship was designed to approximate: Instead of allowing overtures between the sexes it thwarts any rapprochement. However, it would not be sufficient to say that Lennox mocks the strategy to entangle the admirer in an argument to test his feelings and to provoke compliments which is held to be a strategy typical of gentlewomen. When Glanville presumes that every woman is pleased by the passionate way of talking, he only reproduces a cliché often used to seduce a lady against her will. Though there can be no doubt that Arabella's argument is not consistent, there is a lack of self-criticism in Glanville's application of the rule he refers to. In this respect, the meta-discourse displays a malfunction of gender marking and gendered role playing. Observing the argument, the reader cannot miss the absurd effect of an etiquette that leads to inauthenticity and hypocrisy. Men and women are damned to perform with respect to concepts or scripts that cause severe misunderstandings and offend sensibilities that were induced by literature alone.

Despite her unwise behaviour, Arabella is not a dull character. Similar to Cervantes's hero, Lennox' heroine is more enchanted or bewitched than insane. Therefore, a priest is able to persuade her to abandon the spell of romantic literature when she becomes very ill. Whereas Don Quixote passes away after he has converted to reality, Arabella recovers and, luckily, becomes her cousin's wife. If the conversion of the protagonist is a formula that links the novel written in the manner of Cervantes with its counterpart, one major transition from the picaresque novel of the 17th century to the semi-picaresque novel of the 18th century is the loss of ambivalence. In *Lazarillo de Tormes* (1554), *Guzmán de Alfarache* (1599/1604), *El Buscón* (1603/1626) and in *Simplicissimus* the conversion is either a lip service or ineffective and momentary. Often, the rogue only tries to escape punishment so that the reader must doubt his motives. The case with Lady Arabella is fairly different; she really changes her mind. In fact, she has no practical needs at all. Whereas the picaresque novel questions the social ranking Lennox questions the gender marking in the discourse of one privileged class. As long as Arabella, with the assistance of her personal maid, a female Sancho Pansa, perverts every sign of affection she is deprived of reason. But as soon as she is in control of her wits, a happy ending is very likely to happen. If the picaresque hero and the picaresque heroine display the stereotypes of gender performance by demarking them and by switching between roles normally reserved for one sex exclusively, Arabella carries the exclusiveness of the stereotypes much too far: she excludes herself from the experience of love by overplaying the role of the graceful lady who demands constant proof of compassion before she is willing to accept a lover.

Lennox wrote her novel under the supervision of Samuel Johnson and Samuel Richardson. Richardson's *Pamela*, published in 1741 was parodied in Fielding's *Shamela* (1742). Developing his own branch of comic romance, Fielding managed to write a narrative like *Tom Jones* (1746-48) with a plot hard to exceed in complexity and a hero hard to outdo in terms of mislead kindheartedness. Yet, it was the aim of American novelist John Barth to produce "a plot that was fancier than *Tom Jones*" (Ruth 1984: 107) and a character mislead even further than Fielding's protagonist. This anti-hero is, naturally one might say, a poet, named Ebenezer Cooke. Cooke really did exist in the early 18th century and wrote a satire that was mistaken to be a praise of Maryland. Merging the picaresque and the Cervantesque mode of narration in a manner that is really hard to surpass, the revised version of *The Sot-Weed Factor* (1967) exploits two clichés opposed to the concepts that were tested in *The Female Quixote*, namely:

THE MALE VIRGIN AND THE HOLY WHORE

Being raised by Henry Burlingame, a trickster-like character who unites the features of a quick-change artist with those of a trained philosopher, the unworldly Ebenezer Cooke meets the prostitute Joan Toast. Refusing to pay money for an act which he believes should be an expression of true love, Ebenezer protects his innocence but hands over the girl to a cruel world of betray and disease. After a series of grotesque adventures that unfolds on hundreds of pages and contains, among other digressions, a deconstruction of the famous Pocahontas-myth, Ebenezer and Joan meet again. Finally, after witnessing her death, the foolish poet takes responsibility and mourns the fatal course of events that reflect the worldview of the picaresque novel. Thrown into "a nest o' wolves and vipers" (Barth 1967: 710), the hero's task is to become an author while the fancy plot directs the reader to take *The Sot-Weed Factor* for a meta-novel.

When Ebenezer and Joan meet for the first time, their dialogue displays the absurd effects of role switching and gender de/marking. I quote only the most significant lines:

'Come along now, sweet,' Joan said presently, and turned to him entirely unclothed. 'Put the guineas upon the table and let's to bed. [...]'
'I cannot pay thee," Ebenezer declared. [...]' 'I have the five guineas and more. But how price the priceless? How buy heaven with simple gold? Ah, Joan Toast, ask me not to cheapen thee so! Was't for gold that silver-footed Thetis shared the bed of Peleus, Achilles' sire? Think thee Venus and Anchises did their amorous work on consideration of five

guineas? Nay, sweet Joan, a man seeks not in the market for the favors of a goddess! [...] What I crave of thee cannot be bought.'
'Aha,' smiled Joan, 'so 'tis a matter o' strange tastes, it't? I'd not have guessed it by the honest look o'ye, but think not so quickly 'tis out o' the question. [...]'
'Dear girl, I swear to thee now I am a virgin, and as I come to thee pure and undefiled, so in my mind you come to me; what'er hath gone before, speak not of it. [...] Joan Toast, I *love* thee! [...] Speak no more of your awful trafficking, for I love thy sweet body unspeakably, and that spirit which it so fairly houses, unimaginably.'
'Nay, Mr. Cooke, 'tis an unbecoming jest ye make, to call thyself virgin', Joan said doubtfully.
'As God is my witness,' swore Ebenezer, 'I have known no woman carnally to this night, nor ever loved at all. [...] and till this night no woman e'er looked on me with favour.'
'Marry!' laughed Joan. 'Doth the ewe chase the ram, or the hen the cock? Doth the field come to the plow for furrowing, or the scabbard to the sword for sleathing? 'Tis all arsyturvy ye look at the world!' [...]
'Scorn me, Joan, and I shall be a splendid fool, a Don Quixote tilting for his ignorant Dulcinea; but I here challenge thee – if you've life and fire and wit enough, love me truly as I love thee, and then shall I joust with bona fide giants and bring them low! Love me, and I swear to thee this: I shall be Poet Laureate of England!' [...]
'May ye suffer French pox, ye great ass!' Joan replied, and left the room in a heat.
(Barth 1987: 53-59)

The basic joke is as evident as effective. Transferring the concept of the ideal bride to the suitor and making fun of the male virgin, Barth turns Ebenezer into another Arabella until the prostitute leaves the scene. At the beginning, like Glanville, she assumes that Ebenezer plays a joke on her. But behind the simple operation of reversing the stereotypes that are used to demark gender performance lurks another much more complicated practice. If the Cervantesque hero refuses to pay for sex and converts the profane picaresque heroine into a muse, the text parodies the procedure of transfiguration – a procedure often held to be the main task of poetry, especially when the subject is erotic. Showing drastically how this procedure confuses nearly everything and contributes to the overall perversion of the social world, Barth's novel makes an auto-reflexive use of the display function.

Of course, this is not to say, that *The Sot-Weed Factor*'s meaning is limited to literature. Rather, the book questions if there is any reality not based on acts of story-telling and transfiguration, myth-making and projection. It follows that each concept whether concerned with love, sex or gender involves the so called "novelization of world" (Morson & Emerson 1990: 303-305). Probably, literature is not a transcendental form of perceiving. Still, it might be the form every cultural practice takes on since culture is nothing else than the transfiguration of nature. One could even argue that nature itself is inaccessible since every access needs a form, and form, inevitably, is a product of culture. To be more specific: if sexual desire is a gift of nature, it is a common cultural practice and a traditional task of literature to transfigure this desire and to separate true love from carnal pleasure. Since in the Christian world carnal pleasure demands repentance, a prostitute has to suffer hard before she can be transfigured into a respectable person, or even a holy whore. The martyrdom of Joan Toast exemplifies this common practice in such a way that the reader can easily grasp its absurdity. Joan does not speak out as Courage is able to do, but Cooke's renounce of his former attitude towards her says it nearly all. It was his metaphysical misconception of love that caused the physical destruction of a woman which he impressed so much that she desired him, and desperately.

To sum up: The adventures of the ingenious knight, of Lady Arabella and Ebenezer Cooke show how transfiguration works and, anticipating the Pragmatic Maxim, doubt its effects. Whereas a character like Henry Burlingame enjoys many sexual encounters, the Poet Laureate always gets himself and others in trouble. Again and again Barth's meta-fiction displays the disastrous outcome of fictions that serve moral purposes and political interests. History is a fake but true love is really possible if freed from misconceptions. As a product of the spirit prevailing the 1960s, the novel seems to suggest that the sexual liberation of men and women might alter the course of events. If there is no need to mantle desire there would be no reason and, consequently, no chance to suppress, exploit and betray people. My last example, then, is intended to confront this expectation with the gender performance in a society that claimed to treat men and women with equal respect.

REAL WOMEN AND UTOPIAN MEN

In 1974 Irmtraud Morgner (1933-1990) published *Leben und Abenteuer der Trobadora Beatriz nach Zeugnissen ihrer Spielfrau Laura*. A continuation appeared in 1983 under the title *Amanda. Ein Hexenroman*, and a fragment of the last part of the trilogy was edited posthumous in 1998: *Das heroische Testament*. I confine myself to the discussion of the first volume. Like Ebenezer Cooke Beatriz de Dia did exist. But instead of writing a period novel or the travesty of a period novel like *The Sot-Weed Factor*, Morgner moves the heroine from medieval to modern times. After 816 years of sleep Beatriz awakens in 1968 – in the year of the student revolt. The construction of a new highway destroys her castle, and when Beatriz hitchhikes to Paris, a man rapes her. Since this experience is repeated several times her adventures reveal: within the capitalist society a woman is treated either like a prostitute or a confidence trickster. Reading Marx, Beatriz learns that the relation of men and women indicates the degree to which a society has humanized itself: "Der gesellschaftliche Fortschritt läßt sich exakt messen an der gesellschaftlichen Stellung des schönen Geschlechts" (Morgner 1986: 64). This, then, is the standard of comparison the reader should accept. When Beatriz meets a young man from East Berlin, she is told that in the German Democratic Republic men and women have equal rights. So, Beatriz decides to settle in East-Berlin and to own her living as a song-writer.

In the former GDR, the focus of interest shifts from Beatriz to Laura Salman, her relatives and related matters. This is to show that life is a constant trial to bridge the gap between utopian thinking and reality. In an address to the male reader the narrator presumes that the stereotypical way men conceive of women causes all the trouble women have to face every day (Morgner 1986: 98). History is "a male ocean of egoism" ("dieses männliche Meer von Egoismus", Morgner 1986: 26). Accordingly, the 'real existing socialism' seems to be an island worth protecting. Here men and women are treated differently. However, even in the GDR women are denied full self-determination because they have no right to terminate pregnancy (Morgner 1986: 112). As long as it is supposed that women have the 'natural' task of raising children and keeping the house, men remain privileged. Consequently, when a law of abortion passes legislation in 1973, the argument in favour of this law is quoted in the text in full length to reestablish an optimistic attitude towards the GDR (Morgner 1986: 329-335).

Though completely at odds with the doctrine of 'socialist realism', Morgner's novel sticks to the promise of communism, taking it to be a promise of justice and freedom, equal rights and peace. Criticising not only chauvinism and militarism, but also the lack of fantasy that prevent women from self-empowerment, the procedure of transfiguration serves a new function. Morgner questions the traditional distinction between the realistic and the fantastic mode of narration. With a twinkle in the eye, the GDR is announced as the land of the miraculous (Morgner 1986: 7, 167, 447), where everything is possible. Since the 'possible' is identified with the 'thinkable' and since every thought can be transformed into a fable, 'tellability' surpasses wishful thinking. In the realm of the novel, the dream of liberation takes on a form of verisimilitude – not realized yet but likely to be realized soon. Being an operation of dialectics, transfiguration, as understood by Morgner, indicates that there are unsatisfied but justified demands. According to the poetics discussed in the novel, utopian thinking produces models that stimulate practical political action (Morgner 1986: 282). But in the course of action the model has to be transfigured. It follows that the fantastic mode of narration is intended to stimulate action without determining the results. Writing, reading and discussing a novel in public contributes to the overall discourse that, step by step, alters the course of events.

Consequently, many episodes in the novel should be understood as 'counter-images' (Morgner 1986: 218). Either they mirror reality in such a way that the reader can imagine the effects of the common practise not visible yet, or they transcend this practice without demanding imitation. In this frame of reference, love, due to its utopian potential, becomes a stimulus for transfiguration. Love triggers the imagination and reinforces practical action. The reader's task, then, is to confront the fairy tale and the myth, the legend and the fable with the actual demands of politics. If, for example, 'he' reads the embedded story of Valeska who is transformed into a man, the text confronts the male reader with a 'counter-image' of his conscience. Seeing herself in a mirror and looking at her 'penis', Valeska bursts out in laughter:

Valeska fiel in unmäßiges Gelächter. Angesichts des Gewächses, worauf Legionen von Mythen und Machttheorien gründeten. Beweisstück für Auserwähltsein, Schlüssel für privilegiertes Leben, Herrschaftszepter: etwas Fleisch mit runzliger, bestenfalls blutgeblähter Haut. Valeska fehlte die entsprechende Rollenerziehung für den ernsten, selbstbewussten Blick in die Mitte: das Vorurteil (Morgner 1986: 428-429).

Like in the 'literature of carnival' (Bakhtin: 1984), Morgner presents the reader a grotesque body. But whereas in Rabelais and Grimmelshausen the grotesque body is the body of the collective, Valeska is an individual with the conscience of a woman and the physical appearance of a man. She is capable to enjoy carnal pleasures with both sexes. When she sleeps with a woman she performs like a man, but when she makes love to her husband her body takes on a female form, temporarily. Never tempted to engage in the misogyny of men talking about women, disrespectfully, Valeska is a utopian 'counter-image' to the real existing men and their misconception of women (Morgner 1986: 421-444).

Another example belongs to the so called 'stories of wanderlust' Laura is telling. Border crossing Wanderlust, of course, has been an unsatisfied demand in the former GDR. This links this kind of yearning to the wishful thinking that is reflected in the story. Wally, the female protagonist, is willing to sacrifice her demands in favour of her husband Sigmund though she can wear his shoes. That means, she is capable of the same talents and has herself all the potentials required for the career he performs. But there is no chance to do since the gender marking determines the roles of men and women, reciprocally. Whereas the transfiguration of Valeska opens up the mind of the reader, Laura's wanderlust-story displays the frustrated aspiration of women and the promise which is denied fulfilment in the real existing socialism so far (see Appendix).

In fact, one has to say that *The Life and Adventures of Beatriz according to Laura's testimonial* is not a picaresque novel in the strict sense, but it rounds up the picture. Talking about role playing and gender marking as presented in the works of Grimmelshausen, Lennox, Barth and Morgner, the overall impression is that literature reveals the unsatisfied demands of men and women, the oppressive force of society and the practical bearings of its effect, especially the pitfalls of misconception and dissimulation, hypocrisy and misogyny. So, to answer at least some of the questions put on the agenda of this volume I am able to conclude:

1. Masculinity and femininity are depicted as resulting either from affectation or contingent construction.
2. On the one hand transfiguration is criticized as an operation that can cause severe misunderstandings and 'gender trouble'. On the other hand, it is presented as a procedure to overcome concepts that conceivably restrict the discourse and, a fortiori, the performance.
3. Because of its affinity to the grotesque body a picaresque character is able to queer the conventional gender marking. However, this should be seen as part of the display function of satire and not as an ontological statement. To parody gendered behaviour does not necessarily imply a conception bereft of any sexual difference.
4. The inverted world in the literature of carnival is a 'counter-image'. Taken as a model it might lead astray if not scrutinized according to the Pragmatic Maxim and, consequently, transfigured.

Bibliography

Bakhtin, Michail. *Rabelais and his world*. Tr. Hélène Iswolsky. Bloomington 1984.
Barth, John. *The Sot-Weed Factor*. [1967] New York et.al. 1987.
Bauer, Matthias. *Der Schelmenroman*. Stuttgart, Weimar 1994.
Fielding, Henry. *The History of the Adventures of Joseph Andrews and of his friend Mr. Abraham Adams & An Apology for the Life of Mrs. Shamela An-*

drews. Edited with an introduction by Douglas Brooks-Davies. [1742] Oxford 1991.

Fielding, Henry. *The History of Tom Jones*. [1749] Ed. R. P.C. Mutter. London 1985.

Grimmelshausen, Hans Jacob Christoffel. *Simplicissimus Teutsch*. [1668] Ed. Dieter Breuer. Frankfurt a.M. 2005.

Grimmelshausen, Hans Jacob Christoffel. *Courasche* [1670] / *Springinsfeld* / *Wunderbarliches Vogelnest I und II* / *Rathstübel Plutonis*. Ed. Dieter Breuer. Frankfurt a.M. 2007.

Kehlmann, Daniel. *Kommt, Geister. Frankfurter Vorlesungen*. Reinbek bei Hamburg 2015.

Lennox, Charlotte. *The Female Quixote or The Adventures of Arabella* [1752]. Ed. Margaret Dalziel with an Introduction by Margaret Anne Doody. Chronology and Appendix by Duncan Isles. Oxford 1998.

Morson, Cary Saul/Emerson, Caryl. *Mikhail Bakhtin. Creation of a Prosaics*. Stanford 1990.

Morgner, Irmtraud. *Leben und Abenteuer der Trobadora Beatriz nach Zeugnissen ihrer Spielfrau Laura. Roman in dreizehn Bänden und sieben Intermezzos* [1974]. Darmstadt, Neuwied 1986.

Peirce, Charles Sanders. *Philosophical Writings of Peirce*. Selected and ed. with an Introduction by Justus Buchler. New York 1995.

Pratt, Mary Louise. *Toward a Speech Act Theory of Literary Discourse*. Bloomington 1977.

Reed, Walter L. *An Exemplary History of the Novel. The Quixotic versus the Picaresque*. Chicago 1981.

Ruth, Wolfgang. "'Meager Fact and Solid Fancy': Die Erfindung der Vergangenheit in John Barths *The Sot-Weed Factor*." *Anglistik und Englischunterricht* 24 (1984): 97–116.

Appendix: *Zweite Fernwehgeschichte der Spielfrau Laura*
Schuhe: Es war eine Frau, Walli mit Namen, die bevorzugte kleinwüchsige Männer. Mit ihnen erschien ihr die Liebe kurzweiliger: der Rollentausch einfacher. Sie heirate einen Mann namens Sigmund. Er konnte ihre Pullover tragen, sie seine Oberhemden. In den Flitterwochen gaben sie der Sehnsucht, der andere zu sein oder ihn bei sich haben zu wollen, nach, indem sie Kleidungsstücke tauschten. Die symbolische Handlung und der im Stoff gefangene Geruch des begehrten Körpers tröstete, beruhigte und erregte sie. Den Vorteil, daß auch ihre Schuhmaße nicht differierten, erkannte die Frau später. Sie nutzte ihn nach der Geburt ihres ersten Sohnes, als die große freudige Erschütterung dieses Ereignis-

ses von der Aufmerksamkeit verdrängt wurde, die ihre nun gewählte Beschäftigung als Sekretärin erforderte. Dem angestrebten langjährigen Medizinstudium hatte sie aus familiären Rücksichten entsagt. Sigmund, der gleichzeitig mit Walli das Abitur an der Arbeiter-und-Bauern-Fakultät abschloß, mit um einen Grad schlechterer Note als sie, studierte Maschinenbau. In Dresden, er besuchte die in Leipzig verbliebene Familie fast jedes Wochenende. Walli konnte seine Hilfe entbehren, sie war eine kräftige Frau. Beim Abitur hatte sie ungeachtet der Wehen, die sich während der Russischklausur einstellten, die Prüfung sorgfältig erledigt, war überhaupt Arbeiten von Haus aus gewohnt, sie entstammte einer bäuerlichen Familie. Um die Trennung leichter zu ertragen, kaufte Walli sich ein Paar braune Schnürschuhe und übergab sie Sigmund mit der Bitte, das Schuhwerk gelegentlich in Dresden zu tragen. Sobald er das Staatsexamen abgelegt hatte, wollte sie sich an der Philosophischen Fakultät der Karl-Marx-Universität für ein slawistisches Studium bewerben. Nach Büroschluß, wenn der Sohn aus der Krippe geholt, abgefüttert, ins Bett gebracht und die Hausarbeit getan war, las sie energisch russischsprachige Bücher. Als der Sohn fast drei Jahre alt war, gebar sie eine Tochter. Sigmund bestand das Staatsexamen mit der Note 2 und fand eine Anstellung als Ingenieur in Karl-Marx-Stadt. Dort und auf Dienstreisen trug er Wallis Schuhe, sooft er sich unbeobachtet fühlte. Wenn er Löcher in die Sohlen und die Absätze schief gelaufen hatte, ließ Walli sie beim Schuster reparieren, wobei sie darauf achtete, daß gutes Material, möglichst Leder, verarbeitet wurde. Das slawistische Studium schlug sie sich aus dem Kopf und strebte statt dessen eine Ausbildung als Unterstufenlehrerin an, sobald die Tochter, die den Tageskrippenaufenthalt gesundheitlich nicht vertrug, das Kindergartenalter erreicht haben würde. Nach der Geburt des zweiten Sohnes freute sich Walli, endlich die beinahe vierjährige Hausfrauentätigkeit beenden und wieder als Sekretärin arbeiten zu können. Zumal der Familie in Karl-Marx-Stadt eine Wohnung zugesprochen wurde. Bei kleinen häuslichen Abendgesellschaften, wenn Sigmund und seine anwesenden Arbeitskollegen dem Wein zusprechen und Dienstreiseerinnerungen austauschen und die anwesenden Ehefrauen zu Konfekt und Strickzeug greifen, zieht Walli gewöhnlich die Schuhe an und verschränkt die Arme über der Brust. Sonst verwahrt sie die Schuhe, wenn der Mann sie nicht trägt, in der Wohnzimmervitrine neben Kristall und Porzellan.
(Morgner 1986: 270-271)

Picaresque Narrative and Gender Construction in Wilhelm Raabe's *Lorenz Scheibenhart* (1858) and *Aus dem Lebensbuch des Schulmeisterleins Michel Haas* (1860)

HANS-JOACHIM JAKOB

I.

The writing of picaresque narratives in German-speaking countries in the 19th century appears to be something of an oddity. The German picaresque novel reached its highpoint in the 17th century. After the appearance of Christian Reuter's *Schelmuffsky* (1696-1697), this literary tradition seems to have disappeared for the time being (Bauer 1994: 72-140). No significant texts of this genre seem to have been passed down from the 18th Century. We can speak of a lack of the picaresque novel in German 18th century literature (Jacobs 1983: 75). Possible candidates from the following century in each case placed a great strain on, what is in any case, a not exactly consistent theory of the genre (Guillén 1969). Are the relevant works from the period of the flourishing reception of the Baroque in the early 19th century precisely picaresque tales or novels or not? This is an issue that arises at least in relation to Ludwig Tieck's text *Ein Tagebuch* (1798) or to Adelbert von Chamisso's *Peter Schlemihls wundersame Geschichte* (1813), and also to Friedrich Christoph Weisser's *Schalkheit und Einfalt. Oder der Simplicissimus des siebzehnten Jahrhunderts im Gewande des neunzehnten* (1822), probably to the works of Jeremias Gotthelf, as well as to Victor von Strauss und Torneys *Westfälischem Schelmuffsky* (1861) (Koeman 1993: 103-136 and Martin 2000: 248-256); on Chamisso Michaelis 2013; on Weisser Meid 1995; on Gotthelf Mahlmann-Bauer 2014; on von Strauß und Torney Bartels 1992). On the contrary, Jürgen Jacobs also makes the case for Heinrich Heine's fragment *Aus den Memoiren des Herren von Schnabelewopski* (1834) as a singular text from the 19th century. At best we can say that picaresque elements may be found in autobiographies of the late 18th and early 19th centuries (Jacobs 1983: 85-96; furthermore Seiler 1986 and Bauer 1994: 88-89). Finally the question remains as to whether we can agree with Hans J. Hahn that Fanny Lewald's travel novel *Diogena* (1847) is a "Schelmenroman des Vormärz" (2011: 187) and that the character who gives the novel its title can be said to be a pícara. The industrially prosperous 19th century with its economic rise of the bourgeoisie no longer appears to have had the right type of interest in enigmatic itinerants and their memoirs of their adventures on the margins of society.[1]

In contrast to the above-mentioned texts, the analysis of Wilhelm Raabe's early story *Aus dem Lebensbuche des Schulmeisterleins Michel Haas* (1860) appears surprisingly unambiguous.[2] The older research into Raabe had over-hastily dismissed this early work of the author from Brunswick as being 'trivial' and had consistently tried to ignore it where possible. Heinrich Detering's initiative in 1986 to subject the Haas text to a consistent re-reading with the programmatic subtitle "Picarisches Erzählen im bürgerlichen Realismus" must therefore appear all the more remarkable.[3] Detering (1986) is fully aware of the methodological difficulties arising from the different, sometimes contradictory attempts to define the limits of the picaresque. Detering refers to Bader (1972) and Jacobs (1983): "Dem *Baader-Jacobs*schen ‚Idealtypus' nun entspricht Raabes Erzählung in jeder Hinsicht" (Detering 1986: 91). He is nevertheless able to form a basic

---

[1] Cf. as an explanation Jacobs (1983: 88-89): "Der Grund für die Abwendung vom Schelmenroman scheint vor allem darin zu liegen, daß die Figur des Picaro für bürgerliche Autoren und Leser keine Möglichkeiten der Identifikation bot, ja daß sie vor allem Vorbehalte und Ablehnung herausforderte. Denn die pikarische Lebenstechnik des parasitären Sich-Durchschlagens mit Hilfe moralisch bedenklicher Praktiken wie Betrug oder Gelegenheitsdiebstahl mußte vom Standpunkt wohletablierter Bürgerlichkeit her als Angriff auf die sittliche und ökonomische Ordnung erscheinen. Auch daß der Schelm außerhalb fester sozialer Bezüge in einer Art Vagabunden-Position steht, widersprach den bürgerlichen Harmonie- und Ordnungsvorstellungen."

[2] The information below is based on the following edition: Raabe 1951 et sqq. It is predominantly the second volume, which has been used for reference: Raabe 1992. – *Michel Haas* can be found in: Raabe 1992: 435-473, commentary 614-625.

[3] This states that it was Hermann Pongs who first identified the picaresque elements of the text (1958: 142). "Raabe öffnet sich vielmehr dem naiven Realismus des Schelmenromans, also dem Typus Lazarillo, Simplizissimus, Schelmuffsky; als Querschnitt durch das ‚Landläufer'-Leben des ‚Präzeptors' im achtzehnten Jahrhundert".

framework structure of a picaresque narrative out of all the confusion: It is a fictitious autobiography written from a great distance in time involving frequent changes in location, the clear social advancement of the hero, namely the pícaro, who is forced to work as the servant of many, not very conciliatory employers, his enforced transition from a victim to a perpetrator, constantly changing and not very beneficial relationships with women, and life-threatening illnesses which serve as warnings that he should reconsider his previous lifestyle. In addition, Detering is also able to identify the presence of another narrative model, which stands in contrast to the picaresque confessional biography. It is that of the pietistic short biography of the 17th and 18th centuries (1986: 98). In his study Detering once again outlined the contours of the religious aspects of the biography even more clearly (1990: 27-42). Thus this life story of the schoolmaster, which cannot be unambiguously categorised, is classified as belonging to some model or other of the picaresque narrative. It rather derives its tension from the hiatus between farcical and violent stories which are picaresque in character and the constantly expressed trust in God, for example, in allusions to the Bible which are of Pietistic provenance.

The co-existence of competing text models reminds us perhaps of the best known of the early modern exponents of the picaresque novel in German – Hans Jacob Christoffel von Grimmelshausen and his *Simplicissimus Teutsch* (1668). The main text is complemented by the so-called 'off-shoot novels' of the ten-book-cycle such as *Courasche* (1670) and *Springinsfeld* (1670). The first novel *Simplicissimus* has characteristics of a picaresque novel (Althaus 2007; Honold 2007; Watanabe-O'Kelly 2015) but it also has characteristics of a confessional novel, a satirical novel and even those of a *bildungsroman*. For good reasons, however, the research into Raabe has so far denied the possible existence of any lines of influence between the books about *Simplicissimus* and Raabe's stories.[4] None of the Baroque author's works has been found in Raabe's collection of books. In his works themselves there is only one allusion to the *Simplicissimus* novel, in the text *Eine Grabrede aus dem Jahre 1609* (1863) (Raabe 1974: 59-

---

4   See the valuable contribution of Hohl-Trillini (1997: 123, note 2) on the progress of research: "Unbedingt einen *Einfluß* festzustellen, kann natürlich nicht der einzige Zweck des Vergleichs sein [...], zur Zeit kann eine These zum Einfluß Grimmelshausens auf Raabe allenfalls durch stilistische Untersuchungen *vorbereitet* werden, da die Belege für Raabes Lektüre noch nicht zugänglich sind, wie Prof. Hans-Jürgen Schrader mitteilt [...]." Hohl-Trillini then examines also – without necessarily starting from the influences – the character portrayal of Courasche in Grimmelshausen's novel of the same name and of Doris Radebrecker in Raabe's *Die Innerste* (1876).

83). Nevertheless there do seem to be parallels to Grimmelshausen's work in Raabe's early work, in relation to the elements of the actions, the assignment of locations and the characteristics of individual characters from the ten-book-cycle. However, these are probably only accidental and random. Nevertheless there is a particular charm in making a comparison of both the male and female characters in Grimmelshausen's works with those of Raabe. Thus, Simplicius, Courasche and Springinsfeld all embody different types of picaresque lifestyles. For example, the confessional life story of the pícara Courasche serves as a furious pamphlet against her former lover Simplicius.

With the intense reception of Baroque literature in early 19th century, the identification of Grimmelshausen as the author of *Simplicissimus* in the early 1830s and the subsequent efforts to explore his works, allow us to identify a certain tradition of discourse which firmly binds Simplicissimus as an adventure and pícaro novel within the Thirty Years' War. The absence of picaresque narratives from the literature of the 19th century, which could have perhaps continued the tradition of the stories of a precarious life in times of war, is surprising. At least in the dominant form of discourse of historicism, the period from 1618 to 1648 was the topic of countless fiction and non-fiction texts. On the reception of Grimmelshausen see Wald (2008: 441-452). Raabe, too, announces a certain penchant for the early modern period in the selection of the historical material for his writings and here times of war and the periods leading up to wars, as well as the consequences of war, all play an important role (Chopin 2000; Stöckmann 2009 and Meierhofer 2010). The Thirty Years' War is explicitly present in the short stories *Lorenz Scheibenhart* (1858) and *Else von der Tanne* (1865) (Radcliffe 1969). Especially in relation to *Lorenz Scheibenhart* we find a way of accessing the text, which interprets both the course of the action and the range of characters as the constituents of a "narrative experiment". Detering had already used this concept to describe more closely the religious models in Raabe's narrative universe. In the current context the 'narrative experiment' therefore initially revolves around the inclusion of the Thirty Years' War in *Lorenz Scheibenhart* and the possible parallels with Grimmelshausen. The *Scheibenhart* story does not in fact satisfy the requirements of a picaresque narrative as a genre[5] but it

---

5   Pongs also suggests – even if cryptically – a possible imitation of the picaresque narrative: "Stimme eines Simplizius, Spiegel deutscher Volksnot; nur ist die Sprache noch von den Klischees des Historismus nicht frei, und wo versucht ist, eine Liebesgeschichte in das Landknechtsbild hineinzuzeichnen, spürt man die flache Gefühligkeit des Bösenberg-Stils" (Pongs 1958: 118). Dr. Max Bösenberg is the main character in Raabe's text *Die Kinder von Finkenrode* (1859).

does, however, compile and arrange the building blocks of a retrospective war narrative. Here the male image of the 'warrior' is of great relevance. As a second stage it is intended that *Michel Haas*, which is a fully validated story of a pícaro, is studied once again in its relationship to Grimmelshausen, and even also as a parody of the journeys described in the Baroque novel.[6] Unlike in *Scheibenhart*, in *Michel Haas* we find manifested in a complex, multi-layered way, the fragile masculinity of the eternally roving "itinerant" who never succeeds in settling down anywhere. Here the male secondary characters both reflect and exaggerate the hardships of the main character. The female characters are drawn in a much more rounded way than they are in *Scheibenhart* and there is even an episode devoted to the battle between the sexes.

II.

Lorenz Scheibenhart[7] is subtitled "a life story from a barbaric time". Immediately in the first lines of the tale, the story seems – like *Michel Haas* – to be taking a Pietist turn: "In the name of the Father, and of the Son and of the Holy Spirit! Amen!"[8] Born in 1595 in Brunswick, Germany, the first-person narrator Scheibenhart is thrown out into the world at the age of nine. His father is suspected of being involved in a conspiracy against the Town Council and is beheaded on the Brunswick Hagenmarkt Square. His father's property is confiscated and his wife and son are banished from the town. On the history of Brunswick see Bertschik (1995: 58-61). On their way to Wolfenbüttel the mother and her child go past the "site where witches were once burnt alive" and where "the

---

6 On Grimmelshausen and *Michel Haas* see Hohl-Trillini (1997: 130, note 20): "'Aus dem Lebensbuch des Schulmeisterleins Michel Haas' (Anfang 18. Jahrhundert) spielt zwar nicht im Krieg, beschreibt aber einen ausgesprochen wechselvollen Lebenslauf, dessen Darstellung alle wesentlichen Merkmale des Pikarischen zeigt und so wieder mit dem kriegsgeschüttelten Leben vieler Grimmelshausen-Helden vergleichbar ist."

7 Raabe (1992: 305-337, commentary 575-587). On *Lorenz Scheibenhart* see Brewster (1983: 197-211).

8 "Im Namen Gottes, des Vaters, des Sohnes und des heiligen Geistes! Amen!" (Raabe 1992: 307). See also: "Ja, ja, alles hat seine Zeit: Pflanzen und Ausrotten, Würgen und Heilen, Brechen und Bauen, Lieben und Hassen, Friede und Streit – und uns ist das Letztere vor allem zugefallen – Gottes Wille geschehe!" (308, a quotation of Pred 3, 1-8).

screams of the human torches" can still be heard.⁹ Scheibenhart's going out into the world is not nearly as spectacular as that of Simplicius, whose parental farm is devastated by mercenary foot soldiers (Grimmelshausen 2005: 27-30). Nevertheless it is important to remember that in *Lorenz Scheibenhart* arbitrariness, brutality and deadly superstition determine the everyday life some fourteen years before the war broke out. When the family arrives in Wolfenbüttel they are invited to stay at the house belonging to the local tax official Franz Algermann. At school Scheibenhart shows slight picaresque impulses. Despite the fact that Scheibenhart had spent his time at school "playing many amusing pranks, though I did also learn a little Latin",[10] Algermann educates the unruly pupil to become a scribe.

Standing as a complementary figure to Scheibenhart, there is the historically authentic Levin Sander, in a similar way to the way in which Simplicius represents an antagonist to the scribe (!) and, later, robber and murderer Olivier, who is not very choosy in his choice of methods (Grimmelshausen 2005: 192-195). Sander embodies the unscrupulous professional soldier *par excellence*.[11] He steals Scheibenhart's girlfriend Susanna from him and provokes him into making a vow to take revenge on Sander. Once again Scheibenhart has to go out into the world. He is robbed by highwaymen in the Harz Mountains – attacks by tramps were everyday events for Grimmelshausen –, and seized by a troop of armed horsemen. He signs up to become a mounted soldier for the city of Goslar. Just after this and during the key year of 1618, and still as a mounted soldier he becomes involved in all sorts of combat actions. Even though the reports of fighting and slaughter are in places phrased in quite an emotional tone, they at no point suggest that there is any sense in all this fighting. Scheibenhart's perspective is that of a "history from below" (Schrader 1973: 33, 39). Sometimes with noticeable sympathy, then again only enumerating the casualties, he describes

---

9   "Eilenden Schrittes, ohne sich umzusehen, zog mich meine Mutter vorüber an der Hexenbrandstätte, mitten durch die mit wilden Gesichtern, starren Augen, offenen Mäulern gaffende Menge, mitten durch die singenden Pfaffen, die Reiter, die wehende Asche und das Geheul der Menschenfackeln" (Raabe 1992: 311).

10 "Ich aber wurd auf die Schul getan, wo ich viel tolle Streiche trieb, jedoch des Lateins ein wenig lernte" (Raabe 1992: 312).

11 "War im Sommer ein Reiter eingeritten in das Neuetor und hatte vorher an der Schenk 'Zum springenden Roß' angehalten und sich einen Trunk reichen lassen aufs Pferd; der hieß mit Namen Levin Sander und war damals ein schmucker Bursch und ein landfahrender Abenteurer, der Dienste nehmen wollt bei dem Herzog. Ist später ein kaiserlicher Rittmeister und berufener Parteigänger worden" (Raabe 1992: 316).

the devastated landscapes and cities. The concise passages about the war remind us less of similar sequences in *Simplicissimus*, but far more of the life story of Springinsfeld in the novel of the same name (Grimmelshausen 2007b: 212-295; Raabe 1992: 325-327, 333-336). The national war becomes a sequence of victories and defeats; first for one and then for the other warring party. Even the people at the top of the military hierarchies are not immune to death and destruction. Christian the Younger of Braunschweig-Lüneburg, still known in the military jargon as the "Mad Christian",[12] loses an arm and dies of the plague at the age of 27 (Raabe 1992: 327). Scheibenhart joins the Protestants under Gustav II. Adolph and is present at the fateful battle of Lützen. Severely wounded in the leg, Scheibenhart then encounters the corpse of the Swedish warlord, who is now lying in the moonlight, shorn of all his legendary grandeur: "By the light of the moon I gazed upon a naked, plundered corpse with a face covered in blood – Gustavus Adolphus!"[13] After this dramatic encounter, Scheibenhart's war comes to a premature end the next day when his wounded leg is sawn off. It is perhaps here that the parallels to the figure of Springinsfeld can be most clearly seen. Springinsfeld also took part in the battle of Lützen, even though he did not suffer any major wounds or injuries (Grimmelshausen 2007b: 235-239). This hardbitten mercenary does not lose his leg until after 1648 when it is blown off by an exploding mine on the island of Crete. Here too the leg had to be amputated (283-286). Scheibenhart construes his image of true masculinity *nolens volens* from the example of Levin Sander. Scheibenhart's break out into the world takes the form of his learning to use the tools of the soldier's trade in order to prepare him for a fatal confrontation with the "Partisan" and the performance of his act of personal revenge on him. The respectable scribe transforms himself into an armed horseman because he thinks that in this position he will have sufficient legitimacy and armour for a final confrontation.[14] Typical of the pícaro novel in the way in which Grimmelshausen writes them, the copyist from Wolfenbüttel

---

12 "Wie biß der tolle Christian die Zähne zusammen, wie schüttelte er den zerbrochenen Degen gegen das Geschütz Tillys und das spanische Fußvolk Cordovas da drüben!" (Raabe 1992: 326). On Christian the Younger of Braunschweig-Lüneburg see Bok (2000).

13 "Eben tastete ich an den Körpern der Gefallenen umher, da fiel ein schwaches verschleiert Mondlicht durch die Wolken. Bei seinem Schein blickt ich in einer nackten, geplünderten Leiche blutbesudelt Gesicht – Gustavus Adolfus!" (Raabe 1992: 336).

14 "An den tückischen Levin dachte ich zumeist, da schoß mir ein Gedanke durch die Seele – ha, ihn vor die Klinge kriegen, ihn niederhauen im ehrlichen Gefecht!" (Raabe 1992: 324, cf. Bertschik 1995: 115-116).

exchanges the role of the victim for that of the perpetrator. The final confrontation with Sander never takes place, however. In Stadtlohn Scheibenhart is unable to find Sander and instead he is struck down by a musket ball (Raabe 1992: 327). He misses him again in Lützen (335). His constant thinking of Sander and the urgent desire for revenge on him extend even beyond his actual life. In the "Postscriptum" (337) we therefore learn of Sander's death, "because he was as strong as iron in his love for the use of the gun, the sword and the dagger, he had been struck down with axes hooks and hammers".[15] Scheibenhart, however, finds his true masculinity only at an advanced age when he is able, even though still severely disabled, to triumph over his enemy's grave: "May God have mercy on his [Sander's] poor soul; but may dogs keep watch over his grave during the day and owls by night!"[16]

The only female character described in any detail, Susanna Rodin, remains, almost stereotypically, in the role of the victim. Even if, at least initially, she has the rudimentary characteristics of a *femme fatale*, her social decline begins with her liaison with Levin Sander and a resulting child born out of wedlock with the descriptive name „Herzeleid" (Raabe 1992: 330). Her father had cursed Susanna, "when the water as high as a pike has washed over my grave to wash away my dishonour, I shall be forgiven."[17] This is what happens. When Wolfenbüttel is flooded by the troops of Gottfried Heinrich zu Pappenheim's army, Susanna drowns. Herzeleid dies of the effects of hypothermia and malnutrition. Here too, the first-person narrator also suggests there is a divine judgment for the mother and child, "it was a horror like those in the days of the Flood."[18] It therefore

---

15 "Der Levin Sander ist bis vor Hildesheim an den Galgenberg zwischen den Pferden mitgeführet, daselbst aber ist er, weil er für Geschoß, Hieb und Stich eisenfest gewesen, mit Äxten, Haken und Hammern niedergeschlagen worden" (Raabe 1992: 337).

16 "Gott sei seiner armen Seele gnädig; aber über seinem Grabe sollen Hunde bei Tag und Eulen bei Nacht wachen!" (Raabe 1992: 337).

17 "Mein Vater ist tot; er hat mich verflucht: wenn das Wasser pikenhoch über meinen Leib weggegangen ist, die Schmach zu waschen, soll mir vergeben sein; meine Mutter ist tot, wenn mein Kind nicht wär, wär ich auch längst gestorben und hätt die Schand gesühnt; lasset uns hier, Herr!" (Raabe 1992: 330)

18 "In Kähnen, auf zusammengebundenen Brettern schwammen die elenden Leut umher; bald neigten und senkten sich die Häuser und stürzten zusammen; dazwischen donnerte das Geschütz rings von den Höhen um die Stadt – es war ein Grauen wie in den Tagen der Sündflut" (Raabe 1992: 332). On Susanna Rodin cf. Bröhan (1981: 76): "Zusammengerafft in eine kurze Novelle vollzieht sich auch hier die Wertung nach weiblichem Tugendideal und patriarchalischer Disziplin, wobei eigenbestimmtes Handeln

seems as if in *Lorenz Scheibenhart* we have some of the ingredients of a picaresque narrative against the background of the Thirty Years' War in the tradition of Grimmelshausen. However, we can neither speak of a picaresque narrative process here, nor of Scheibenhart as being a pícaro figure. The bitter recollection of the many tribulations in life has little in common with the cheerful confessional autobiography of Simplicius which often draws on the memory of farcical episodes. The honest, and despite all his experience of war, upright Scheibenhart, who on the contrary pursues his desire to murder people, also, as a character, has little in common with Grimmelshausen's Springinsfeld. The experienced mercenary does not care about victory or defeat and looks instead, preferably on the margins of the fighting, for ways to enrich himself to the best of his ability.

III.

Although it conforms to the model of the pícaro story, compared with the works of Grimmelshausen, *Michel Haas* seems in many ways to be a parody of the Baroque picaresque novel. The folly of the action of the fighting in the Thirty Years' War has by now disappeared as Haas was born in 1697. However, the times in the 18th century are also not exactly peaceful. Violence in all its forms determines human interactions. Haas' profession as a wandering tutor does not correspond with the adventurous life as a mercenary experienced by Simplicius or Springinsfeld. Finally, the distance covered by Haas, who describes himself as being a "Landläufer" (Raabe 1992: 473) or itinerant vagrant in his memoirs, appears to be absurdly short. If in the *Simplicissimus* novel and its *Continuatio*, Simplicius made a complete round, the world trip – which also included an additional remote island – Haas nonetheless remains in a narrow radius of certain towns in today's Eastern Westphalia and South Lower Saxony (Detering 1986: 92, note 45). In the rest of the story any possible relationship with Grimmelshausen is manifested in a decidedly loose and unsystematic way. Simplicius finds a refuge in the Westphalian town of Lippstadt, in order to continue the interrupted course of his education and to read romance stories. It was also in Lippstadt of all places (Raabe 1992: 439) that Haas received the rudiments of his school education. Simplicius also uses his stay in Westphalia for fitting in some amorous escapades with the daughters of respectable local citizens. Haas starts to do this just one stop down the line in the environs of the grammar school in Detmold

---

der Frau nur Unglück nach sich zieht und zum Scheitern verurteilt ist." See furthermore Maierhofer (2005: 206-208) on *Lorenz Scheibenhart*.

(442).[19] As in Grimmelshausen Haas' amorous advances to members of the other sex tend to be made on a level which does not entail any commitment. These incipient relationships are in general ended by the furious intervention of the young woman's parents or legal guardians.

The other building blocks of a picaresque confessional life story, as found in the works of Grimmelshausen, for instance, undergo significant variations. At the heart of the *Simplicissimus* novel are a number of humorous "little episodes" ("Stücklein"). In these humorous episodes the main character plays all sorts of pranks with cunning and deception, sometimes on unsuspecting and naive, sometimes on his extremely unpopular and cunning contemporaries. The 'episode' about catching and selling the fish in *Michel Haas*, however, is given a decidedly theological dimension. It is precisely in Easter Week that Haas catches a large number of carp in the Senne region, which he wants to sell profitably in Paderborn. The fish die on the way there. A cunning landlord with the meaningful name of "Deuvel" (Raabe 1992: 452) advises Haas to rub the carp with urine so that they look a little fresher. The attempted sale of the carp on Good Friday turns into a fiasco. Detering interprets the contaminated fish as representing a concealed desecration of the Sacrament, because during the Easter season the fish represents the traditional symbol of the Crucified One (Detering 1986: 103). The superficially amusing picaresque story turns into a terrible blasphemy.

In *Michel Haas* the course of the discourse on the fool is once again different from that found in Grimmelshausen. Simplicius is condemned as a fool and forcibly dressed in a fool's costume. It is only with a lot of trouble and cunning that he can escape from this role which has been forced on him. Later on it is a sign of his own rise in society that he is given, as it were, his 'own' fool. On the highway, Simplicius picks up the dreamer Jupiter who explains to him his highly eccentric plans to bring peace to the warring society (Grimmelshausen 2005: 252-266). Haas, however, meets, following the fish-selling episode, a certain Herr von Bock who, to the distress of his wife, displays all sorts of foolish behaviours. Even a nine-year stay in prison does nothing to diminish his delusions. The most pronounced expression of his madness significantly once again revolves around fish. Von Bock constantly digs holes and ditches in the house's garden so that he can release "Häringe" (Raabe 1992: 456) into them. Von

---

19 A further, looser parallel to Grimmelshausen can be seen in the fact that the local parish priest and Simplicius are discussing his novel *Keuscher Joseph* (Grimmelshausen 2005: 318-321). After moving on to Lemgo, Haas now makes allusions to the Biblical story of Joseph when he finds himself subjected to persecution by the oldest daughter of a baker (Raabe 1992: 445).

Bock's madness is highlighted by the fact that he is releasing these herrings into the holes and ditches in the hope that they will breed there! Haas dissuades him from continuing with the senseless undertaking with a remarkably simple method. He tells von Bock that the King of England has arranged for his digging tools to be collected (457). In doing so, Haas mentions several times that this inspiration only came to him by Divine aid: "The dear Lord also granted that he [Bock] fell for this!"[20] All the previous attempts to combat Herr von Bock's debilitating melancholy had been condemned to failure.[21]

This successful curing of the fool, which is not found in the *Simplicissimus* novel (Grimmelshausen 2005: 461-477), again points indirectly to the main character himself. In contrast to much more robust pícaro figures, Haas sees himself as being subject to many temptations by the Devil.[22] His short-term and extremely casually mentioned transformation from victim to perpetrator does not provide him with any remedy here.[23] In comparison to Scheibenhart, Haas is often afflicted by life-threatening illnesses (Raabe 1992: 440-441; 449-450; 454; 468-469).[24] In the *Simplicissimus* novel the flaring up of illnesses, such as the one after the infamous *beau alman* episode, serve as warnings that Simplicius should reconsider his previously immoral life (Grimmelshausen 2005: 370-373). After each of his stays in hospital, however, Simplicius, generally blithely continues his previous way of life. The worst illness to afflict Haas, however, does not have any organic causes such as those in *Simplicissimus* and they point back

---

20 "Schenkte auch der liebe Gott, daß er sich endlich dreingab" (Raabe 1992: 457).

21 "Wie nun der Mann neun Jahre im Zuchthaus gewesen, supplizierte sie [Frau von Bock] so viel, daß sie ihn endlich losbekam, und tat sie ihn nach Hildesheim zu einem Doktor, daß er ihn heile von seiner Melancholey" (Raabe 1992: 455).

22 "Gott behüte uns dafür, denn es ist eine böse Anfechtung des Teufels" (Raabe 1992: 472).

23 "An diesem Orte bin ich zwei und ein halb Jahr gewesen; aber ich war zu hitzig, dachte wunder, was für eine große Kreatur ich sei, prügelte den alten Kalefaktor, daß sie ihm zwei Tage den Buckel einschmieren mußten, und die Herrschaft lag leider Gottes im Fenster und sah den ganzen Lärm an" (Raabe 1992: 462).

24 Ironically it is one of his illnesses which prevents Haas from joining the horsemen, as Scheibenhart does, and as is appropriate to a picaresque hero: "Ging also wieder gen Detmold und ließ mich unter die Preußen annehmen als Reiter, sintemalen der Graf Karl von der Lippe damals ein Reiterregiment kommandierte zu Königsberg. Als wir aber grade zum Schwören ausmarschieren sollten, da faßte mich Gottes Gewalt und warf mich aufs Krankenbett, daß ich lange, lange auf den Tod lag und nicht vermeinte, wieder davonzukommen" (Raabe 1992: 449-450).

to Herr von Bock (Detering 1990: 37). Even if Haas is latently dissatisfied with his unsteady and unsettled life, the most devastating visitation of illness on him arrives suddenly and completely without warning. The "malo hypochondriaco" (Raabe 1992: 468) strikes him and transforms the tough tutor, who had always found ways to satisfy the grumpiest and most difficult-to-please employers, into a fear-ridden and emotional wreck who is always close to tears. It is now that the masculine identity of the flexible itinerant vagrant is available to him with the greatest vehemence.[25] Once again, and this time in a particularly serious way, Haas sees himself as being in the hands of God and being forced to rely on His mercy and help. He interprets the terrible hypochondria as a punishment and a warning for his infamous picaresque actions:

No one would be able to describe this dangerous illness because it can take you from life to death, if you do not cling tightly onto God and show deep remorse for your sins and confess them sincerely, as David, Manasseh and Jeremiah all did in the past. Without God's help no one can survive this illness for even one year.[26]

Almost right at the end of the story Haas does the same thing as Simplicius and takes his own life in a remote location. This place "in the Senne and out in the wild, where you see nothing but wild horses and game"[27] is where his hypo-

---

[25] One possible way of fighting hypochondria is to stay at a spa. Extended stays at spas, such as in Sauerbrunnen, also allow the characters in the Simplician novels to recover their battered health (Grimmelshausen 2005: 467-474). Haas stays in the scarcely less famous spa town of Bad Pyrmont: "Respondebam: 'Ja!', nahm Abschied, reisete ab, und brauchte drei Wochen lang die Kur und das Bad und wurde allmählich besser, aber nicht ganz gesund" (Raabe 1992: 471).

[26] "Diese gefährliche Krankheit zu beschreiben, ist kein Mensch imstande; denn sie gehet vom Leben zum Tode, wenn man sich nicht fest an Gott hält und seine getane Sünde herzlich beichtet und bereuet, wie David, Manasse, Jeremias pp. auch getan haben. Ohne Gottes Beistand kann sie kein Mensch ein Jahr lang aushalten" (Raabe 1992: 471).

[27] "Mit erleichtertem Herzen fuhr ich wieder aus in die Welt und kam zum Leutnant Schmidt, der ein Freigut hatte mitten in der Senne und der Wildnis, wo man nichts als wilde Pferde und Wild zu schauen bekam, wo die Menschen gar selten waren" (Raabe 1992: 472). In the *Scheibenhart* tale, the remote location is pure imagination: "O wie schad ist's doch, daß es nicht mehr an der Zeit ist, ein hären Gewand anzutun und hinzuziehen in eine thebaische Wüste und sein Hüttlein zu bauen fern von den Menschen bei den Tieren der Wildnis..." (Raabe 1992: 317).

chondria should now completely disappear. The Simplicius' renunciation of the world should, however be understood as being action which is intended to take his leave of a humanity which is characterised by its vices and sins. In the *Continuatio*, Simplicius' departure from the world allows him to lead a pious life on the "Cross Island" far from the general tumult of war. Haas, however, is unable to bear solitude for very long and returns as quickly as possible to human society. Even before this, however, his recovery from his hypochondria had been announced. Haas comes across two women brawling in the most foul-mouthed way, one of whom he had desired a decade ago.[28] The genre scene throws light on the conception of the female characters in the narrative. Even if neither of the female figures is described in any great detail, they are both distinguished by the fact that they self-confidently take whatever they want. The contrast with Susanna Rodin from the *Scheibenhart* narrative and her role as a victim could not be greater. Haas, on the contrary, has his masculine identity called into question by the constant female invectives against him and he not infrequently reacts by leaving and taking flight. Even if Haas' interest in a conductor's daughter was returned by her (Raabe 1992: 442), a baker's daughter from Lemgo shows that she was already an experienced temptress (444-445). In addition, there are rather inconspicuous female characters such as Frau von Bock, who is fully occupied in coping with the unpredictability of her foolish husband. The end point is reached when Haas encounters his childhood sweetheart, Anna Marie, whose appearance has visibly changed in the decades, which had passed since he had last seen her, and which once again caused this itinerant to seek to flee.

The battle between the sexes is also played out in the Haas story. One feels, however, that this passage is but a weak reminder of the much more dramatic episode in Grimmelshausen's *Courasche*. The pícara is forced by her short-term partner, a lieutenant, to fight with him using clubs, to decide which of them should be allowed to wear the trousers (Grimmelshausen 2007a: 46-50). In this fight it is the over-hasty lieutenant who receives a vicious beating from the experienced fighter Courasche. Haas has an "Amtmeyer" (Raabe 1992: 445) as an employer and who partakes of alcohol to excess. Late one night he demands that Haas sings a large number of hymns for his edification. The resulting loud noise gets well and truly on the nerves of the *Amtmeyer's* wife. When the oil lamp goes out, the woman is not prepared to provide any more fuel for it. The *Amtmeyer* utters two pithy sentences to Haas, telling him who should wear the

---

28 "'Anna Marie?!' rief ich und schlug die Hände über dem Kopf zusammen und wußte in diesem Augenblick nichts mehr von meinem malo hypochondriaco" (Raabe 1992: 470).

trousers in the household and how to deal with rebellious women.[29] The master of the house blocks the chimney in the kitchen and puts some old brooms and rags into the burning fire in the hearth. In no time at all it is impossible for anyone to see their own hands in front of their face because of all the smoke in the room. The entire housekeeping staff is in uproar and runs into a huddle. The *Amtmeyer's* wife decorates the face "of this poisonous cat"[30] and the excitement is endless. It is significant that – and in contrast to the scenes in Grimmelshausen – there are neither winners nor losers in this raw fight for supremacy. According to Detering this burlesque scene gains theological significance from the fact that the edifying mood created by the description of the singing of a hymn, together with the first lines of the hymn which was sung before it, is used as a contrast to the later sequence of the battle of the sexes saturated in fire and smoke. This is now clearly to be seen as being the work of the Devil, especially because the smouldering stuff causes "the stench of Hell".[31]

IV.

The picaresque adventures of itinerant vagrants find themselves put into the strange perspective of the historicist narrative tradition of the mid-19th century. The pícaro, with his uncertain and insecure world governed by Dame Fortune, appears highly dysfunctional against the historico-philosophical foundations of historicism (Bertschik 1995: 1-22; Grätz 2006: 431-444). In the narrative of the itinerant vagrant there is precisely no historically significant personage striding through the space of *historia* and subjugating the world to himself. Raabe uses various strategies in his refusal to bow to the postulates of a meaningful historiography and all its aesthetic literary remodelings. Faced with the horrors of the

---

29 "'Sie will nicht, Michel', sagte mein Prinzipal und stieß mir den Ellbogen in die Seite. ‚Siehet Er, das ist das Vergnügen beim Freien; merk Er's sich. Hab bemerkt, daß Er nach meiner Ältesten schielt – da hat Er ein Exemplum, wie's mit dem Weibsvolk ist" (Raabe 1992: 447-448). "Merk Er's sich, Präzeptor: Manneshand gehört oben" (449).

30 "Hu, wie fuhr die Meisterin gleich einer giftigen Katze herum, mir und dem Herrn mit zehn ausgespreizten Klauen vor den Augen herum!" (Raabe 1992: 449)

31 "Alle alten Besen des Hauses, drei wollene Socken und ein zerlumpter wollener Frauenrock glimmeten und qualmeten darauf nach Herzenslust, daß man durch den Rauch nicht durchsehen konnt, und der Schornstein war fein sorgsam verstopft, daß ja nichts verlorenginge von dem Höllenstank" (Raabe 1992: 449; cf. Detering (1986: 100-101; 1990: 34).

Thirty Years' War, it is not possible for any form of picaresque narrative to be used in any section of *Lorenz Scheibenhart*, even though this work contains an ensemble of characters which has many similarities of those in the Simplician novels. Scheibenhart himself is unable to carry out his intended actions as an avenger and is forced to withdraw from all the fighting as a disabled veteran. In the final analysis *Michel Haas* therefore in many respects represents an atypical, if not actually travestying picaresque narration. The life's journey of the schoolmaster encompasses, unlike the Baroque journey around the world, a geographical area which is full of provincial narrowness. The 18th century of the early Enlightenment, does indeed remain largely unaffected by fighting in war, however, there is even in peacetime still a bitter free-for-all fight in a mean world.[32] The funny 'little episodes' about selling the fish and the battle between the sexes, which are intended to add charm to a picaresque story in the first place, turn out to be scenes of blasphemy against the Sacrament and a vision of Hell *en miniature*. Haas sees himself threatened in his male identity, almost constantly and from all sides – by life-threatening diseases, self-confident women, melancholy, and the worst affliction of all – by his hypochondria. Haas emphasises several times, and with the utmost clarity, that human existence, and especially a person's life's journey, are and will continue to remain in God's hands.[33] It is precisely this pious conclusion, which might have been an appropriate ending to a piece of Baroque devotional writing, which must have been more than surprising to people in the mid-19th century.

BIBLIOGRAPHY

Althaus, Thomas. "Konzeptuelle Brüche. Grimmelshausens *Simplicissimus* und die Tradition pikaresken Erzählens." *Simpliciana* XXIX (2007): 41–55.
Baader, Horst. "Typologie und Geschichte des spanischen Romans im ‚Goldenen Zeitalter'." Ed. August Buck et al. *Neues Handbuch der Literaturwissenschaft. Vol. 10, II. Renaissance und Barock*. Frankfurt a.M. 1972. 82–144.

---

[32] "So muß die Unschuld Angst und Not ausstehen in dieser bösen Welt!" (Raabe 1992: 466)

[33] A verse from a hymn in the Brunswick hymnal almost acts as the motto of the story: "Alles hat ja seine Zeit, / Freud und Leid. / Gut Gewitter, böse Stunden / Werden wechselweis erfunden. / Dennoch geht es, wie Gott will, / Halte still!" (Raabe 1992: 441, 451, 473). "Wenige Texte Raabes nehmen ein so frommes Ende wie diese fiktive Autobiographie" (Detering 1990: 27).

Bartels, Ulrich. "Der *Westfälische Schelmuffsky* von 1861. Zur Schelmuffsky-Rezeption im Thienhäuser Kreis." *Simpliciana* XIV (1992): 197–209.

Bauer, Matthias. *Der Schelmenroman.* Stuttgart, Weimar 1994.

Bertschik, Julia. *Maulwurfsarchäologie. Zum Verhältnis von Geschichte und Anthropologie in Wilhelm Raabes historischen Erzähltexten.* Tübingen 1995.

Bok, Marten Jan. "Christian von Braunschweig in den Niederlanden." Ed. Niels Büttner. *Der Krieg als Person. Herzog Christian d. J. von Braunschweig-Lüneburg im Bildnis von Paulus Moreelse.* Ausstellung im Herzog Anton-Ulrich Museum Braunschweig 16. März bis 14. Mai 2000. Braunschweig 2000. 14–39.

Brewster, Philip James. *Wilhelm Raabes historische Fiktion im Kontext. Beitrag zur Rekonstruktion der Gattungsproblematik zwischen Geschichtsschreibung und Poesie im 19. Jahrhundert.* Ph.D. Ithaca, NY 1983.

Bröhan, Margrit. *Die Darstellung der Frau bei Wilhelm Raabe und ein Vergleich mit liberalen Positionen zur Emanzipation der Frau im 19. Jahrhundert.* Frankfurt a.M., Bern 1981.

Chopin, Isabelle. "Die Topographie des Krieges in Erzählungen Wilhelm Raabes." *Jahrbuch der Raabe-Gesellschaft* (2000): 52–73.

Detering, Heinrich. "Der Landstörzer Michel Haas. Picarisches Erzählen im bürgerlichen Realismus." *Jahrbuch der Raabe-Gesellschaft* (1986): 83–106.

Detering, Heinrich. *Theodizee und Erzählverfahren. Narrative Experimente mit religiösen Modellen im Werk Wilhelm Raabes.* Göttingen 1990.

Grätz, Katharina. *Musealer Historismus. Die Gegenwart des Vergangenen bei Stifter, Keller und Raabe.* Heidelberg 2006.

Grimmelshausen, Hans Jacob Christoffel von. *Simplicissimus Teutsch* [1668]. Ed. Dieter Breuer. *Grimmelshausen. Werke I.* Frankfurt a.M. 2005. 9–551.

Grimmelshausen, Hans Jacob Christoffel von. *Courasche* [1670]. Ed. Dieter Breuer. *Grimmelshausen: Werke I, 2.* Frankfurt a.M. 2007a. 9–151.

Grimmelshausen, Hans Jacob Christoffel von. *Der seltzame Springinsfeld* [1670]. Ed. Dieter Breuer. *Grimmelshausen: Werke I, 2.* Frankfurt a.M. 2007b. 153–295.

Guillén, Claudio. "Zur Frage der Begriffsbestimmung des Pikaresken." Ed. Helmut Heidenreich. *Pikarische Welt. Schriften zum europäischen Schelmenroman.* Darmstadt 1969. 375–396.

Hahn, Hans J. "Lewalds *Diogena*, ein Schelmenroman des Vormärz." Ed. Christine Ujma. *Fanny Lewald (1811-1889). Studien zu einer großen europäischen Schriftstellerin und Intellektuellen.* Bielefeld 2011. 187–202.

Hohl-Trillini, Regula. "Stimmengewirr aus schwierigen Zeiten. Erzählen über schlimme Frauen bei Raabe und Grimmelshausen." *Jahrbuch der Raabe-Gesellschaft* (1997): 123–146.

Honold, Alexander. "Travestie und Transgression. Pikaro und verkehrte Welt bei Grimmelshausen." Ed. Christoph Ehland and Robert Fajen. *Das Paradigma des Pikaresken. The Paradigm of the Picaresque.* Heidelberg 2007. 201–227.

Jacobs, Jürgen. *Der deutsche Schelmenroman. Eine Einführung.* München, Zürich 1983.

Koeman, Jakob. *Die Grimmelshausen-Rezeption in der fiktionalen Literatur der deutschen Romantik.* Amsterdam, Atlanta, GA 1993.

Mahlmann-Bauer, Barbara. "Jeremias Gotthelf und die Tradition des Schelmenromans." Ed. Bernhard Jahn, Dirk Rose and Thorsten Unger. *Ordentliche Unordnung. Metamorphosen des Schwanks vom Mittelalter bis zur Moderne.* Heidelberg 2014. 265–300.

Maierhofer, Waltraud. *Hexen – Huren – Heldenweiber. Bilder des Weiblichen in Erzähltexten über den Dreißigjährigen Krieg.* Köln, Weimar, Wien 2005.

Martin, Dieter. *Barock um 1800. Bearbeitung und Aneignung deutscher Literatur des 17. Jahrhunderts von 1770 bis 1830.* Frankfurt a.M. 2000.

Meid, Volker. "Friedrich Christoph Weissers *Schalkheit und Einfalt* (1822), oder: Der literaturkritische schwäbische Simplicissimus." Ed. Wilhelm Kühlmann. *Literatur und Kultur im deutschen Südwesten zwischen Renaissance und Aufklärung. Neue Studien.* Amsterdam, Atlanta, GA 1995. 315–327.

Meierhofer, Christian. "Im Schutt der Geschichten. Frühneuzeitliche Denk- und Schreibweisen in Raabes historischem Erzählen." Ed. Dirk Göttsche and Ulf-Michael Schneider. *Signaturen realistischen Erzählens im Werk Wilhelm Raabes.* Würzburg 2010. 159–181.

Michaelis, Sarah. "Pikaresker Peter Schlemihl – Intertextualität zwischen Chamissos *Schlemihl* und Grimmelshausens *Simplicissimus*." Ed. Marie-Theres Federhofer and Jutta Weber. *Korrespondenzen und Transformationen. Neue Perspektiven auf Adelbert von Chamisso.* Göttingen 2013. 259–277.

Pongs, Hermann. *Wilhelm Raabe. Leben und Werk.* Heidelberg 1958.

Raabe, Wilhelm. *Sämtliche Werke. Im Auftrag der Braunschweigischen Wissenschaftlichen Gesellschaft.* Ed. Karl Hoppe and Jost Schillemeit. Freiburg i.Br., Braunschweig 1951.

Raabe, Wilhelm. *Sämtliche Werke. Vol. 9/1. Erzählungen. Das letzte Recht* […]. Ed. Karl Hoppe and Rosemarie Schillemeit. Göttingen 1974.

Raabe, Wilhelm. *Sämtliche Werke. Vol. 2. Die Kinder von Finkenrode. Erzählungen* […]. Ed. Eberhard Rohse. Göttingen 1992.

Radcliffe, Stanley. "Wilhelm Raabe, der Dreißigjährige Krieg und die Novelle." *Jahrbuch der Raabe-Gesellschaft* (1969): 57–70.

Schrader, Hans-Jürgen. "Zur Vergegenwärtigung und Interpretation der Geschichte bei Raabe." *Jahrbuch der Raabe-Gesellschaft* (1973): 12–53.

Seiler, Bernd W. "Der Schelm, der nur noch gibt, was er hat. Adolph von Knigge und die Tradition des Schelmenromans." Ed. Friedrich Kienecker and Peter Wolfersdorf. *Dichtung – Wissenschaft – Unterricht*. Paderborn et al. 1986. 300–322.

Stöckmann, Ernst. "Der erzählte Krieg als Sinnkritik der Weltgeschichte. Zur Ästhetik des betroffenen Subjekts in Raabes Kriegserzählungen der mittleren Zeit." *Jahrbuch der Raabe-Gesellschaft* (2009): 82–99.

Wald, Martin C. *Die Gesichter der Streitenden. Erzählung, Drama und Diskurs des Dreißigjährigen Krieges, 1830 bis 1933*. Göttingen 2008.

Watanabe-O'Kelly, Helen. "The picaro as narrator, writer and reader: The novels of Hans Jakob von Grimmelshausen." Ed. J. A. Garrido Ardila. *The Picaresque Novel in Western Literature. From the Sixteenth Century to the Neopicaresque*. Cambridge 2015. 184–199.

Masks to Mock the Light

The Authentic Pícara in Marivaux's *La Vie de Marianne*

ALEXANDRA SCHAMEL

In recent years, the picaresque novel has been an intensely debated issue that has received increasing attention. However, the highly questionable topic of the gender of the picaresque protagonist was hardly considered. Referring to this desideratum, Enrique García Santo-Tomás mentions in his article *The Spanish female picaresque* the "absence of gender as a discursive category" (Santo-Tomás 2015: 63) as one of the features that have traditionally been considered essential to the genre. This paper focuses on the ways how the 18th century French novel, namely Marivaux's *La Vie de Marianne*, adopts the picaresque tradition in the social frame of Enlightenment and its anthropological patterns. The reactivating of picaresque features can be illustrated in the function of constructing the self by masking it. I will describe this strategy as 'mask of authenticity'. Within this heuristic frame, my central question is whether and to what extent this strategy is gendered. Is the mask of authenticity used in particular by the female subject in order to fend off the normative discourses which Enlightenment has produced as a sight-dominated regime? The normative discourses mostly seem to represent a male authority, for example the patriarch (Frömmer 2008: 28-40). In addition to the discussion of the aspect of gender, my argument highlights the fact that the picaresque genre is not to be understood as a homogenous system of features, but that the different components of picaresque writing are adopted and continued in a great diversity and must always be related to cultural, social, and mental constellations. The evolving dynamics can even be directed against each other. A quite fitting conceptual metaphor to describe this complex, even paradoxical process is the "rhizomatic ramification" (Lickhardt 2014: 5).

My paper will concentrate on the text and its anatomy as a starting point for further theoretical suggestions. At the beginning of my argumentation, I would like to call attention to the very ambivalence of the picaresque body, that can be considered as being authentic and at the same time protean and involved in a permanent transformation. This ambivalence is based on a cognitive function of the body.

THE AUTHENTIC BODY OF THE PÍCARO

Lazaro's experience of being initiated into the real world of cruelty and avarice consists in his being suddenly pushed against the bull made of stone (Lazarillo 2003: 7-8). This push, given by the hand of the blind beggar, aligns the sustained injury and Lazaro's sudden capacity to see in a causal relationship. Through the push, Lazaro is enabled to open his eyes as someone who is waking up. He recognizes his own homelessness as an existential condition of man, the metaphysical power of providence being an illusion. The wound in his body testifies to the confrontation of the pícaro with reality. It is the painful sign of resistance and suffering, but also the sign of an act of recognition in the sense of *desengaño*, which figures as the essential aspect of the picaresque nature. The wound in the body proclaims the very self-conscience of the pícaro *opposite* the world, and this juxtaposition implies a mental autonomy as well as a "corporeal" one. This autonomy implies the very consciousness of having a body, or even: of receiving a body in the birth-like process of cognition: "[...] después de Dios este ma dio la vida" – "[...] after God, he gave me life" (Lazarillo 1992: 24; Lazarillo 2003: 8). By suffering the wound, the pícaro discovers his body as an aspect of his selfhood. By wearing the marks of *desengaño*, the body figures as an indicator of the combative picaresque identity, his extraordinary capacity to survive in the great ocean of life:

[...] y también porque consideren los que heredaron nobles estados cuán poco se les debe, pues Fortuna fue con ellos parcial, y cuanto mas hicieron los que, siendoles contraria, con fuerza y mana remando, salieron a buen puerto (Lazarillo 1992: 11).

[...] like people who are proud of being high born, to realize how little this really means, as Fortune has smiled on them, and how much more worthy are those who have endured misfortune but have triumphed by dint of hard work and determination (Lazarillo 2003: 4).

It is this capacity to survive that ennobles the pícaro over the brutal but ignorant crowd. The picaresque body is marked by auratic wounds, that not only testify to the epistemological capacity of the pícaro, but also shall be seen or proudly be shown to the world. The wounds can be considered the authentic testimony of the hard earned, but precious life experience as its material evidence. So, in its anthropological dimension, the construction of the picaresque nature presupposes the integration of mind and body. This unity is the anthropological subtext of the pícaro's life, of his unique misery and laborious solo-run. As the corporeal experience of initiation induces the capacity to see as a skill of reason that has then been enlightened by the beggar's brutal act – "y siendo ciego me alumbró y adestró en la carrera de vivir." (Lazarillo 1992: 24) – "and though he was blind he revealed things to me and made me see what life was about" (Lazarillo 2003: 8) – the *desengaño* structure seems to be one of the first articulations of the paradigm of visibility leading to the epistemological ideology of the Enlightenment.

THE PROTEAN BODY

The authentic body of the pícaro, marked by suffering, is at the same time a quite solid and versatile body. By means of his body the pícaro permanently dissimulates his identity. The admirable body control implied in this art of dissimulation is an essential element of the picaresque protean nature. This art has been discussed as an air of adaptation or subordination under the rule of social structures. In this respect, the pícaro would figure as *subiectum* in the proper sense of the word (Wehr 2007: 25-44). On the other hand, in a perspective that emphasizes the connection between picaresque and carnivalesque according to Bachtin, this permanent dissimulation can be considered as a gesture of empowerment and authorization of picaresque sovereignty with respect to the ruling semantic order represented by the feudal system (Bachtin 1987: 47-60). By means of physical (mimic and gestural) dissimulation, the pícaro eludes the discursive control. His protean body articulates the cyclical dynamics of the carnival as a permanent playful subversion, which questions the system of semantics. The play of the pícaro is of a "hilarious relativity, it denies conformity, clearness and one's dull identity with oneself" (Bachtin 1987: 90) and inaugurates an enigmatic power in contrast to the established discourses. The pícaro is free because he constantly changes.

With the impulse of thinking the otherness of the existing world, an epistemological paradigm is articulated that works as a game using the body. The rogue, presenting his versatile body in an endless series of different roles, illustrates the superior capacity to see 'behind the scenes' and proves to be someone who knows absolutely about the changeability of social roles and world-structures. The pícaro represents one of the first figures generated by the paradigm of knowing as seeing, and this paradigm will be continued until the Enlightenment. But in the middle of the 16th century, the concept of the pícaro still integrates the body in the capacity to know as it expresses semantic otherness as a game: as a mimic and gestural act of dissimulation which reveals the superior capacity to think otherness (Ehrlicher 2010).[1] So Lazaro praises the wit of the blind beggar, especially focusing on his artful voice while praying in the church and on his fine humble and pious look (Lazarillo 1992: 25-26, Lazarillo 2007: 8). The purely playful and relativistic aspects of the picaresque acting are naturally to be seen in tension with the attempt of the early epistemological paradigm to articulate "truth," a didactic doctrine or moral meaning (Kinzkofer 2003: 36-55).

THE CHANGE OF THE PARADIGM OF VISIBILITY BY DESCARTES

We remember that the *Lazarillo de Tormes* underlies the moment of initiation as an act of a sudden recognition provoked by a physical experience (being hurt), with metaphors of seeing and light ("alumbró" in the Spanish original). Lazaro wakes up, which means: He opens his eyes, and in the time to come, he must even better open his eyes. By hurting him in this brutal manner, the blind beggar "has enlightened his reason". The German translation of Lazarillo de Tormes (1614) actually uses the attribute "enlightened" to characterize Lazaro's state of mind after the brutal initiation: "und ob er schon blind war, hat er mir doch meinen Verstand erleuchtet" (Lazaril 1979: 15). In fact, the epistemological paradigm we observe in the structural moments of *desengaño* and initiation in *Lazarillo* and that binds together the intellectual capacity to see or recognize the truth and the corporeal experience, seems to be the very beginning of the epistemological paradigm which leads to the Enlightenment and already transports its conviction of the intelligibility of the world, of man and nature. But the form of this paradigm will be deeply transformed by Descartes's method of gaining knowledge.

The *Discours de la méthode* (1637) was essential for the European Enlightenment, and Descartes was born in 1596, only a few decades after the first publication of the *Lazarillo de Tormes* in 1554. Descartes's method exposes the see-

---

[1] Ehrlicher also refers to the Erasmian base of this interrelation between dissimulation and cognition as well as to the Platonist implications working here (Ehrlicher 2010: 142-160).

ing which *Lazarillo de Tormes* combined as an act of recognition *and* corporeal experience as the *only capacity* to produce evidence. In this context, Cassirer proposes the conceptual metaphor of the *tableau*: a plain area completely illuminated by reason, where the relations within the scientific object are shown to be evident and intelligible (Cassirer 1998: 30-33). Thus, the philosophy of recognition in *Lazarillo* articulates an epistemological paradigm of visibility which seems to point to Descartes. But this paradigm of visibility will be significantly modified by the Cartesian assumption of the dualism of the two substances of body and mind. Descartes clearly distinguishes between mental and physiological functions, and in doing so he creates the precondition for man becoming the scientific object himself in the stage-like anthropological area dominated by reason and its penetrating views (Deneys-Tunney 1992: 31-40). For example, in the *Discours*, the function of the human heart is explained to an uninformed audience as a logical and self-adjusting series of causes and effects (Descartes 2011: 80-94). Involved in the discussion, his epistemology provoked about the lost unity of the person, Descartes develops in his *Principia* the relationship between mental and physiological processes using the conditional pattern "If x, then y" (Perler 2006: 180-187). The Cartesian dualism of the substances blocks the dynamics of self-constitution, which is based on an experience of one's own body. Instead, the method isolates the capacity of seeing in its epistemological function, while the body is completely excluded from the cognitive faculty and – in the best of cases – serves as the scientific object itself. So, Descartes's method declares the anthropological concept of the *machine mouvante* to be a collective imagery. In the Cartesian tableau, the human body becomes entirely readable, but its signs can no more base the authenticity or uniqueness of the subject in its very body. Descartes instead defines the corporeal signs as indices of affective qualities. They have to be demonstrated first and foremost for scientific reasons. Authenticity gives way to the necessity of evidence.

The indexical body based on the Cartesian epistemology can be considered to be the very fundament of the aesthetic arenas, constructed in literature at the end of the 17th and during the long 18th century, which attempt to illustrate the nature of man. This can be seen, for example, in Diderot's *drames bourgeois* (Graczyk 2004: 77-116). In the preface for *Le père de famille*, Diderot compares the agitations and dynamics of the human heart with the spectacles of nature: "Le cœur de l'homme est tantôt serein et tantôt couvert de nuages; mais le cœur de l'homme de bien, semblable au spectacle de la nature, est toujours grand et beau, tranquille ou agité" (Diderot 2005: 114). The sensibility (*sensibilité*) is used as the central anthropological concept that stages the Cartesian conditional patterns of body and mind as a scheme of impulse and reaction, for example blushing as a sign of shame, tears as a sign of deep emotion or the holding of hands as a sign of fondness, friendship or tender love, as well as fainting due to great excitement of the female heart in particular. The tradition of the romance of gallantry, for example Honoré d'Urfée's *Astrée* (1607-27) and Madame de Scudéry's *La Carte de Tendre* in *Clélie, histoire romaine* (1654-1660), makes available a great number of patterns which constitute a scheme of virtue, and virtue is essentially coded by the signs of the body. The patterns of 'indexically readable virtue' developed by the literary imagination create – in a social function – strict normative patterns of identity for the upcoming middle-class.

THE PICARESQUE IN MARIVAUX

Most of the studies about the picaresque tradition in France consider Sorel's *Histoire comique de Francion* (1623, 33) and Scarron's *Roman comique* (1651-57) as early representatives of the genre, whereas Lesage's *Gil Blas de Santillane* (1715, 24, 35) is mentioned in the context of the 18th century. The affiliation of Marivaux's *La Vie de Marianne* (1731-41) to the picaresque genre does not seem to be obvious, even though, as Jenny Mander (2015: 157-183) points out, it does display some of the genre's typical features: the proof of the authenticity of the text by means of a fictive editor (who pretends to have found the manuscript in an old mansion in Brittany), the conceptualization of the text as a set of memoirs using the epistolary form; the unknown origin of the protagonist Marianne, who claims to be a countess, but whose noble birth remains doubtful throughout the story; the battle for survival in the metropolis of Paris in the middle of the 18th century; and finally, Marianne's romantic relationships with various gentlemen of the upper class, such as Climal and Valville, the popular narrative scheme of gendering the original picaresque constellation of master and servant (Kinzkofer 2003: 74-75).

In the following, I will demonstrate how Marivaux deals with the picaresque tradition in *La Vie de Marianne* as he reflects the reintegration of the body in order to create a concept of personal authenticity. The author foils the enlightened discourses of knowledge in the 'regime of visibility' by means of the older, playful and corporeal strategy of the roguish mask. My hypothesis can be formulated as follows: Marivaux activates the carnivalesque function of the roguish mask to construct semantic otherness in the anthropological dimension. With the mask/masque, the subject empowers himself as a protean being over the established discursive order and its indexical codes.² In this self-enactment, the subject regains authenticity (Straub 2012: 9-12).³ The authentic empowerment is based on a masquerade that is to be illustrated as an intentional act executed on one's own body; it reintegrates the body of the subject in the process of self-construction. Perhaps we could put it in other terms: In Marivaux, we can observe an intentional masquerade which reappropriates the body to the subject, but – in the regime of visibility – this reappropriation and authentication is necessarily paradoxical, as it takes place by becoming another one by dissimulation and mask, by becoming different to the readable schemes of reason. This mask/masque of authenticity continues the picaresque function to transgress and to subvert the established discourses and breaks their claim to create a normative and binding power.

MASK/MASQUE IN MARIVAUX

The putting on of the mask in Marivaux can be considered as an act of self-constitution by which the body is concealed and withdrawn from interpretation. It is delivered from the normative conceptualizations of the anthropological discourse and is set into relation with one's very own and unnamable affective reality. In this subversive game, the subject regains an area of freedom of action in relation to its anthropological obligations. The mask/masque constitutes an area that transgresses the completely readable, indexically marked identity (marked as a fixed semantic relation between body and mind) in the regime of visibility. The masquerade rather opens this showroom to a personal identity and performs it as a presence. This presence is – to describe it with Maurice Merleau-Ponty – already interspersed with absence, interwoven with otherness (Merleau-Ponty

---

2 In the argument, mask is also coded with masque and masquerade. This connotation is in most of the cases explicitly indicated by the notation "mask/masque". The double coding seems plausible, because the physiognomic set in 18th century anthropology is quite fixed and approaches the quality of material masks. The act of dissimulation always includes the putting on of a different physiognomic mask. Charles Le Brun's physiognomy was still the great authority (Le Brun 1980: 93-131; Graczyk 2004: 90-91).

3 For the notion of personal "authenticity" created by mask/masque, the study refers to recent approaches which elucidate the paradoxical impact of authenticity, as it seems to represent an unidentifiable dimension and "sends off signals both of immediacy and mediation, genius and performance, spontaneity and staging" (Straub 2012: 10).

1964: 170-201).[4] Relating to the problem of gender, there remains the question of whether this mask/masque of authenticity is in any way used by the female subject in particular, specifically by Marianne. And how is Marianne – the concealing one – then depicted in comparison to the pícaras of the early picaresque context? In the novels of Scarron and Sorel, the pícara is, in most cases, a prostitute, a mistress or an actress for comedy. These characters, who openly show their bodies and give themselves up to the gaze of male society and the sexual desires of men, represent the tradition of the older, body-inspired discourse of the picaresque and also imply the old pathos of showing, namely the signs of hard reality, which should be denounced. The early Spanish pícaras, for example Úbeda's *Pícara Justina* (1605) and Delicado's *Lozana Andaluza* (1528), wear the disfiguring "wounds" of their trade, the scars of syphilis, in their own faces (Mander 2015: 180; Kinzkofer 2003: 77-78).

In Marivaux, the situation is already different and more complicated: When we consider Marianne as a pícara, there must be respect for the strong tradition of the *romance* that derives from medieval times and lives on in the classical age.[5] The *romance,* an epic form deployed in the European context in different national variations, cannot be denied as a decisive influence even in the times of the Enlightenment. The rough pícara of the early texts has been integrated in this tradition and has been – in a manner of speaking – mainly 'domesticated' within the sublime but rigid codes of courtly gallantry in speech, gestures and facial expressions (Steigerwald 2009: 51-73). The old epistemological paradigm transported by the picaresque pattern that combines the (self-)cognition and the corporeal conscience of the outlaw, is superimposed by the post-cartesian paradigm of indexicality and total visibility. This excludes individual corporeal experience in favor of generally valid evidence and social compatibility.

The described dynamic corresponds to a process that already characterized the social reality of 17th century France. The mistress, originally a prostitute,

---

4 See in particular the notions of "insertion réciproque" and "entrelacs de l'un dans l'autre" (Merleau-Ponty 1964: 180, 181). Merleau-Ponty, in his reception of Husserl's phenomenology, refers to the correlation of temporality and subjectivity.

5 *Romance* originally means "written in a romance language," in contrast to Latin. The term is also used for the *romance,* a popular epic form of courtly literature which has been adopted in the European context since the 11th century, for example the *chansons de geste* and the later *roman courtois* in France. For the tradition of the Spanish *romance* (*el romance*) and its structural components, see Hesse (1992). For the *romance* as a form living on in the European context, see Bodmer (1955: 7-10). For the *romance* in France, see Raynaud de Lage (1976), and Köhler (1978).

gains a great deal of influence at the French court, lives close to the king and the political affairs, but is at the same time deeply involved in the rigid representative system of the court. Furthermore, it is the particular French cultural condition of *la cour et la ville* that has prepared the ground for the described continuum of gallant patterns from the classical age to the Enlightenment (Auerbach 1951: 12-50). Even in the age of Enlightenment, when the courtly tradition is rejected as a kind of slavery of mind, the courtly and gallant codes keep their binding function in society and articulate a definite gender model, as will be seen in Marivaux's novel. The cocotte or the mistress represents the public discourse of legitimated prostitution, constellating man and woman as subject and object of concupiscence.

LA VIE DE MARIANNE: UNUTTERABLE LOVE AS OPPOSED TO GENDER DIFFERENCE

In the following, I will present a discussion of a central passage in Marivaux's *La Vie de Marianne* in order to illustrate my previous reflections and hypothesis.[6] The passage includes the first encounter of Marianne and Valville in the church (Marivaux 2007: 122-142; Marivaux 1743: 62-83). The erotic reality between both remains vaguely expressed as "quelque chose de plus sérieux qui se passait entre lui et moi" (Marivaux 2007: 122) – "There was between him and me a Secret; and much more serious and earnest Intercourse" (Marivaux 1743: 62). *Eros* communicates itself *ex negativo*, as it shows exclusively in the disturbing effects on the interplay of will and behavior. This dual dynamic of the erotic reality is inscribed in Marianne's looking back in the moment when she is leaving the church. She looks behind herself, towards Valville and the place of the first encounter, as she feels a certain absence:

Enfin on sortit de l'Église, et je me souviens que j'en sortis lentement, que je retardais mes pas ; que je regrettais la place que je quittais ; et que je n'en allais avec un cœur à qui il manquait quelque chose, et qui ne savait pas ce que c'était. [...] [E]n m'allant, je retournais souvent la tête pour revoir encore le jeune homme que je laissais derrière moi ; mais je ne croyais pas me retourner vers lui (Marivaux 2007: 122).

---

6   The playful, enigmatic game seems also to be conserved in some ways in Marivaux's concept of the *je ne sais quoi*. *Le Cabinet du philosophe* explains the *je ne sais quoi* as a mere form, extremely flexible but not available for any interpretation (Marivaux 2001: 350-351).

At last the Service was over, and I remember I came out of the Church without either Life or Soul in me. I flackened my Pace, and much regretted the Place I had just left. In short, I dragged myself as it were along, with a heavy Heart that wanted something, though it knew not what it was. [...] For as I went I often turned my Head again, to look at the young Gentleman behind. But I did not suspect it was on his Account I did it (Marivaux 1743: 62).

On the one hand, this look back refers to the attribute of the erotic reality as being a reality "afterwards" which cannot but be already absent. Love will always be progressing and cannot be completely explained or be fully looked at; in a manner to speak: you can only look after it. On the other hand, this look back at Valville indicates the spontaneous impulse to fix a semantic value of the erotic encounter, to locate it in a substitutive place: the pew or the beloved himself.

The experience of the inexplicable lack of something unutterable obviously creates in the concerned lover the strong intention of signification, namely to fill the absence with some supplementary meaning: it is the intention to grant a possibility for the erotic reality to express itself, to adopt a communicative form or materialization, even if the ongoing dynamics of the transformative erotic reality must at the same time break down this semantic frame. So, Marianne confesses: "mais je ne croyais pas me retourner pour lui." The central conflict of the passage arises from the fact that the paradox dynamics of love are embedded in a society of omnipresent visibility, evidence and obviousness. Such a society is dominated by various discourses of knowledge that define man and his nature by means of different semantic patterns, similar to a scientific object. These discourses are the discourse of gallantry and the implied system of morals and virtue represented by Valville himself and the medical discourse represented by the doctor who examines Marianne's hurt leg (Marivaux 2007: 125-127; Marivaux 1743: 65-67). These discourses of knowledge articulate the traditional gender-constellation of the *romance,* the main source of gallant discourses in the early modern period: In contrast to the active men, the female protagonist takes on a passive, object-like status and indicates a need. As a cocotte, Marianne acts using the facial expressions and gestural vocabulary of gallantry in front of her admirers in the church with the purpose of appeasing her need for social and sexual appreciation. Russo even induces this need of the cocotte for recognition in an existential dimension when she points out: "The cocotte needs to be seen in order to feel that she exists" (Russo 2007: 80). As a hurt woman, Marianne depends on the chivalrous help of Valville, who arranges for her quick transport to his house (Marivaux 2007: 123-125, Marivaux 1743: 63-64). As a sick and virtuous woman, she undergoes the medical examination by the doctor, who represents the qualified and critical look of the medical authority. The text marks this authority of the benevolent doctor as a male, even patriarchal power.

The regime of visibility, which is constituted by the mentioned discourses lacks a sign for the unutterable erotic reality between Marianne and Valville. The ever-fleeing *eros*, however, attempts to find possibilities for expression, and requires a specific sign. This sign points to an inexplicable meaning. It has a signified (*signifié*) that cannot be fixed (made "dingfest" according to Hamacher [1988: 11]) and by this, would refute the dogma of evidence and intelligible truth. The question is: How is this central conflict handled? How does Marivaux manage to mediate or communicate the unutterable erotic reality, as this reality – a permanently transformative one – would reject any fixation of gender-semantics? To what extent is this permanent transformative signified of *eros* in relation to the picaresque substratum of the novel? Referring to the *novela picaresca*, Schlickers (2014: 49-55) points out, that *eros* can be understood as a medium *between* all gender-attributions.

THE PICARESQUE DISSIMULATION: MASKS/MASQUES OF AUTHENTICITY

In the mentioned dilemma, the strong intention generated by the lost origin of love initiates a solution: The indexical signs legitimated by the ruling discourses are recoded. This recoding or masking can be regarded as a subjective act of breaking away from the established social codes, and by this, as an act of sovereign disposal or enactment of the own body. The body is delivered from the discursive conceptualizations and reintegrated into the intentional scope of the subject; by dissimulation, the subject uses his body in his own right in order to articulate his unique and unutterable inner reality. The dissimulation or masking creates a covered area of "darkened semantics". This area cannot be penetrated by the light of reason or interpretation.

The "mask/masque of authenticity" seems to reactivate the carnivalesque mask of the pícaro in the social and cultural context of the 18th century. Bachtin attaches to the carnivalesque mask the function of an outlet in a "monologic" society of rigid codes. In medieval society, the mask of the rogue has a function first and foremost of opening the monologic semantics and of unlocking an area of changing perspectives (Bachtin 1990: 47-60). In Marivaux, the mask of authenticity serves to cover or to hide an area from the official views (and the social control represented by them), and, by this, to regain an invulnerable personal area in the regime of visibility. For this regime attempts to completely take over the body of the subject in order to produce evidence, for example in the form of moral sense, and to clear up the nature of man by articulating the indexical relation between mental and physiological processes. The concealing power of the mask of authenticity which shields the body from the penetrating reason and its procedures of interpretation, implies an unexplainable dimension, and, by this, exhibits a potential of authenticity. With the opaque mask, the subject authenticates his inner reality as it becomes unreadable by the ruling discourses. The mask of authenticity enables the subject to achieve the emancipation of his distinctive personality.

Having a glance at Marivaux's text again, we can extrapolate the strategy of putting on the mask of authenticity. On her way home from church, Marianne daydreams, and as she does not pay attention as she walks, she is involved in an accident in which her leg is hurt (Marivaux 2007: 123; Marivaux 1743: 63). This structural moment at the level of the *énoncé* activates the traditional model of virtue and gallantry: The chivalrous man brings help to the woman who finds herself in a situation of distress. Acting according to this gallant scheme, Valville arranges the transport of Marianne to his house. During the transport, Marianne's shrewd analysis opens a semantic dimension "behind" the obvious signification of Valville's behavior and facial expression: "À travers le chagrin qu'il en marqua, je démêlai pourtant que le sort ne l'avait pas tant désobligé en m'arrêtant." (Marivaux 2007: 123) – "However, I soon perceived, that, for all the Concern he seemed to be in, Chance had pretty well favoured his Desires by stopping me" (Marivaux 1743: 63). With this observation, the facial expression of grief can be read as a mere mimic mask of *eros*, and *eros* is, in contrast to the physiognomic marks of worry and grief and their clear conceptualizations, exclusively evoked by a paraphrase, that means: *ex negativo*. Love and its unutterable desire break the clear gender-specification of the surface because it disposes Valville and Marianne in an *equal* manner to playful dissimulation, to semantic masquerade.

This masquerade, that delivers the own body from the discourses of knowledge and power, evokes the carnivalesque masquerade of the pícaro. His masquerade is generated by the playful use of his own body, the body approaching the quality of mere form. This form cannot be fixed as a significative pattern but undermines the signification of the performed gesture and permanently withdraws it into the distance of irony. In the context of the changed cultural conditions of the Enlightenment, Marivaux recapitulates this originally carnivalesque and picaresque "discovery," namely "that man possesses also a body", as Bauer points out (1993: 65). In the end, this resistant body eludes his being taken over by the semantic ideology and in this rejection becomes the sign of the opaque relation between body and mind. The dissimulating body paradoxically indicates authenticity by contradicting the fetishism of evidence so typical for the enlightened anthropology.

Furthermore, the mask/masque of authenticity cannot be read at the level of the *énoncé*, but exclusively at the level of the *énonciation*: Marianne and Valville are playing, in solidarity with the reader, with the indexical codes of the established discourses. They seem to be actors at the margin of the fictive world, at the margin of valid gender-attributions. Through their communicative community, they surpass the level of the *énoncé*. They have the capacity to control their bodies and prove themselves to be authentically feeling persons in contrast to the puppy-like characters of Marianne's admirer, Climal (Marivaux 2007: 143-145; Marivaux 1743: 83-84), the doctor and other persons of evident authority, such as the matron of the convent in the third part of the novel (Marivaux 2007: 216-225; Marivaux 1743: 151-163).

THE HURT LEG: PICARESQUE GAME AS OPPOSED TO *ROMANCE*-LIKE SHAME

The text furthermore reveals the picaresque heritage to construct a discourse of authenticity which in contrast to the completely enlightened evidence of anthropological truth reintegrates body and mind to the unutterable unity of the person. The doctor's request to uncover and to expose the hurt leg evokes an intense flushing on the part of Marianne – the undeniable indexical sign of shame. This ethical concept is used in order to mask the sensual desire of the protagonist: "À cette proposition, je rougis d'abord, par un sentiment de pudeur; et puis, en rougissant pourtant, je songeai que j'avais le plus joli petit pied du monde." (Marivaux 2007: 125) – "This Proposal put my Modesty to the Blush; but nevertheless I reflected, that I had the prettiest Food in the world." (Marivaux 1743: 65). Hidden under the identical signifier (flushing), using this signifier as a semiotic niche or a masque, the desire is developed as a reflective act of becoming aware of one's own body. Marianne discovers that *her* body can be used for her own intentions, which means in our context: to express her affection of love towards Valville. So the strategy seems to be clear: Marianne and Valville use the ethical semantics and their indexical appearance in order to express their mutual desire in the regime of visibility. In this context, the semantic cover of virtue and its indexical catalogue transport a quite clear gender-conception: Coded as female is Marianne's bashful flushing at having to uncover her leg; coded as male is the authority of knowledge represented by the doctor as well as by the caring affection of the chivalrous Valville for the hurt woman. This construction of gender is illustrated by an obvious spatial separation of male and female: Marianne is helped by the housemaid in uncovering her leg, whereas Valville and the doctor are waiting in the corner of the room (Marivaux 2007: 126; Marivaux 1743: 66). The playing field, however, that Marianne and Valville open up behind the mask of moral discourse, constitutes the essential area of communication between the two lovers. In this communicative area, the intentional dynamics of unnamable desire break fixed attributions of gender. In the superior control of their bodies, Marianne and Valville are equal in their authenticity, unfolding their unutterable personalities.

THE AUTHENTICITY OF CRYING

The last part of the passage also illustrates how the picaresque substrate, that is, the roguish masquerade, opens up a discourse of authenticity. This discourse of authenticity seems to reject any gender-attribution. The catalyst of the conflict, that brings the picaresque dynamics to the surface of the text, is the problem of Marianne's going home; in the broader sense: her dark origin, as implied by residence at Madame Dutour's, the owner of a laundry (Marivaux 2007: 127-134; Marivaux 1743: 75-83). Initially, the picaresque masquerades of Marianne and Valville first and foremost attempted to create a masked area of signification. In the end, the dynamics of the unnamable *eros* and the values of the regime of visibility provoke an open conflict. This conflict is, in the context of Marianne's origin, articulated as a conflict between *amour-propre* (vanity) and love. On the one hand, *amour-propre*, as an essential value of the regime of visibility, requires the covering of the dark spot, which cannot serve the dogma of evidence. On the other hand, love demands that this dark spot is to be revealed in order to enable Valville to pay visits to Marianne and to express his love towards his beloved. More and more, this dilemma complicates the strategy of the protagonist of using the causalities of virtue for the construction of a quite favorable picture of herself. In the end, Marianne is trapped: She tries to fulfill the reduction procedure, which is imposed by the anthropological discourse. She evaluates and quantifies her affects and translates them into appropriate schemes of behavior. But these attempts are condemned to failure and culminate in the sudden and anxious question of the protagonist: "A quoi donc étais-je réduite?" (Marivaux 2007: 139) – "To what an Extremity was I then reduced?" (Marivaux 1743: 79). Marianne cannot master the complex work of interpretation and translation as required in the code system. In this situation of failure, Marianne suddenly starts to cry: "[...] excédée de peines, de soupirs, de réflexions, je pleurai, la tête baissée." (Marivaux 2007: 138) – "Overwhelmed with my own Sighs, Reflections and Grief, I was crying, with my Head cast down" (Marivaux 1743: 77-78). The crying seems to be the effect of the final breakdown of the protagonist, the "succomber" (Marivaux 2007: 139). Marianne's tears indicate a disturbance in the semiotic practice of enlightened anthropology and its indexical system. The tears represent a sign of the body which cannot be interpreted *within* the existing codes, as this sign represents the collapse of the system itself. The tears can be regarded as a sign that covers the body and makes it opaque. It is delivered from interpretation, from the necessity of being intelligible. The crying effectuates a relief for Marianne, and she feels free from the pressure of *amour-propre*, which always requires the hidden meaning to be unmasked: "il [= mon découragement] me soulagea, il me mit à mon aise, il affaiblit ma vanité, il me défit de cet orgueilleux effroi que j'avais d'être connue de Valville. Voilà déjà bien du repos pour moi." (140) – "For in the first Place it eased me, and alleviated my Troubles. It abated my Pride, and freed me from the Apprehensions I was under, left Valville should know me. This was a main Point of Ease recovered" (Marivaux 1743: 79).

Marianne's tears seem to be quite spontaneous, indicating a sudden emotional outbreak. But are these tears in fact authentic in the sense that they completely remove all masks? This assumption is contradicted by Marianne's comment: "[I]l n'y avait peut-être pas de meilleur expédient pour me tirer d'affaire, que de pleurer [...]. Notre âme sait bien ce qu'elle fait, ou du moins son instinct le sait pour elle." (Marivaux 2007: 139). – "And there was perhaps no better Way of easing my Heart than by crying [...]. The Soul knows perfectly well what she does, or at least her secret Apprehensions know it for her" (Marivaux 1743: 79). The initiation of the crying is attributed to the soul in some sort of management of the affects, as if the soul has instructed the tears and the crying to serve a certain intention. The involuntary instinct, that served as the operator of the model of the *machine mouvante*, is thus reintegrated into the intentional scope of the subject. Through the attribute of being intended, the crying receives the connotation of dissimulation and mask. The mask seems to be put on in order to create an area that is unavailable to interpretation. As the tears do not point to a positive meaning, but to the negation of all meaning, they figure as an opaque sign of the body: They disguise their meaning and are accentuated in their quality of being mere form, even the unremovable mask of something unutterable. By this, the tears paradoxically amalgamate artificiality and authenticity. The carnivalesque masquerade of the rogue suggested by Bachtin transports a model of semantic otherness which Marivaux reactivates as a strategy of authentication, of masking the unutterable self and its affective universe in the enlightened regime of visibility.

The body control of the pícaro, who performs the permanent transformation of sense and signification, seems to me the prototype of Marianne's sovereign gesture: to put on the mask of crying. This putting-on of the mask validates an act of regaining the body, of recreating its integrity. The opaque mask covers the body and turns it to the otherness of reason, so that the body becomes unattainable to the indexical dynamics of interpretation and instead inaugurates the integrity of the subjective affective reality. The central concept in this procedure is the "soul" or the "heart". Both concepts are used in several metaphors of masking and hiding, for example, on Valvilles "petites façons" (Marivaux 2007: 126) – "little Artifice" (Marivaux 1743: 66) and his sublime dissimulations: "[...] car le cœur est bizarre, il y a des moments où il est confus et choqué d'être pris sur le fait quand il se cache" (Marivaux 2007: 127) – "For the human Heart is very odd and strange. There are Occasions in which it is confounded and ashamed to be discovered in the Fact, when it strives to be concealed" (Marivaux 1743: 66). The hiding of the heart implies these paradoxical dynamics of masking the self as an authentic one.

THE UNNAMABLE IS BEAUTIFUL

We have now to ask if the strategy of masking authenticity which seems to be of picaresque origin has any attribution of gender. Marianne's tears seem to be quite powerful in their effect, as Marianne points out:

C'est que cet abattement et ces pleurs me donnèrent, aux yeux de ce jeune homme, je ne sais quel air de dignité romanesque qui lui imposa, qui corrigea d'avance la médiocrité de mon état, qui disposa Valville à l'apprendre sans en être scandalisé (Marivaux 2007: 140).

My Tears and Discouragement gave me in the Eyes of that young Gentleman a romantic kind of Dignity, which awed him, and which, by making previous Amends for my indifferent Station, prepared Valville to hear of it without being shocked (Marivaux 1743: 79).

The very attribute of tears of being not available to any interpretation grants to the protagonist a quality of ethics, of dignity. These ethics are, of course, borrowed from the genre of the *romance* with obvious irony. The epistemic darkness, however, effectuated by Marianne's mask of authenticity receives – in contrast to the ideology of evidence and visibility – a *positive* value. The opaque mask constitutes an area of vision ("aux yeux de ce jeune homme"), where the inexplicable dimension of the person can be realized as a crucial fact. The masked crying connotes a theatrical staging which imposes a great impression on Valville and brings him into a mood of inclination and even more tenderness towards Marianne. This mood levels out the inferiority of her social status, or, as it is stated later on, it adds a beauty to it ("[I]ls [= cet abattement et ces pleurs] viennent d'ennoblir Marianne dans l'imagination de son amant" [Marivaux 2007: 140]). – "They ennobled Marianne in the Opinion of her Lover." (Marivaux 1743: 80). The staging area constituted by Marianne's mask of authenticity cannot be understood any more as the fully illuminated area of evidence and the penetrating view of reason, but as an area that is opened to the auratic *persona*. This *persona* has at the same time an aesthetic potency. Marianne seems clearly superior to Valville, who is the attracted one. She initiates the masking and expels the man to a lower position: her admirer. This trace of gender-constellation is also implied in Marianne's partisanship for the disadvantaged woman:

> Et ne vous embarrassez pas d'ignorer ce que vous êtes née ; laissez travailler les chimères de l'amour là-dessus ; elles sauront bien vous faire un rang distingué, et tirer bon parti des ténèbres qui cacheront votre naissance. Si une femme pouvait être prise pour une divinité, ce serait en pareil cas que son amant l'en croirait une. À la vérité, il ne faut pas s'attendre que cela dure ; ce sont là de ces grâces et de ces dignités d'emprunt qui s'en retournent avec les amoureuses folies qui vous en parent (Marivaux 2007: 141).

And never be uneasy about unknowing your Birth. Do but let Love's chimerical Fancy work for you; that will soon give you a noble Extraction, and make the best Advantage of the Darkness with conceals your Birth. If any Woman could be taken for a Goddess by her Lover, it would surely be in such a Case. 'Tis true, you must not expect that Things will last long so. These are borrowed Charms and Qualifications, which vanish with the tender Extravagancies that gave them Birth (Marivaux 1743: 80).

The disadvantaged woman receives the authority to construct her own identity by means of masking her authentic self. These masks disguise her dark origin and lend to the woman an unassailable beauty and power towards the man and his regiment of vision and knowledge, but also towards the naive imagination (nurtured through the reception of *romances*) that is attributed to wide-eyed Valville. The discussion may be continued about the topos of idealization of the masked woman implied in this lecture, as well as of the mask, for example in the form of clothes, necessarily becoming a fetish.

On the one hand, we observe a certain upgrading of the female position with respect to the male. On the other hand, the male position is strengthened nevertheless, as the text articulates in the ongoing passage. As Marianne's mask of authenticity has managed to establish her dark origin as an esthetical and quasi-ethical value, there is no more reason to disguise this epistemic darkness. So Marianne confesses her lodging at Madame Dutour's (Marivaux 2007: 143; Marivaux 1743: 83). Even if this confession once more causes worry and concern in Marianne regarding Valville's reaction, his esteem for Marianne seems to be stable. His repeated question "Voilà donc ce que signifiaient vos pleurs?" (Marivaux 2007: 143) – "This was the Occasion of your Tears [...]" (Marivaux 1743: 83) is combined with the *participe présent* "serrant," the gesture of tenderly pressing her hand. Valville, in fact, turns towards Marianne's body, even if he cannot read this body. By touching the unreadable body, Valville validates the lack of signification that the body has received by masking it and breaks away from the male-dominated discourse of knowledge. The touching of the unreadable body is obviously not a grasping in the sense of intellectually understanding by reason. This touching rather concedes to the unreadable body a right of being far from being like a body-machine. This being is not "used up" by its visible and intelligible physiology but holds another dimension of being invisible to the eyes. The being of the unreadable body indicates a presence that remains interwoven with absence. A personal encounter in this cell of communication which finds the "you" in the unexplainable unity of body and mind is then possible. This encounter appears in fact authentic to the reader. Marianne's and Valville's love appears to be true.

The reactivation of the picaresque in Marivaux seems to react to the dogma of evidence in the regime of visibility. Following the early prototype of the epistemological paradigm which will lead to the Enlightenment, the non-readable mask/masque of authenticity reintegrates the body as an aspect of the self. The personal integrity effectuated by this mask/masque exceeds gender-dichotomies, which are operating on the *romance*-like and moral cover of the text.

BIBLIOGRAPHY

Alpert, Michael (Tr.). *Lazarillo de Tormes and Francisco de Quevedo – The Swindler (El Buscón). Two Spanish Picaresque Novels*. London 2003.

Anonymous. *Leben und Wandel. Lazaril von Tormes. Und Beschreibung, was derselbe für Unglück und Widerwärtigkeit ausgestanden hat*. [1614] Ed. Manfred Sestendrup. Stuttgart 1979.

Ardila, J. A. Garrido. *The Picaresque Novel in Western Literature: From the Sixteenth Century to the Neopicaresque.* Cambridge 2015.

Auerbach, Erich. "La cour et la ville." Ed. Erich Auerbach. *Vier Untersuchungen zur Geschichte der französischen Bildung.* Bern 1951. 12–50.

Bachtin, Michail M. *Rabelais und seine Welt. Volkskultur als Gegenkultur.* [1963] Ed. Renate Lachmann. Frankfurt a.M. 1987.

Bachtin, Michail M. *Literatur und Karneval. Zur Romantheorie und Lachkultur.* Frankfurt a.M.1969.

Bauer, Matthias. *Im Fuchsbau der Geschichten. Anatomie des Schelmenromans.* Stuttgart 1993.

Bodmer, Daniel. *Die granadinischen Romanzen in der europäischen Literatur.* Zürich 1955.

Cassirer, Ernst. *Die Philosophie der Aufklärung.* Hamburg 1998.

Deneys-Tunney, Anne. *Écriture du corps. De Descartes à Laclos.* Paris 1992.

Descartes, René. *Discours de la Méthode.* [1637] Tr. Christian Wohlers. Hamburg 2011.

Diderot, Denis. "À Mme La Princesse de Nassau-Saarbruck." [1614] *Le fils naturel, Le Père de famille, Est-il bon? Est-il méchant?* Ed. Jean Goldzink. Paris 2005. 109–115.

Ehland, Christoph. Ed. *Das Paradigma des Pikaresken – The Paradigm of the Picaresque.* Heidelberg 2007.

Ehrlicher, Hanno. *Zwischen Karneval und Konversion. Pilger und Picaros in der spanischen Literatur der Frühen Neuzeit.* München 2010.

Frömmer, Judith. *Vaterfiktionen. Empfindsamkeit und Patriarchat in der Literatur der Aufklärung.* München 2008.

García Santo-Tomás, Enrique. "The Spanish female picaresque." Ed. J. A. Garrido Ardila. *The Picaresque Novel in Western Literature. From the Sixteenth Century to the Neopicaresque.* Cambridge 2015. 60–74.

Graczyk, Annette. *Das literarische Tableau zwischen Kunst und Wissenschaft.* Munich 2004.

Hamacher, Werner. "Unlesbarkeit." Ed. Paul de Man. *Allegorien des Lesens.* Frankfurt a.M. 1988. 7–26.

Hesse, Christiane. "Textsorten/Typología textual." Ed. Günter Holtus, Michael Metzeltin, Christian Schmitt. *Lexikon der romanistischen Linguistik (LRL),* VI,1: Aragonesisch/Navarresisch, Spanisch, Asturianisch/Leonesisch. Tübingen 1992. 215–216.

Kinzkofer, Alexandra. *Der Schelmenroman als Anti-Romanze. Frauenbild und Liebesthema.* München 2003.

Köhler, Erich. *Der altfranzösische höfische Roman.* Darmstadt 1978.

Lazarillo de Tormes. Ed. Francisco Rico. Madrid 1992.

Le Brun, Charles. *Conférence sur l'expression des passions. Conférence tenue en l'Académie Royale de Peinture et de Sculpture; sur l'expression générale et particulière*. [1668] Paris 1980.

Lickhardt, Maren. "Vorwort." *Zeitschrift für Literaturwissenschaft und Linguistik* 175 (2014): 5.

Lickhardt, Maren. "Zu Transformationen des Pikarischen – On Transformations of the Picaresque." *Zeitschrift für Literaturwissenschaft und Linguistik* 175 (2014a): 6–23.

Mander, Jenny. "Picaresque itineraries in the eighteenth-century French novel." Ed. J. A. Garrido Ardila. *The Picaresque Novel in Western Literature*. Cambridge 2015. 157–183.

Marivaux, Pierre Carlet de Chamlain de. *Journaux et Œuvres diverses*. Ed. Frédéric Deloffre, Michel Gilot. Paris 2001.

Marivaux, Pierre Carlet de Chamlain de. *La Vie de Marianne*. [1731-1741] Ed. Jean M. Goulemot. Paris 2007.

Marivaux, Pierre Carlet de Chamblain de. *The life of Marianne: the adventures of the Countess of ****. Tr. from the Original French. London 1743.

Merleau-Ponty, Maurice. *Le visible et l'invisible*. Paris 1964.

Perler, Dominik. *René Descartes*. Berlin 2006.

Russo, Elena. *Styles of Enlightenment. Taste, Politics, and Authorship in Eighteenth-Century France*. Baltimore 2007.

Raynaud de Lage, Guy. *Les premiers romans français*. Geneva 1976.

Schlickers, Sabine. "Cherchez la femme: Genealogie und Entwicklung der spanischen *novela picaresca* – Cherchez la femme: Genealogy and Evolution of the Spanish *novela picaresca*." *Zeitschrift für Literaturwissenschaft und Linguistik* 175 (2014): 49–64.

Steigerwald, Jörn. "Galanterie als Kristallisations- und Kreuzungspunkt um 1700: eine Problemskizze." Ed. Daniel Fulda. *Galanterie und Frühaufklärung*. Halle 2009. 51–73.

Straub, Julia. "Introduction: The Paradoxes of Authenticity." Ed. Julia Straub. *Paradoxes of Authenticity. Studies on a Critical Concept*. Bielefeld 2012. 9–12.

Wehr, Christian. "La Vida de Lazarillo de Tormes und die Form der Invidualität im Roman." Ed. Christoph Ehland. *Das Paradigma des Pikaresken – The Paradigm of the Picaresque*. Heidelberg 2007. 25–44.

Virile Maturity, Female Linearity, and the Transformation of the Picaresque Novel
Tobias Smollett's *Roderick Random* and Daniel Defoe's *Moll Flanders*

JENS ELZE

Daniel Defoe's *Moll Flanders* (1722) and Tobias Smollet's *Roderick Random* (1748) are probably the two canonical texts that come closest to a continuation of the picaresque genre in eighteenth-century Anglophone Fiction. As such they share many similarities: both feature orphans that in their younger years meander through the precarious landscapes of the emerging commercial society of Great Britain; both feature a repeating change of profession or occupation with occasional descents into delinquency and roguishness – though much more nuanced in *Moll Flanders*. Both are narrated by themselves from the supposed end of their peregrinations, which depicts them from a position of relative bourgeois stability and material security. They also both clearly relate to the narrative scripts of the very first picaresque, *Lazarillo de Tormes* (1554), certainly channelled in *Moll Flanders*'s case through the popular criminal biographies of the late seventeenth and early eighteenth century, and in *Roderick Random*'s case through the bourgeois French version of the picaresque, especially, Alain-Rene Lesage's *Histoire de Gil Blas de Santillane* (serially published between 1715 and 1735) which Smollett had translated into English prior to writing *Roderick Random*. Upon closer scrutiny, however, both texts, despite these striking similarities open up surprisingly different trajectories for the picaresque novel and for the development of the modern novel in general. Therefore, they also relate differently to the Spanish picaresque tradition and emphasize and develop upon varying and distinct aspects of their precursor *Lazarillo de Tormes*.

In scholarship the picaresque has often been reduced to a literature of roguery or delinquency emblematic in the titles of Frank Wadleigh Chandler's jumpstart to picaresque scholarship *Romances of Roguery* in 1901 all the way into the late 1960s to Robert Alter's *Rogue's Progress* and Alexander A. Parker's *Literature and the Delinquent*. While this sociological reduction to delinquency has at times proven to be a conceptual problem for the literary history and typology of the picaresque, both *Roderick Random* and *Moll Flanders* for large parts do in fact fit in to this tradition of picaresque delinquency. They do however, arrive at completely different modes of detaching themselves from roguish life through different – and I will argue differently gendered – possibilities of maturity that also have severe implications for the development of literary form.

Roderick Random's concluding gentility, for example, takes up Lazarillo de Tormes's proposed closure to his unsteady life-narrative through marriage and employment as town crier and adds to its stability. Therein Smollett's novel almost approaches the tautological structure of the epic or the novel of ordeal and the detached viewpoint of satire. *Moll Flanders*, on the other hand, more clearly continues the open syntagm and the on-going precariousness that lurks behind Lazarillo de Tormes' rhetorical unreliability and its picaresque "sisyphus-rhythm" (Wicks 1986: 242), and develops those aspects of the modern novel, that emphasise the open-endedness and problematicity of human self-actualization. Gender, this paper will suggest, is obviously a, if not *the*, determining factor in these trajectories and socially determines the various formal solutions that the novels project.

Despite their lapses into delinquency, the protagonists of both novels ultimately aspire towards the same goal of becoming a gentleman/gentlewoman, though they originally endow this non-profession differently. For the very young Moll 'gentlewoman' at first denotes the opposite of its official social semantics: for her it means to earn her living *independently* through needle-work, as opposed to the more comfortable but less independent occupations and remunerations associated with in-house-servanthood. Only when she shortly lives in a wealthy household, does she change her conception towards the official tenets of genteelness and aspires to get rich without work. Her course of action to achieve that is now marriage, rather than raising herself through accumulating and investing wages or payment. This is of course the opposite of her previous course of action, as it signifies enduring dependence on the patriarch of a household. Her first attempt to marry the heir of a family she has worked for since being a young girl fails miserably: She is deceived and exploited and finally ends up with the second son of the estate, who in a context of primogeniture is of course not an heir awaiting a fortune. Accordingly, they live but moderately and after his early death she is soon thrown into indigence. After this disappointment, the subsequent portion of her life, which spans well more than half the novel, is devoted to various schemes of achieving success through marriage. All of these unions fail to gain her permanent security and comfort, though some men prove to be good husbands, while other relations are even romantically and platonically successful, such as the marriage to her 'Lancashire Husband'. On the other hand, the episodicity of the novel obscures the fact that these arrangements do, however, often cover significant periods of time, which means that there are moments of permanence underneath this paradigmatic surface of constant change. Her final marriage with the banker, for example, lasts five years in which she lives comfortably, but not ostentatiously. Whenever Moll is married, she, like Defoe's other famous heroine Roxana goes into "a kind of sleep or temporary retirement" (Kahn 1991: 80) that finds its formal expression in the temporal condensation of these episodes. The novel could have focused on the domestic moments of these marriages and Moll's psychological development within them, but instead emphasises the volatility that defines the transitions between them. This is of course significant: as a wife and a woman despite occasionally experiencing enduring content she always at the very least remained precariously tied to the contingency of death that may incur on her husbands and that would leave her utterly unsupported materially: "if he died I was undone" (189).

It has been argued that this last and largely satisfactory marriage with the banker, which she achieves in her early 40s, is the "psychological and structural middle of the novel" (Novak 1983: 90), where Moll is at her most balanced. After her youthful ambitions have tempted her to a life at the margins of social acceptance, she has sobered from these aspirations and settled for the securities and ethics of bourgeois marriage. But this bourgeois compromise proves impossible to sustain: her 'retirement' remains temporary. Therefore, after five years – not of marital bliss, but of content and compromise – her husband falls sick and she is faced with the prospects of poverty. Maximilian Novak has made clear that "she watches his decline with terror" (1983: 91).

Terror is not even an exaggerated concept in this context, because this death disrupts her entire previous existence: not only has she lost her husband and the security associated with his profession and income, but it also dawns on her that the relatively dependable series of marriages, which secured her income for close to three decades can probably no longer be sustained. For this reason the assumption of a 'psychological middle' is a problematic notion, because it suggests that somehow a regression in her psychological development leads her to abandon this arrangement, while it clearly is brought on by the utter contingency of social reality. The novel at this point overcomes the circularity of picaresque episodicity, but not in order to plausibly and productively transpose the protagonist to a better social place and end the narrative with a sense of maturity and continuity, but rather in order to include the linearity of female aging into the picaresque paradigm. A prospect that would afflict a woman who has lived off of her looks since early childhood most severely. With the possibility of mature marital compromise foreclosed and the linearity of female aging introduced into the framework, not even the precarious picaresque 'sisyphus-rhythm' of unsuccessfully taking up the same profession in a series of seemingly endless iterations remains an option. Next to her marriage schemes, she has also intermittently spent a few years working as a prostitute. This profession as well as her marriage schemes obviously rely on both her personality and on her concrete person, that is, her body. She is considered – so she repeatedly tells us – physically attractive, which leads to her continued success on this career path throughout the first half of the novel. This path is ultimately unsustainable, not only because it is never rendered permanent through enduring marital happiness, but also unsustainable, because in a highly contested marriage market she may no longer be a tradable commodity after having reached her middle age. In fact, what follows this fifth marriage to the banker is the most precarious instance of her life narrative and one of the few, in which she even approaches the material scarcity of *Lazarillo de Tormes* and the Spanish Picaresque by having to go hungry or at least feeling sincerely on the verge of going hungry (190).

After all of her resources have been spent following the death of this fifth husband, she moves to the city of London, desperate to find a way to make her living otherwise. She resorts to her initial idea of sustaining herself by the work of her hands, which she does by first taking up again the manual occupation of needlework, but soon, and more importantly, by resorting to theft. Paradoxically, needlework and stealing are in many respects similar: both require manual skills, both signify a mode of subsistence in which she takes care entirely of herself unsupported by husbands, benefactors, or society and both are professions in which she acts largely invisibly, either outside the public space or clandestinely within it. Unlike in marriage schemes and prostitution, her personality does not enter into the equation. In fact, she relies on a complete absence and discontinuity of personality in order to be successful in a clandestine profession that is fully unlike prostitution – which involves at least one – and marriage, which typically involves and affects two of the aspects of personality and body. When those forms of institutionalized female dependency seem no longer available to her, delinquency becomes the only autonomous response to increasing deprivation, at least as long as she remains in England.

This turn towards self-sustaining manual labour as I have argued, is significantly gendered. When she moves to London she is 48 years of age. Her physical *maturity*, therefore, somewhat disenables her dependence on marriage-schemes, for which younger (female) partners are often preferred for social and libidinal reasons. The marriage market was also becoming highly disadvantageous because it was a sellers' market in imperial England, where men were decimated by and caught up in wars, sea-faring, and trade. At the same time, her middle age is what only enables the possibility of thievery, which relies not only on a lack of personality, but also on non-suspiciousness, inconspicuousness, and, thus, a degree of invisibility that is often problematically associated with middle aged women in a libidinal economy of male gazes. With her thievery she became wildly successful as she herself states: "We not only grew Bold, but we grew Rich" (202). She continues with this career for many years even though she repeatedly reflects that "Those distresses were now relived, and I ... had so good a Bank to support me why should I not now leave off, as they say, while I was well" (203).

She is finally caught stealing and is arrested, when she is already sixty years of age, which in the context of 18th century life expectancy probably also meant having left behind the invisibility of middle age. She is ultimately sentenced to transportation together with her third husband – Jemy, the Lancashire husband – whom she reunites with in prison and with whom she had had the romantically most fruitful relationship. In Virginia, she can finally invest the clandestine and unproductive money that she has saved and fully devote her famous self-interested industriousness to start a new life outside the narrow confines of English society, geography, and property relations. She and her husband make a fortune as farmers and after their sentences return to England rich, where they still live at the end of the novel, aged 68 and 70. Despite this ultimate success, it took her almost her whole life to reach that status of legally sanctioned prosperity, for which from a biological perspective there does not seem to be too much duration left. Before arriving at this "safe harbour" – at the end of the novel, not in its middle as she had hoped (188) – her life has been presented as a constant trial, a constant eruption of contingency, a constant effort at self-actualization, regardless of the moral status of her responses. This on-going exposure to uncertainty certainly reflects the historical material possibilities of women in the 18th century, in which "property became more concentrated in the hands of a patriarchal elite" and which witnessed a "general growth of anti-female sentiment" (Ramsbottom 2008: 211-212). It also, however, reflects a clear gender bias in the transhistorical notion of maturity. A notion that is so important to the closed *form* of the novel, but that Georg Lukács significantly termed a "*virile* maturity" (84; emphasis added). Psychological or ethical maturity for Moll was achieved in the settling down in compromise with her financial advisor husband, a compromise that also would inform the end of the sobering trajectory of "accommodation" of many novels of formation (Buckley 1979: 17-18). In her case, it did, however, not occur at the end of the novel to close the text together with the trials and tribulations of youth. Indeed she had hoped to have "landed in a safe haven" – explicitly evoking the "salieron a buen puerto" (11) of Lazarillo de Tormes – that would deliver her from "the Stormy Voyage of Life past" (188). Instead, however, her arrival occurs in the middle of the novel and proved unattainable and unsustainable, because it is thwarted by the incursion of her husband's death. In the case of Moll Flanders, ethical maturity also coincides with the problem of physical aging and with a lack of personalized bourgeois property, which are no issue in later 'virile' novels of formation. This gendered relation between social heteronomy, physical aging, and psychological maturity infuses uncontained physiological and social linearity into her life-narrative. Socially this entails a further criminal escalation; formally, it prevents the ultimate closure of her life into a linear process of emergence and self-actualization through established and cyclical social mechanisms like inheritance, property, or marriage.

Therefore, *Moll Flanders* opens and ends precariously. Already at the outset of the novel, she points, if not to a potential continuation of her criminal career, then at least to the fact that some of her crimes may not have yet been discovered by the authorities and may not have been considered when her sentence was originally commuted to transportation, rather than death. Even in the legitimate material security in which she now lives at 70 years of age in the frame narrative there are "some Things of such Consequence still depending there" (8) to make her future remain strangely open. Her previous transportation had been the condition of possibility for the wealthy life that she leads towards the end of the novel, not only because it kept her alive, but also because the vast spaces of America offered her the possibility of channelling her industriousness and ambitiousness into the accumulation of property through the transformation of common nature that John Locke, in his *Second Treatise on Government*, saw as the ethical and material base of all legitimate property. This transformation of the commons and its modes of acquiring property through industry, labour, and merit that happens in America may not have been available to her in the insular early modern narrowness of an already commercial society in England. But even in the closing legitimacy of natural law, she admits that she cannot publicise all aspects of her crimes and cannot reveal her real name until after her death, which obviously tempts the reader to constantly fill the gaps that her narrative might leave to insert more severe crimes and thus the text requires urgently what Matthias Bauer has termed a "Komplementärlektüre", a complementary reading (Bauer 1996: 25). Even at the very end of the text, the closure of her life narrative, therefore, only hinges on the non-guaranteed term "resolve" (343), which points to a projection of continuity but cannot rule out potential future reversions and contingencies, that may still shatter the stability of her bourgeois existence.

In Hans Blumenberg's theory of the novel this irresolvable uncertainty of the future is precisely what defines the novel and the concept of reality from which it emerges. According to Blumenberg, the novel originates in the context of an emerging modern concept of reality. In this modern concept of reality, reality is a "consistent context" that structures and regulates the world. Reality is no longer the guaranteed material surface of the earth, nor the Platonic ideas that lie behind it, but the notions that mankind has created and is creating about the world as well as the institutions, values, and structures, with which it has replaced divinely ordained nature in a process of open-ended actualization. Correspondingly, the novel is also marked merely by a "progressive certainty [...] that might contain elements which could shatter previous consistency and so render previous 'realites' unreal" (Blumenberg 1979: 33).

Moll Flanders has clearly extended the openness of the picaresque novel into such a linear "progressive certainty". In her final gesture of sincerity ("we *resolve* to live in *sincere* penitence"; 343, emphasis added) she renders the unending contingency that Lazarillo still tries to deny through his re-inscription into the feudal hierarchies, into the official principle of her life narrative and the world in which it unfolds. Her perpetual social instability is here not only a historicist question of specific social context and *content*, to be denigrated by scholars interested in formal questions of literature. Rather, the representation of social content clearly structures the necessities of form and our perception of it. Moll's narrative makes clear – and may even exploit – what Blumenberg has said of the open-endedness of the novel: Closure, in his estimation, is merely a formal "irritation" that limits the principal infinity of the novel and the infinite and conflictual process of human actualization. This open-endedness is certainly more readily visible in contexts of social instability in which settling down and the outlook of continuity and closure, which it affords, is highly unlikely. This formal affinity – or rather informal tendency – of the novel is probably why the emergence of the modern novel also coincided with a turn in attention towards the lower classes, which clearly originated with *Lazarillo de Tormes* and the Spanish picaresque novel. It also makes clear that "actualization" is hardly ever about the transparent and immanent intersubjectivity with which male, white, bourgeois humans allegedly create the world sovereignly with the help of science and reason, but also about the endless self-actualization and self-responsibility with which the lower classes are increasingly tasked since early modernity. Blumenberg was aware that this concept of reality quickly turned to one of paradox in which the transformative and intersubjective potential of humanity are contained by new worldly and social – rather than divine – structures of dominance and transcendence (1979: 34). These containing structures undermined the ideal of intersubjectivity and transparency in human world making, but not the linearity and un-endedness of self-actualization with which most individuals were confronted, particularly since the advent of early capitalism and modernity. Especially for women in the eighteenth century, this meant "growing female responsibility *and* continued subjection" (Ramsbotton2008: 209; emphasis added).

In *Moll Flanders* this lack of closure, therefore, clearly has to do with the protagonist's gender. Interestingly, one of the more influential comments regarding her gender has been Ian Watt's assertion that "the essence of her character and actions is [...] essentially masculine" (1957, 113). Clearly Watt wants to emphasize the disobedient character of Moll's personality that transgresses traditionally female roles. This designation of Moll's masculinity, however, not only contradicts with the very different social options actually available to masculine semi-pícaros in some of the canonical texts of the eighteenth century but also disregards the social nexus of femininity, aging, and precariousness and their relation to notions of formal linearity and cyclicality. I am not much interested in programmatically contradicting Watt's self-admittedly subjective position on this issue and posit Moll as essentially female. It is, however, not debatable that the novel includes stagist and linear conceptions of biological femininity, like puberty and climacteria and that female aging and its implications as they are presented in the text, insert a degree of linearity that is unmatched in its biological and social determinism by male picaresque protagonists in eighteenth century British Fiction. Even at the end of the novel when her material maturity is safely rooted in the tenets of Lockean natural law and when she is not only matured but significantly aged, she still continues to live contingent upon potential discoveries about herself by the legal system of England and other uncertainties that Moll is not fully prepared to rule out, before her life is not yet finished and her peregrinations thereby ultimately arrested. Her life remains indomitably precarious, even when the only further incursion that may be reasonably expected is physical death through old age.

Roderick Random's life trajectory functions quite differently than the one of Moll Flanders. He is not of lowest, but of genteel birth and despite the absence of parents has relatives that initially care for his bringing up and he even receives a formal education and training as an apothecary. Typical of the picaresque, his narrative also starts *ab ovo*, even though his precarious peregrinations do not start as early in his life as Moll Flanders', but only in his youth, when he decides to go to London. After a lengthy section that depicts his obstacle-laden way to the capital, his career subsequently leads him through the lower regions of the London underworld. Later, he is forced onto a man-of-war, where he works as a surgeon and even shows some moments of heroism. In terms of his roguery, he is never the active agent but often on the receiving end of tricks, which in some instances attests to an inability to learn and plot reality, quite in contrast to the accumulative and synthesizing consciousness that Scottish enlightenment thinkers, such as David Hume, proposed around the same time. When he is a little more mature – as in no longer a youth – he returns to England from his involuntary global voyages and *now* attempts to marry his way into the upper class, quite like Moll did. Significantly, however, for him this scheme becomes an option somewhat later in his natural life and especially much later in the structure of the novel.

Roderick eventually marries successfully and happily only after having found some modest material success as a trader and businessman himself. His wealthy wife is significantly called Narcissa, so that the material and psychological affects of his marriage clearly and ironically point to his bourgeois self-recognition. His conversion from roguishness and his economic success is even further strengthened by the discovery of his lost father who acknowledges him as his rightful son and heir (413). His father was the disinherited first-born son of a wealthy landowner in Scotland, who then disappeared and who returned to his rightful social place by using his inalienable genteel talents to become a rich trader. This entrepreneurial success may be a slight at the property relations expressed in primogeniture, but rather than disrupting the timeless hierarchies of inheritance and blood, it also points to a stable relation between genealogy and self-realisation that is typical of the narrative structure of romance and the novel ordeal (Bakhtin 1986: 23sq.).

A similar trajectory is experienced by Roderick himself. Not incidentally do his economic success, his marriage, and his recognition by his father coincide with his age of maturity – he is probably in his late twenties by that time. This *anagnorisis* indubitably arrests the potential revocability that has loomed over Moll Flanders even after she had accumulated significant property and reached old age. Roderick's life narrative not only closes without residues of future contingency, but it ends as he enters an age conventionally associated with psychological, intellectual, and ethical maturity. The text also leaves a much larger expected portion of his life in which this stability may iteratively unfold before the incursion of death, thus formally containing the novel's principles of linear consistency and progressive certainty, in favour of a *very closed form*. Unlike the novel as envisaged by Blumenberg, at the end of *Roderick Random* we do not have any legitimation to feel that the future might "contain elements which could shatter previous consistency" (1979: 33). The impending birth of his first son at the end of the novel even elevates him to the privileged generational middle-position and genealogically secures his position into the future, whereas Moll's eight children have not had any impact on her maturation and have served as markers of precariousness, rather than as guarantors of future stability. Roderick Random's future is now determined by the genteel essence he acquired and discovered, which resembles the stability of the epic and the stable relation between actualization and genealogy that also defines the novels of Henry Fielding: After Roderick has been wrongfully confined to the peregrinations among the low life, his recognition safely positions him and guarantees his stability for the rest of his life. No suspicion of change, not even the suspicion of an incurrence of death – from which he is decades removed – is left at the end, but only the notion of the permanence and legitimacy of matured and immortal gentlemanliness. For Roderick Random physical and psychological maturity is the end of history, for Moll Flanders it was the beginning of precarity that can only be survived – not overcome – by relying on industriousness and the invisibility that female middle age affords. Moll often reflects on her looks and her body, changed due to pregnancies and due to age, which is certainly not only a chauvinistic move to display female vanity on Defoe's part, but relates female physicality and physical aging to a marketplace for marriage and to strict regimes of (in)visibility.

For Roderick Random, on the other hand, physical aging is not an issue. In fact his whole body and countenance is not an issue but he is defined as a gentleman precisely by a characterless, bodiless, and faceless handsomeness that also eludes any manifestation of aging: he always fits into every random piece of clothing that he finds and his facial features are never described. Hence, his psychological and material maturity fully recasts the circularity of picaresque roguery and youthful immaturity as a "neoclassical indeterminacy of the man of the world" (Lynch 1996: 83; emphasis added). His gentlemanly 'virile maturity' – which much more literally resonates with this ill-termed concept than the metaphysical, at times utopian, insight that Lukács actually had in mind – ends both the endless linear progression *and* the repetitive circularity of the novel at a point at which physical decline has not yet set in, keeping the progressively deathly linearity of the novel as an idea safely out of its already narrow frame. What needs to be overcome for Roderick Random to arrive at a safe haven is an untamed youthful vivacity of spirit, while for Moll it is the very contingency and linearity of life itself.

Of course pragmatically *Roderick Random* is also a satire and the self-evaluations of the protagonist should be seen with a grain of salt. There is, however, nothing about the end of his peregrinations that leaves any doubt as to its ensuing stability. The satiric language pertains largely to the adventurist and panoramistic part of the narrative in which he surveys the condition of England and assembles a satiric anatomy of his times, types, and landscapes. Satire needs such a largely stable viewpoint from which to assert itself and through which it can panoramistically frame the effects of this hostile world. It assesses the status of the world from a position of moral and intellectual superiority that the disinterested viewpoint of the gentleman affords, who now belongs to "those qualified to observe", while his younger self still belongs to "those who are objects of others' observation" (Lynch 1996: 82). In the pseudo-autobiographical novel – that lacks the detached third person narration of Fielding's *Tom Jones* – the possibility of satire is intricately related to maturity. Maturity here is the departure and disentanglement from the referential world of satire to the Olympian viewpoint from which to assess the world and one's own development in it. Ian Watt in his seminal study on the rise of the novel aptly termed this novelistic strand of the eighteenth century – defined by Fielding and Smollett – "realism of assessment" that needed to come to a sense of stability and generality in order not to dissolve into the utter perspectivity of the modern novel and of legalistic casuistry. While Smollett's protagonist is not infallible and is himself not fully exempt from authorially implied satiric scorn, his quasi-epic life trajectory is nonetheless the affirmative formal and biographical counterpart to his rhetorical and satirical negativity. Satirical pragmatics, do therefore not change the fact that those novels strongly contained the linearity and perspectiveness on which the later modern novel relied. These quasi-epic life trajectories may have been tied to the imperative of the gentlemanly accumulation of experience – as Roderick's unwilling, but inevitable military career displays – and self-recognition, but they ultimately remained secured by the structures of entrepreneurial social emergence available to able *men* and further guaranteed, tamed, and dignified through the recognition of bourgeois genealogy.

It is perhaps not incidental that a female protagonist was able, or condemned, to extend the novelistic propensity towards unending actualization well beyond the moment of psychological maturity that *forms* the end of *Roderick Random* and later of many a *novel of formation*, at least those that tend more towards the classificatory pole of the *bildungsroman*'s double tendency of transformation and classification (Moretti 1987: 8). Maturity, in terms of discovering operational ethical principles and being able to live by them, is always foreclosed for Moll Flanders, even if her ethical meandering is certainly treated ironically. In opposition to the universalizing "realism of assessment", Watt termed this casuistic tendency of Defoe's the "realism of presentation" that found its fullest expression in the novels of Samuel Richardson, which also usually featured female protagonists (Watt 1957: 293). In the eighteenth century the tendencies of realism of assessment and realism of presentations remained distinct and only came together in nineteenth-century realism in the wake of Jane Austen, when their balanced handling became the signature of the modern novel, which had to "combine into a harmonious unity the advantages both of realism of presentation and realism of assessment" (Watt 1957: 297). Unlike most of his critics, I do not question Watt's literary history for the heuristics of overemphasizing a dialectical trajectory at the expense of the continuities between romance and realism that Michael McKeon has succinctly summarized (1985: 2 sq.). Rather, I doubt that the realism of assessment is as important to what has become the modern novel. Even if one shares Lukács' dictum that the ethics of the author is the aesthetical problem of the novel (110 sq.), for a modern reader an excess of assessment – regardless whether it is deployed through commentary or obtrusive counterpointing – is more difficult to digest than an excess of presentation, as the comparatively low – and often whimsical – popularity of Dickens' moralistic satirical novels in academia seems to attest. While the novel as the result of an actualization of linear consistency was always an illusion due to the necessities of form and the conflictual nature of perspectivity and self-actualization, closure nonetheless tends to be unresolved or ambivalent in most 'serious' – or 'grownup' to use Virgina Woolf's term – modern fiction and assessment remains provisional and implicit at best.

Assessment in Watt's terms also points towards a stability in handling the world and its representations that seems to exclude potential counterperspectives to a tendency of patriarchal bourgeois common sense. This common sense is often conflated with a universal rational spirit and neutrality accessible to gentlemen but that remains inaccessible to women. It also points towards a sense of closure and inoculation that seems at odds with the endless nature of the modern novel. Closure in the novel, in Blumenberg's estimation, is merely the "irritation that aesthetic form cannot escape" (1979: 42). This closure in *Roderick Random* is obviously and literally a greater "irritation" and nuisance than in *Moll Flanders*. It sets the formal limits of a narrated human life so much narrower and does so not even out of the onto-epistemological necessities of first-person narrative or the aesthetic limits of form, but rather by embracing the pseudo-developmental paths of quasi-epic bourgeois male self assertion. In the hostile world of satire, the superior and characterless protagonist must be allowed to close himself off from any further incursions and needs to isolate himself from the temporalities, perspectiveness, and contextuality of human self-assertion to assume his rightful place atop a hierarchy that is still based in land-ownership, birth, and inheritance. The 'virile' novel has considered the open-endedness of self-realization only unto the point in life in which gentle*manly* maturity is achieved. After this, developmental temporality – and typically the text – ends in order to arrest change and dynamism in the containable time-space of youth. *Moll Flanders* of course also had to ultimately give in to the "irritation" of form, but in her case the "biographical form" that usually "overcomes ... 'bad' infinity" (Lukács 1971: 81), stretches the narrative towards the physiological and onto-epistemological limits of the representation of human life. This predisposition to stretch the first person novel to its utmost formal ends is rooted in her lower social birth, but perhaps even more so in her gender, that does not allow for propertied resignations at any turn.

Moll Flanders, the narrator, thus emphasizes that representational aspect of *Lazarillo de Tormes* that relies on the never ending thrownness under "fortunas y adversidades", that Lázaro only pretends to escape by claiming to close off the syntagm of picaresque meandering, through "hard work" and marriage (4). By admitting the impossibility to ever escape adversity even at the end of a very long and ultimately successful life – and in the genre of conversion narrative – she extends the problematicity of *Lazarillo*'s ending and, therefore brings the picaresque closer to the modern novel in terms of emphasizing the linearity of development and its open-endedness. *Roderick Random*, on the other hand, expands the quasi-epic and satirical aspects of *Lazarillo de Tormes* in which he tries to isolate himself from his meandering and anticipates those aspects of the *bildungsroman* that emphasize the classificatory arrival over the continuous and potentially transformative search. Even though *Moll Flanders* precedes *Roderick Random* by more than a quarter of a century it is much closer to both the material precarity of the Spanish picaresque *and* the metaphysical uncertainties of the modern novel. Early on in the life of the novel, this discrepancy of form in the historical trajectory of the novel is firmly embedded in the social and legal possibilities associated with the genders of the protagonists.

Of course Daniel Defoe may not necessarily have been interested in uttering a critique of the social conditions of women. Moll's propensity towards continual openness may also quite problematically hint towards a casuistic anti-idealism that was emerging in England from the end of the seventeenth century, which assumed that an "ethical problem must be approached on its own terms and decided on its own merits" (Starr 1971: 7). Maximilian Novak has confirmed that on the level of fictional rhetoric "*Moll Flanders* includes a central character who assumes not merely the particularity of an individual character but also the generality that makes up for the prototype of the eternal female, which is often related to casuistry" (1983: 95). This essentializing connection between femaleness and casuistry is certainly problematic and feeds into the purely and explicitly male conception of a holistic, immovable, and neutral classicist *spirit*. At the same time, however, it also makes the gender affinities of the origin of the modern novel even clearer, as casuistry relates intricately to the difficulty to arrive at guaranteed principles and pertains very much to the contextuality, openness, perspectivity, and precarious intersubjectivity of "reality as the result of an actualization". As such, it is also the legalistic principle that best fits the "linearity" of modern novelistic form in which the tenets of law may always be shattered by contingencies and events that fall outside its classificatory purview. Satiric forms on the other hand have a more uneasy relation to casuistry. They also acknowledge the inappropriateness of the letter of the law, but mostly because it allows certain subjects to elude the governing realm of its spirit, thereby mourning its limited range of formalisation and execution. Casuistry, and even more so antinomianism, conversely assumes that laws, in letter, may simply be inapplicable in certain circumstances because they contradict the necessity to social survival, while their spirits have originated in the context of specific sociocultural possibilities that camouflage as neutral and universal. Despite occasionally and implicitly including the protagonist-narrator and his bourgeois genteelness among the objects of satire, *Roderick Random* nowhere displays the 'female' casuistry of Moll's narrative or the fully antinomian legitimations of delinquency that were typical of eighteenth century lower working class self-assertion (Linebaugh 1991: xxi).

From this perspective of a feminine and unprincipled casuistry, Defoe's plot structure may have been read as anything but well meaning: The fact that Moll Flanders is unable to acquire the *properties* to help her ascend to the status of disinterested observer that enables detached satire or the "firm and immovable" (Goethe 1875: 59) principles of the classical and classificatory *bildungsroman* is a highly problematic notion. The lack of such a detached perspective, however, renders *Moll Flanders* into a much more consistent continuation of the precarious picaresque form and its critical 'atopy' (Mecke 2000). Furthermore, her casuistry is certainly not inaccurate descriptively, especially if it is seen as the correlate of the "legal conventions that made women's ownership of property tenuous" (Lynch 1996: 85). Even if Defoe had not been an avid casuist himself – which he was – and even if he was not interested in pointing out the social precariousness of women – which he well might have been – in patriarchal society, his moral standpoints would not effect the importance of the formal innovations that this gender choice of protagonist afforded. Even if it had been the symbolic channelization of anti-casuist prejudice and not a form of social critique, *Moll Flanders*' decidedly female continuation of the picaresque novel would still be an indispensable opener for the trajectory and the possibility of the modern novel.

Bibliography

Bakhtin, Mikhail. "The *Bildungsroman* and its Significance in the History of Realism (Towards a Historical Typology of the Novel)." *Speech Genres and Other Late Essays*. Austin, TX 1986. 10–60.
Bauer, Matthias. *Der Schelmenroman*. Stuttgart 1996.
Blumenberg, Hans. "The Concept of Reality and the Possibility of the Novel." *New Perspectives in German Literary Criticism*. Ed. Richard E. Amacher and Victor Lange. Princeton, NJ 1979. 29–48.
Buckley, Jerome. *Season of Youth: The Bildungsroman from Dickens to Golding*. Cambridge MA 1974.
Defoe, Daniel. *Moll Flanders*. Oxford 1971.
Goethe, Johann Wolfgang. *Wilhelm Meister's Apprenticeship*. Tr. R. Dillon Boylan. London 1875.
Kahn, Madeleine. *Narrative Transvestism: Rhetoric and Gender in the 18th Century English Novel*. Ithaca, NY 1991.
La Vida de Lazarillo de Tormes: y de sus fortunas y adversidades. Ed. Francisco Rico. Madrid 1990.
Lazarillo de Tormes. Tr. Michael Alpert. Harmondsworth 2003.
Linebaugh, Peter. *The London Hanged: Crime and Civil Society in the Eighteenth Century*. London 1991.
Lukács, Georg. *Theory of the Novel: A Historico-Philosophical essay on the forms of great epic literature*. Tr. Anna Bostock. Cambridge MA 1971.
Lynch, Deidre. *The Economy of Character. Novels, Market Culture and the Business of Inner Meaning*. Chicago 1996.
McKeon, Michael. *The Origins of the English Novel*. Baltimore, MD 2002.
Mecke, Jochen. "Die Atopie des Pícaro: Paradoxale Kritik und dezentrierte Subjektivität im Lazarillo de Tormes." *Welterfahrung – Selbsterfahrung. Konstitution und Verhandlung von Subjektivität in der spanischen Literatur der frühen Neuzeit*. Ed. Wolfgang Matzat and Bernhard Teuber. Tübingen 2000. 67–94.
Moretti, Franco. *The Way of the World. The Bildungsroman in European Culture*. London 1987.
Novak, Maximilian. *Realism, Myth, and History in Defoe's Fiction*. Omaha 1983.

Ramsbotton, John D. "Women and the Family". *A Companion to Eighteenth-Century Britain.* Ed. H.T. Dickinson. Malden, MA 2008. 209–222

Smollett, Tobias. *The Adventures of Roderick Random.* Oxford 1979.

Starr, G. A. *Defoe and Casuistry.* Princeton, NJ 1971.

Watt, Ian. *The Rise of the Novel: Studies in Defoe, Richardson, and Fielding.* London 1957.

Wicks, Ulrich. "The Nature of Picaresque Narrative: A Modal Approach." *PMLA* 89:2 (1974). 240–249.

Contributors

Matthias Bauer is Professor of Literary Studies at the Department of German at the University of Flensburg (Germany).

Anne J. Cruz is Professor of Spanish and Cooper Fellow in the Humanities, Emerita, University of Miami (Florida).

Hanno Ehrlicher is Professor of Romance Literatures at the University of Tübingen (Germany).

Jens Elze is Junior-Professor of British Literature and Culture at the University of Göttingen (Germany).

Frank Estelmann is Lecturer of Romance Literatures at the University of Frankfurt am Main (Germany).

Hans-Joachim Jakob is Lecturer of German Literature at the University of Siegen (Germany).

Timo Kehren is Research Assistant at the Department of Romance Languages and Literatures at the University of Mainz (Germany).

Maren Lickhardt is Assistant Professor of German Literature at the University of Innsbruck (Austria).

Alexandra Schamel is Lecturer of comparative literary studies at the University of Munich (Germany).

Gregor Schuhen is Professor of Romance Literatures at the University of Koblenz-Landau (Germany).

Hans Rudolf Velten is Professor of Medieval German Literature at the University of Siegen (Germany).